The Law Market

The Law Market

Erin A. O'Hara and Larry E. Ribstein

UNIVERSITY PRESS
2009

OXFORD
UNIVERSITY PRESS

Oxford University Press, Inc., publishes works that further
Oxford University's objective of excellence
in research, scholarship, and education.

Oxford   New York
Auckland   Cape Town   Dar es Salaam   Hong Kong   Karachi
Kuala Lumpur   Madrid   Melbourne   Mexico City   Nairobi
New Delhi   Shanghai   Taipei   Toronto

With offices in
Argentina   Austria   Brazil   Chile   Czech Republic   France   Greece
Guatemala   Hungary   Italy   Japan   Poland   Portugal   Singapore
South Korea   Switzerland   Thailand   Turkey   Ukraine   Vietnam

Published by Oxford University Press, Inc.
198 Madison Avenue, New York, New York 10016

www.oup.com

Oxford is a registered trademark of Oxford University Press

Library of Congress Cataloging-in-Publication Data

O'Hara, Erin A.
The law market / Erin A. O'Hara and Larry E. Ribstein.
    p.   cm.
Includes bibliographical references and index.
ISBN 978-0-19-531289-8
1. Venue—United States.   2. Forum shopping—United States.   3. Forum selection clause—United States.
4. Conflict of laws—Jurisdiction—United States.   5. Domicile—United States.   6. Tax havens.
7. International business enterprises—Taxation—United States.   8. Income tax—United States—Foreign
income.   I. Ribstein, Larry E.   II. Title.
KF8858.R49 2009
340.068'8—dc22   2008018395

9   8   7   6   5   4   3   2   1
Printed in the United States of America
on acid-free paper

Acknowledgments

Thanks to

Stanimir Alexandrov
Daniel Barham
Margaret Blair
Chris Brummer
Frank Buckley
Henry Butler
Christopher Drahozal
Larry Helfer
India Johnson
Bruce Kobayashi
Geoffrey Miller
Richard Nagareda
Patricia Shaughnessy
Bo Rutledge
Jeffrey Schoenblum
Suzanna Sherry
Stephen Ware

for helpful advice, comments, and ideas. Thanks to Daniel Nixa and
Jacqueline Schall for valuable research assistance.

Contents

The Law Market

I

Introduction

Once a state or nation produces a law, people and firms connected with the polity must obey the law or suffer consequences. But people and firms increasingly have another choice, that is, to move beyond laws' reach. These moves are becoming easier with faster communication and transportation and freer trade. Parties, in effect, can shop for law, just as they do for other goods. Nations and states must take this "law market" into account when they create new laws.

Consider, for example, someone we will call Saul Shipman, an operator of commercial transport ships between the United States and nations throughout the world. The U.S. Congress and the California legislature have passed regulatory statutes that they intend to apply to Shipman's operations in California. But Shipman has incorporated his business in Delaware, located the company headquarters in Virginia, and registered the ships in the Cook Islands. When customers pay Shipman, he places the company assets in an offshore bank account in the Cayman Islands. The company contracts with employees to litigate any disputes in Virginia state courts, and with customers to arbitrate disputes in the United Kingdom. These contracts may enable Shipman to avoid California and federal corporate, tax, labor, antitrust, and environmental regulations. California and the United States might want to impose their laws on Shipman, but they would risk forcing Shipman to move his operations elsewhere. These jurisdictions accordingly must legislate cautiously.

This book explores the market for law that results from the mobility of parties like Shipman. We will show that this market often enables people to find laws that fit their needs, and the market disciplines governments to enact socially beneficial laws. At the same time, however, the law market can inhibit states from enacting desirable regulations. We will consider how to achieve an appropriate balance between these costs and benefits of the law market.

Our analysis of the law market takes us into a largely ignored field of law called *conflict of laws*. These rules are designed to determine which laws should apply when parties, transactions, acts, or events span more than one jurisdiction. (Throughout this book, a generic reference to "state" includes both U.S. states and nation-states.) This "choice-of-law" inquiry seems to be the sort of third-order question that only a lawyer could love, and even many lawyers assume the issue away. Yet a little reflection reveals that choice-of-law problems pervade our lives. What if, for example, that contract into which you have entered while sitting at your home computer in Illinois with a seller in South Dakota is valid in South Dakota but not in Illinois? Or what if that same-sex marriage you celebrated in Massachusetts is invalid under the law of your new home state of Virginia?

If we think about the question of "which law" at all, we're likely to assume that the territorial, or "when in Rome," principle applies: the applicable rules depend on where you are at the time when the law becomes relevant. Thus, people might be subject to criminal law where they act, breach of contract liability where they breach, tort liability where they cause harm, and property laws where the property is located. However, a purely territorial approach to choice of law seems anachronistic in a world shrunk by rapid transportation, instantaneous communication, and free trade. Spouses and children shuffle among multiple homes. Everyday products and services come from every corner of the globe. International firms interact with customers located throughout the world, often through the impersonal Internet. The companies with which we deal are no longer bounded by factory walls, but increasingly "outsource" important operations through global networks of contracts. This mobility of people, assets, and transactions makes deciding which laws to apply to a legal problem increasingly arbitrary.

Uncertainty about what law to apply can be very costly. Not only do judges and litigants need to know what law governs the resolution of disputes, but people and businesses need to know what law applies at the time they act. For example, before a company enters into a contract, it needs to consider whether some of the provisions will be invalid so it can substitute other provisions, take steps to ensure that a different law applies, or avoid the transaction altogether. Individuals confront similar uncertainties when deciding to marry, divorce, write wills, establish trusts, buy or sell property, or enter into contracts.

One solution to this choice-of-law uncertainty is to have clear rules prescribing the law that governs each type of case. But what considerations should guide these rules? Should we inquire into the intent underlying each law that might apply? What if the legislature did not clearly intend anything about the geographic scope of a law? If the legislature's wishes don't govern, what policies should matter?

In the context of contracts, parties might achieve certainty by specifying the governing state's law in their agreement. The parties might then negotiate for the law that best suits their joint needs, just as they negotiate other terms of the contract. Indeed, sophisticated business contracts increasingly include choice-of-law clauses that state the law that the parties wish to govern their relationship. In addition to settling uncertainty, these clauses might enable the contracting parties to circumvent those states' laws they deem to be undesirable.

The contracts that consumers make every day—credit card agreements, stock and mutual fund investment terms, consumer product warranties, and insurance contracts—also routinely include choice-of-law clauses. In these situations, the insurance company, manufacturer, or mutual fund has effectively chosen the law. The consumer participates in this choice only to the same extent that she participates in any choices related to mass-produced products and services, that is, by deciding whether to buy the product or service. And it is safe to assume that the company's choice of law is not random. A company incorporates in Delaware and the credit card firm chooses to be governed by South Dakota law because these choices serve their interests. This raises the question of whether consumers should be protected from these potentially self-serving, one-sided choices.

Allowing contracting parties to create their own legal certainty thus raises thorny issues. One might wonder why contracting parties should be able to declare that their relationship is governed by the law of one sovereign state and not others. We might expect governments to respond with hostility to the enforcement of choice-of-law clauses. In fact, however, the courts usually do enforce choice-of-law clauses.

Why *Do* the Courts Enforce Choice-of-Law Clauses?

Suppose state A's courts would apply state A law to a contract that was made in A. Assume further that A's law prohibits contracting parties from charging usurious rates of interest (interest rates set above the maximum permitted rate of interest). Now suppose that a firm loans money to a state A resident through a contract that provides for application of state B's law (which does not include a usury statute) to any disputes between the parties. Without the choice-of-law clause, the court would apply state A's law to a case involving enforcement of the debt. Should it enforce the clause?

We might ask why a state A judge, urged by a local lawyer, would ever willingly apply the chosen over the local law, or why the state A legislature would not specify in the statute that a clause choosing some other state's law is unenforceable. After all, these rules were added to state law in an effort to restrict contract clauses. Why should the parties be able to circumvent those limitations merely by adding a choice-of-law clause to their agreements?

One reason that courts and legislatures might not insist on applying local law is that they know in the long run they might not have the last word. To begin with, they know that parties can insert yet another clause in the contract: a choice-of-forum clause, which specifies where disputes will be litigated. For example, the contract might require any suit arising out of the contract to be filed in state B's court, where state B's law is likely to be applied.

One might wonder why a state A court would enforce a choice-of-court clause when this might ultimately result in the enforcement of the state B choice-of-law clause. This question leads us to yet another contract clause— one that requires the *arbitration* of disputes. As discussed in chapter 5, the Federal Arbitration Act mandates enforcement of these clauses by state and federal courts. If state courts must let arbitrators decide cases, they might as well let other courts decide them too, particularly since courts would at least provide litigants with certain basic procedural protections that are absent in arbitration. Enforcing choice-of-court clauses also allows courts to remove complex commercial litigation from their crowded dockets and saves them from having to make the difficult choice between enforcing the contract and enforcing their own law. On the other hand, courts that prefer to keep cases on their dockets may be able to do so only by enforcing choice-of-law clauses.

A company also can avoid state A law by not doing business in state A. If the firm completely avoids A, the U.S. Constitution as well as state juris-diction statutes would protect the firm from being sued in state A's courts.

As we explain, if the firm declines to establish its home office or other local operations in state A, other states handling litigation can more easily decline to apply state A's law under general choice-of-law rules. Either move could inflict economic harm on state A—by making it harder for consumers to buy products they want, diverting potential jobs and clients to other states, and reducing taxes and investments in the state. While state A's failure to enforce choice-of-law clauses might help some pro-regulatory interests in the state, it hurts other local interest groups, which incur costs when firms avoid state A.

The regulating state could simply repeal the offending regulation rather than retain the regulation but enforce choice-of-law clauses. But it might want to keep the regulation for purposes of binding purely local parties for whom it may be impractical to completely avoid the state. Moreover, enforcing the choice-of-law clause offers the parties not just an *escape from* a disfavored law, but also the choice of an *alternative* law, which might still subject the parties to some regulation. The choice-of-law strategy therefore might be a feasible political compromise between interest groups that favor strict regulation and those that favor none.

Courts and legislatures therefore have reasons to enforce choice-of-law clauses *even if* these clauses enable contracting parties to circumvent local law. Parties' *ability* to move gives nations and states an incentive to enforce contracts that let parties legally roam without physically moving—as the B-52s would say, "without wings, without wheels." As discussed further below, this market for law limits the extent to which states and interest groups can regulate parties' contracts. To be sure, the forces that favor enforcement of choice-of-law and -court clauses can be overcome. Groups that favor local state regulation sometimes are able to persuade lawmakers not to enforce these clauses even if this means that some firms and people will avoid the jurisdiction. But the law market has, in several different contexts, proven to be a powerful mechanism for avoiding government regulation of contracts.

Should Courts Enforce These Clauses?

Party mobility does not necessarily prevent courts from enforcing local rules. Thus, in addition to considering the effect of mobility, we need to also address the normative policy question of whether contracting parties *should* be able to opt out of the law that would otherwise apply in favor of the law they choose in their agreements. What if the law that the contract evades was intended to protect one of the contracting parties or third parties from harms imposed by the contract? And what if enforcing the choice-of-law clause enables the parties to opt out of rules they would not be permitted to rewrite directly in their contracts? If a state can prohibit businesses from entering into certain kinds of contracts, it seems odd that firms should be able to avoid this law simply by the sleight of hand of contracting for a different law.

In considering this normative issue, it is important to keep in mind that choice-of-law clauses serve several valuable functions. First, the clauses enable parties to protect themselves from state regulation that imposes costs in excess of its benefits to society. A strong local interest group may favor a law that hurts parties outside the state, including foreign firms, their owners, and consumers in other states who may be forced to pay higher prices as a result of this regulation. For example, notorious "litigation havens" like Madison County, Illinois,[1] thrive on class actions brought under Illinois tort law and procedural rules that bring enormous benefits to local trial lawyers but inflict costs on out-of-state corporations. Although litigation-attracting locales in effect "sell" their legal rules, this is not the sort of law market we have in mind. Litigation havens sell their laws to plaintiffs, who unilaterally choose the location of the lawsuit after the dispute arises. In contrast, we propose facilitating a law market in which law is sold to *both* contracting parties at the time they form their relationship. Our approach could mitigate the problems created by litigation havens because enforcing choice-of-law and -court clauses prevents plaintiffs from selecting the forum, thereby reducing the power of a Madison County judge to, in effect, regulate national firms.

Second, in the real world, choice-of-law decisions are messy, and in many cases it is unclear what law applies without a choice-of-law clause. Choice-of-law clauses reduce uncertainty about the parties' legal rights and obligations and enable firms to operate in many places without being subject to multiple states' laws. These reduced costs may increase the number of profitable transactions and thereby increase social wealth. Also, the clauses may not change the results of many cases because courts in states that prohibit a contract term might apply the more lenient law of a state that has close connections with the parties even without a choice-of-law clause.

To the extent that choice-of-law clauses do enable parties to control which state law governs their activities, one might wonder whether this is the right policy. To answer this question, we must distinguish business-to-business from business-to-consumer contracts. A case in the first category might involve large multinational firms that jointly undertake an international construction project in a developing nation. They may agree to perform their obligations according to the sophisticated commercial law of New York. Surely, there can be little general objection to these parties negotiating through high-priced lawyers over the law that applies to them just as they negotiate other terms. Typically, the clause does no more than simply eliminate a costly source of disagreement in any eventual lawsuit. These clauses might create problems in some contexts, but the general proposition that sophisticated parties should be given some latitude to choose their governing law appears uncontroversial.

Enforcing choice-of-law clauses is more troubling in business-to-consumer contracts, where parties have disparate bargaining power and information. Here, only the business "shops" for law. Consumers never bargain over choice-of-law clauses, probably do not know the clauses are in their contracts, and if they did see them probably would not know what they mean. The contract never explains the clause's true implication—that it negates the legal protection consumers might otherwise receive. Surely, firms should not be able to play this kind of shell game with consumers' legal rights.

But the problem does not seem so bad where markets tend to keep firms honest. While consumers may not bargain over their contracts, they usually have plenty of choice regarding where they spend their money. Moreover, intermediaries can and do constrain a firm's business practices. If a seller chooses the law of some remote country in order to get the benefit of a particularly oppressive rule, some journalist, blogger, or trial lawyer likely will bring the company unfavorable attention and erode the good will it has laboriously built through advertising and customer relations. A firm that hopes to stay in business will not lightly risk its reputation through such a legal trick.

Markets are not perfect, however. Firms in financial trouble could risk their reputations in order to reduce costs, and choice-of-law clauses could deprive consumers of important legal rights. But do the dangers of these clauses justify a broad rule against enforcing choice-of-law clauses that reduce consumers' rights? Even if the clauses may impose costs on consumers in a few cases, somebody has to choose which law applies. Without effective party choice, the parties often race to the courthouse in the hopes of obtaining the first judgment. Naturally, each chooses a court likely to apply the law that it favors. Choice-of-law clauses at least avoid this gamesmanship and provide predictability. Therefore, even where restrictions on enforcing choice-of-law clauses are appropriate, the restrictions should be crafted to preserve the positive effects of contracting for law.

The Impact of the Law Market

Widespread enforcement of choice-of-law clauses powerfully enhances what we call a "law market" whose forces can in turn profoundly affect legal systems. When people can choose their governing laws, a new set of political actors gains influence, and state lawmakers are thereby more effectively disciplined.

These effects can be illustrated by the most pervasive example of a law market: the market for corporate law within the United States. Through the act of "incorporation," the law of the state of incorporation controls matters of the internal governance of the firm, including the legal control and ownership of the firm; the relationships among officers, directors, and shareholders; and the default liabilities of the owners to creditors and to each other. Firms can incorporate in any state they wish, regardless of the location of their headquarters, plants, other assets, or customers. Thus, the act of incorporation is equivalent to a choice-of-law clause that chooses the internal governance law of the incorporating state.

The U.S. courts' ubiquitous acceptance of the choice-of-law rule for internal governance matters provides a sense of what might happen if choice-of-law clauses received comparable recognition. Although firms once needed a state legislature's permission to incorporate, and the states in return imposed many mandatory rules on corporations, that era ended when corporations found that they could choose their place of incorporation and could also cheaply reincorporate in any state they preferred. This choice of place of incorporation in turn helped to bring significant contractual freedom to corporations. Indeed, the state of New Jersey found at the beginning of the twentieth century what can happen when a state tries to impose extensive mandatory rules on its corporations. New Jersey was once the leading jurisdiction for incorporations. When New Jersey governor Woodrow Wilson decided to try to regulate trusts through his state's corporation law, New Jersey swiftly relinquished its lead to Delaware, which remains the incorporations leader today.

The market for corporate law is a very clear, specific example of the general concept of a law market and provides insights into how such a market develops. The incorporation analogy readily applies in other contexts. Most obviously, other types of business associations, such as limited liability companies and limited partnerships, involve corporate-type filings with the same consequence of enabling them to choose the law of the state of organization. If the principle applies to these firms, why not also to other comparably complex long-term contracts, such as joint ventures and franchise arrangements? If so, then other markets for law could develop that would influence the content of state regulation in much the same way as has the competition for corporate law.

The rules of the incorporating state also could apply to other legal problems. Consider, for example, the multiplicity of state professional ethics rules that can apply to a multistate professional firm, including the rules that limit the people who own these firms. Why not apply the incorporating state's law to those issues, rather than forcing far-flung professional firms to comply with the rules in each state in which they have offices? Also, securities fraud and disclosure laws bear on internal governance just as do rules about voting and management. Why not apply the incorporating state's law to these issues rather than forcing the corporation to comply with the state fraud law in each jurisdiction in which an alleged misstatement was made to a shareholder?

For that matter, why cannot parties choose their governing law more broadly in other situations? For example, the traditional choice-of-law rule for real property looks to the jurisdiction in which the property is located. Why should parties not be able to register property interests in *any* state, just as they can for their corporations?

Another example is marriage. The validity of the marriage is typically determined by the law of the place where the couple was married. The courts view this state as having "created" the marriage. But as with corporations, the effect of the creation is simply to apply the creating state's law to the marriage.

Marriage is not quite like incorporating, however. Rules affecting the "internal governance" of a marriage obviously have important effects on society generally because marriage influences social norms. These issues are especially salient now that same-sex marriage has created significant disagreement about the proper definition of marriage. It is one thing to apply California law to its heterosexual marriages, and another to give the same recognition to a California same-sex marriage. Similar problems apply to "covenant" marriage, an option provided in a couple of states which restrict divorce. The television show *Big Love* has drawn attention to plural marriage, and, in some nations, it is legal to take multiple spouses. What happens when these families migrate to the United States?

Despite the difficulties these issues present, enabling a full-fledged market in marriage laws has potential value. A choice-of-law approach lets states recognize local norms by deciding which relationships to sanction, while also encouraging them to enforce at least some aspects of alternative relationships that other states recognize. For example, states could decide to enforce marriage-like property and dissolution rules in "civil unions," but decline to give these relationships all of the state-conferred tax and other benefits of marriage. This allows variation and experimentation in marriage rules. If people are willing to move to states that recognize same-sex marriage, or at least some of its components, then states might compete to attract these residents. A consensus as to acceptable rules might evolve from this competition.

Similar law markets might arise for other contentious social issues. For example, people might choose which state's law applies to their durable power of attorney, which appoints a representative to decide whether continued life support or other end-of-life care will be provided to the drafter. In these and other situations, a market for law may be better than trying to impose a single federal solution.

This book explores the law market across a number of arguably contractual contexts, including business formation, consumer contracts, property laws, and marriage laws. Although the law market can provide beneficial effects, we acknowledge that the law market creates social problems in some contexts and that it may be very difficult to determine when the costs of the law market exceed the benefits. Thus, it is necessary to constrain parties' choice of law, but at the same time very difficult to determine how much constraint is appropriate.

Given the problem of determining the social desirability of choosing any particular law, we propose a procedural tool that promotes choice while enabling states to inhibit the erosion of their laws by choice-of-law clauses. Specifically, our proposal would require the debate over choice-of-law clauses to occur in the legislature, which can provide an effective forum for all relevant interest groups and clearer notice to contracting parties of the applicable rule than is possible through case-by-case adjudication of the enforceability of choice-of-law clauses. Our proposal also would protect the state prohibition of choice of law from erosion by federal courts sitting in diversity.[2] In short, we would achieve a better balance between the law market and state lawmaking power by facilitating party choice in some contexts while also enforcing the preferences of sovereigns where local interest groups in a regulating state convince the sovereign that the law market needs to be shut down.

Beyond the United States

The U.S. federal system enables competition across the states for the provision of state law. Other countries are bound into various kinds of federations that facilitate comparable markets. Most important, the European Union has been moving toward a legal system that has some elements of U.S. federalism. For example, the EU now applies a U.S.-type state-of-incorporation rule instead of the traditional European rule that looks to the corporation's "real seat." This law could be the beginning of broader enforcement of choice-of-law clauses within Europe.

Vibrant international law markets also exist. For example, firms can list their securities on exchanges in the United States or elsewhere outside their home countries, partly to subject themselves to those countries' more stringent rules and thereby reassure their investors. Of course, these firms might *also* be subject to their home country's laws if they continue to trade or have operations there. But it is only a small conceptual step from firms' "opting in" to one country's law to letting them "opt out" of another's. Similarly, because ships can register with any nation and, as a consequence, are subject to that nation's laws, some countries compete with one another for "owner-friendly" ship regulations. And, in a competition for trust funds, some nations have made it easier for wealthy individuals to hide their assets.

Although an international law market has many of the same advantages as a market for state law, the hazards arguably increase. The common Constitution, languages, customs, and history across the U.S. states limit the negative consequences of the choice of a particular law. There may be no such protections in the international setting. Also, extending the law market to the entire globe raises concerns about the extent to which firms can flee to low-tax, low-regulation havens while still enjoying the benefits of the more orderly jurisdictions in which they do much of their business. For example, the relationship of the giant insurer American International Group, Inc., with Bermuda and Barbados called attention to the offshore insurance industry and, more generally, to "corporate havens." In the 2004 election, Senator John Kerry referred to companies that used offshore tax havens as "Benedict Arnolds." If a giant U.S. oil company could "incorporate" one of its deep-sea drilling platforms, a practice known as "seasteading," it might be free of meaningful constraints. Countries may have legitimate interests in regulating such activities as gambling, pornography, spam, and violation of intellectual property rights, all of which can be launched globally through the Web from any place on earth. A viable law market accordingly must accommodate nations' legitimate regulatory interests.

The Politics of the Law Market

A market for law may have significant implications for political theory. Under the traditional view of politics, people who do not like their leaders elect new ones. In other words, they exercise what Albert O. Hirschman has referred to as "voice."[3] However, coordinating the electorate is cumbersome and costly. Moreover, the political marketplace is often dominated by interest groups that can influence politicians with money and votes to act in ways that might not serve the public interest.

Voice is not the only source of political power. People can choose the applicable law by deciding where to live—part of what Hirschman calls "exit." Charles Tiebout famously wrote that the production of so-called public goods—the kind that government supplies—depends not just on what the voters decide, but on the preferences that consumers of public goods reveal by choosing where to live.[4] In other words, Tiebout explicitly recognized a kind of consumer market in governments. There is no reason in principle that this market should not embrace laws which, after all, are an important type of government-provided goods.

The problem with the Tiebout option is that consumers of governments must "buy" the entire bundle of public goods associated with a particular place. They may not be able to find just the right bundle of laws and other public goods. People therefore might have to give up their preferences for laws in order to get their preferred mix of other public goods, or vice versa. Businesses, for example, might like the regulatory environment in Nevada and South Dakota, but not the labor market or the weather.

A law market fueled by party choice solves this problem by letting people choose the law separately from both other government-supplied public goods and other attributes of geographic location.[5] Moreover, a separate market for each type of relationship can form, enabling people and firms to choose the law that suits each aspect of their economic or social lives—that is, Delaware for corporations, New York for commercial contracts, Massachusetts for mutual funds, South Dakota for credit cards—and still live in sunny California, which may have inferior laws in all of these areas but better golf courses and ski slopes.

The law market fundamentally alters the political process to the extent that it makes people "consumers" or "buyers" of laws rather than simply voters. Enhancing the law market with choice-of-law clauses involves more than just a change of perspective, but a real political shift. Politicians care who buys their state's or country's laws for the same reasons they care about other political issues—because they get campaign contributions and votes. But choice-of-law clauses empower different people or groups than would wield political influence in the absence of the law market. For example, if local lawyers lose clients when firms choose the laws of other states, these lawyers will pressure their politicians to enact laws that will be popular in the law market. State legislators will have to produce laws that appeal not just to voters and interest groups in their districts but to people everywhere who bear the costs of those laws by virtue of doing business in the state or owning stock in companies that do business in the state. Empowering these other groups can bring greater balance to the political market. A law market also might serve the interests of smaller groups that the political process otherwise might ignore.

The Jurisprudence of the Law Market

The growth of the law market could significantly affect not just specific rules, but more broadly the nature of legal rules. First consider the market's effect on contract law. If people can contract out of state regulation through choice-of-law clauses, this regulation is no longer really mandatory, that is, it no longer prohibits the parties from entering into certain types of contracts. The law market would create a new category of "quasi-mandatory" rules whose enforcement will depend on the parties' decision to include a choice-of-law clause in their contract. It also invites states to respond with "super-mandatory" laws that effectively instruct state judges not to enforce choice-of-law clauses to the extent that enforcement would enable the parties to avoid the relevant statute.

The law market also has an important constitutional dimension. Without a law market, we face a Hobson's choice between the excesses of local government and those of federal control. Powerful interest groups within an individual state may be able to impose their preferences in ways that threaten individual liberties. The federal government then must step in to protect individual rights. But federal intervention may threaten the diversity of views that otherwise would flourish in a federal system. The law market offers a compromise between these unappealing alternatives by enabling legal diversity while protecting minority views. For example, as discussed above, instead of either compelling or forbidding states to recognize same-sex marriage, some states might forbid locally celebrated same-sex marriage but nevertheless recognize some or all incidents of same-sex marriages created under other states' laws. Recognition of same-sex marriage rights might turn on people's willingness to move to states that provide these benefits. The operation of the law market might persuade the Supreme Court to refrain from using the Constitution to take sides in contentious social debates. We are not suggesting that people should be required to move in order to receive basic legal protections. Rather, the ability to pressure at least some states to provide marriage rights changes the calculus faced by the Court.

More broadly, the law market can preserve an important role for states and other relatively small jurisdictions. As discussed above, courts' determination of which jurisdiction's laws apply seem almost random in our highly mobile society. Worse, businesses and individuals easily might find themselves subject to the laws of multiple jurisdictions and forced to comply with the most stringent law. Federal or uniform law may seem to be the only feasible solution. Indeed, businesses often favor federal law as a way out of the maze of state laws that confronts them. But while federal or uniform laws reduce some problems, they may create others by reducing the diversity of laws and parties' ability to avoid bad laws. The law market gives parties a way out of the tangle of different local laws while at the same time preserving legal diversity.

As already mentioned but deserving of repeated emphasis, the challenge is to foster the beneficial aspects of the law market with enforcement of choice-of-law clauses while simultaneously protecting states' ability to impose reasonable regulation. The challenge is particularly acute given that there is no way to determine objectively which regulations are reasonable and which are not. Chapter 10 proposes a federal contractual choice-of-law statute that would ensure the enforcement of choice-of-law clauses without undermining states' ability to regulate. Our proposal is a procedural mechanism that will tend to contribute to more efficient regulations without requiring the federal government to determine which state regulations are "reasonable."

Outline of the Book

This book begins by describing the general structure of the law market and the extent to which parties can choose their governing law. Chapter 2 discusses the policy arguments for and against a vigorous law market. Chapter 3 summarizes the basic system of conflict of laws in the United States and the rules governing enforcement of choice-of-law clauses. Chapter 4 discusses specific mechanisms and political forces that influence the law market. It focuses on state judges' and legislators' incentives to enable parties to circumvent local law by choosing foreign law. Their incentives depend to some extent on the parties' ability to control who will adjudicate their claim and to move physically when judges do not enforce their contractual choices. This chapter also discusses the incentives of lawmakers and others, including lawyers, to supply a menu of efficient laws from which parties can choose. Chapter 4 includes a discussion of empirical evidence that demonstrates the operation of the law market. Chapter 5 discusses the role of arbitration in promoting a law market.

The book then explores specific applications of the principles of contractual choice of law. Chapter 6 discusses what we view as the paradigmatic case for the law market: the rule applying the law of the state of incorporation to the internal governance of corporations. This chapter can be viewed as setting the stage for the later analysis of the limits of enforcing contractual choice. The basic question is this: if contractual choice can be ubiquitously and strongly enforced in this context, why not in others? Chapter 7 discusses enforcement of contractual choice of law in consumer transactions. Consumer contracts present a significant challenge for law markets because of the arguably unilateral nature of contractual choice. Chapters 8 and 9 move the discussion beyond the traditional contract settings in which choice-of-law clauses have been widely used to consider how party choice might work in the contexts of marriage, surrogacy contracts, living wills, and property law. Part of the reason that we explore these legal areas is to emphasize that party choice has differing implications for differing areas of law. As a consequence, the jurisdictional nexus between the parties and the law that they choose might legitimately differ across these contexts. And, states might legitimately choose to accept the operation of the law market in some of these contexts while attempting to shut it down in others.

Chapter 10 discusses mechanisms for facilitating the law market by enhancing certainty through the enforcement of choice-of-law clauses. Specifically, it discusses coordinating state enforcement of contractual choice of law through uniform, model, and federal laws. It also proposes a specific federal statute for enforcing contractual choice that draws on the examples and theories presented in earlier chapters.

Chapter 11 concludes the book with a discussion of the general implications of our analysis for the future of the U.S. federal system and for contract law.

2

Policy Arguments

Many laws improve our lives. Some, however, serve ends we do not value, while others serve valuable ends but at unjustifiably high costs. The costs and benefits of any particular law are difficult to determine precisely, especially when people profoundly disagree over the goals and values that government should promote. Given this uncertainty, some scholars argue that good laws can best be promoted by ignoring debates about the substantive merits of laws and instead carefully constructing the process by which those laws are enacted, administered, and enforced. Examples of procedural rules that tend to generate better laws include rules designed to increase the diversity of voices represented in the lawmaking process and those that protect the integrity of processes by which we select our public representatives.

Choice-of-law systems are a type of procedural mechanism that can influence the quality of laws. To illustrate, suppose that a consumer is injured in state A while using a product that was purchased in state B but manufactured by the defendant in state C. Which law should apply to determine whether the company is liable to the consumer for a defectively manufactured product? If the law of the manufacturer's principal place of business applies, then manufacturers can shield themselves from liability by locating their operations in places that provide consumers with little protection. States competing for factories might be willing to provide a low duty of care for manufacturers even if some consumers might be hurt, especially when a majority of those consumers reside in other states.

If, instead, the law of the consumer's residence applies to determine the manufacturer's liabilities, then states might end up imposing inefficiently onerous standards of care. Manufacturers cannot force consumers in high-liability states to pay the increased cost of higher liability because goods are mobile, making the residence of an injured owner of a product unknowable at the time that the product is sold. As a result, when some states have low and others high consumer protections, the manufacturer may charge all consumers a price somewhere between the price if all states had low protections and the price if all had high protections. This means that consumers in the low-protection states end up subsidizing the consumers in the high-protection states. This leads consumers in the low-protection states to lobby for the most protective laws in order to reverse the subsidy, and consumer product prices rise further. Each state might then compete with other states in an effort to produce the greatest protections. In the end, perhaps no state's citizens will receive a subsidy but yet all states would provide for excessive liability in the sense that consumers do not value their protections at the market prices.

Finally, if the law of the place of the sale of the product determines the liability level, then each state could provide the protections that its citizens prefer on average while the manufacturer could set different prices in different states, based on the protections provided in each state. Of course, citizens might travel to other states to purchase differing bundles of protection and product price, but presumably these choices reflect those citizens' differing preferences. Of the three choice-of-law options mentioned, the place-of-sale rule has the greatest potential for ensuring that states' product liability laws fit citizen preferences while ensuring that each state's citizens internalize the costs of those protections.

An alternative mechanism for encouraging states to provide desirable laws is to enable parties to contract for the law that they prefer to govern their contract. The parties presumably know better than the state what protections they want and how much they are willing to pay for them. Importantly, choice-of-law clauses enable parties to obtain laws that suit their relationship even better than a particular state's law can, because at best even well-designed rules suit the *average* citizen, not each individual citizen. In addition, choice-of-law clauses enable parties to avoid poorly designed laws. This chapter explains how party choice also can work to prevent lawmakers from enacting bad laws.

Although party choice can create potential benefits, it can also impose net costs where a party is forced or manipulated into agreeing that a state's law should apply or where the chosen law harms others not party to the contract. In each of these situations, party choice can also fail to effectively discipline lawmakers. This book explores both the potential benefits and the limits of creating a market for law by facilitating party choice.

Before describing how the law market operates, this chapter explains more generally why states sometimes adopt inferior laws. This chapter also explains why party choice can help to minimize the costs of those laws and reminds the reader that unbridled party choice can, in certain circumstances, impose harmful effects on society, which makes limits appropriate in certain circumstances. In some cases, limits to party choice are necessary in order to prevent other harmful influences on the lawmaking process.

Why Are There Bad Laws?

This book refers throughout to "bad" laws as those which impose social costs on regulated parties or others in excess of the laws' benefits. Although we may occasionally opine on the desirability of particular types of regulations, it is important to emphasize that our approach to party choice reflects our belief that often it is not possible to objectively evaluate the merits of a law. Because of this indeterminacy, we advocate procedural rules—in this book, rules regarding the conflict of laws—that can work to systematically improve the quality of laws without requiring agreement over their merits. But despite the difficulty of proving definitively that any one law is bad, it is important to understand the general causes of the creation and persistence of bad laws.

To understand the benefits of a law market, it is first necessary to understand why bad laws exist without a law market. Laws can be problematic as a result of two basic problems that plague most legal systems: (1) legal rules are subject to selfish pressures by interest groups and lawmakers; and (2) no single set of lawmakers can provide laws that are perfectly suited to the individuals they govern. Each problem is discussed below.

Interest Groups' Influence on Lawmaking

Individuals and businesses differ dramatically in their abilities to organize, gather information, and mobilize voters, campaign contributions, and other influences on legislators. In general, groups that are better able to organize people and resources are better able to demand that laws reflect their interests, sometimes even at the expense of the electorate as a whole.[1] For example, taxpayers are often too uninformed and disorganized to prevent their tax bills from rising to subsidize investors in particular industries. In contrast, lawyers are very effective advocates for self-serving laws because lawyers are already organized for various purposes: to help develop ethics rules, to discuss matters of mutual interest, and to negotiate collective benefits, such as health and malpractice insurance coverage. They can act collectively for political goals at little additional cost as a "by-product" of their nonpolitical activities.[2]

Groups with fairly homogeneous interests tend to be better able to mobilize politically than those with more diverse concerns.[3] And groups that are based within a state or other political entity often can organize more cheaply and effectively to press for favorable laws from that entity than can groups based elsewhere.[4] Although these factors influence a group's political power, they do not necessarily indicate whether the group deserves legal protection or benefit.

The organizationally disadvantaged will not always lose in the political process. Sometimes, an organized group can indirectly represent the interests of individuals who have little direct influence in the lawmaking process. For example, unskilled teenage workers might not be able effectively to organize and lobby against minimum wage increases, which cost them jobs, but employers in many industries can organize to fight the increase.

In addition, otherwise weak groups sometimes can overcome high organization costs when the potential costs of detrimental laws become sufficiently large. When the subsidies to interest groups get big enough to impose a substantial burden on taxpayers, even this diffuse group, perhaps led by watchdogs, can take effective action. Actual or potential opposition groups therefore may be able to limit wealth transfers from weaker to stronger interest groups. In general, competition among organized interest groups may (but will not always) constrain the enactment of bad laws.[5]

Sometimes, interest-group lobbying focuses on the regulation of particular contract terms. Most contract laws provide only default terms in the sense that the parties can replace them with different rules in the contract if they prefer. For example, courts will assume that the buyer is obligated to pay for a product when it is delivered, but the contract could instead require the buyer to prepay for the product. Because default rules can be varied by contract, they are not worth significant lobbying by interest groups. Interest groups care more about mandatory rules, those that the parties may not bargain around. For example, franchisees have lobbied state legislatures for laws that restrict termination of the franchise, labor unions lobby for minimum wage and maximum hour laws, and shippers advocate imposing competitive restraints on foreign shippers.

Even a mandatory rule may not effectively transfer wealth if a party can somehow undo the transfer. For example, a franchisor restricted in its ability to cancel a franchise presumably could recoup its consequent lost profits by raising the price of the franchise.[6] And an employer that must pay its employees more money per hour might make up the difference by spending less on fringe benefits, bonuses, staff lounges, or office parties. But, mandatory rules do often bite. The party subject to the regulation may be unable to pass the costs along. Moreover, with or without bite, those who benefit from a mandatory term may differ from those who bear the costs. For example, while franchise termination protections may increase the price to all franchisees of obtaining a franchise, those who otherwise would have been terminated are still better off with the legal protections than without them.

Lawmakers' Limited Knowledge

Even legislators who are perfectly motivated to provide efficient laws can nevertheless produce or retain bad laws because it is often difficult to know what laws are appropriate for all of the people who are subject to them. Consider some of the questions a well-motivated lawmaker might need to answer before passing a law to rectify an apparent problem:

1. How much will it cost to comply with the law?
2. To whom, and to what transactions, should the law apply?
3. What effects might the law have on contracts or market devices?
4. Is the market likely to better adjust on its own without regulation?
5. Might technologies or market devices be developed in the future to deal with the problem if the law is enacted? What if the law is not enacted?
6. Under what, if any, circumstances should people be able to opt out of the law?
7. Should the law have a "sunset" provision so we can see how it works before making it permanent?

Some legislatures, such as the U.S. Congress, have large staffs and committee structures that enable them to address these questions effectively. Many state, local, and even national legislatures often lack this luxury. Moreover, while expert staff can better equip a legislature to respond to these complicated questions, deference to this expertise can provide an opening for interest-group influence on the experts.

Can Judges Constrain Bad Laws?

Judges have tools to help constrain the costs of bad laws. First, they can interpret ambiguous laws to promote the public interest rather than the interests of the narrow interest groups responsible for its promulgation.[7] Often, a law passed to benefit a narrow interest group will claim in its preamble that it benefits the public interest. These proclamations are intended merely to enable legislators to provide benefits to the interest group without suffering political damage. But the courts can minimize interest-group wealth transfers by taking the legislators at their word and interpreting the statute consistently with its stated purpose. Alternatively, they can interpret bad laws narrowly to cabin the situations in which they impose inefficient costs. Finally, if they cannot negate bad laws through interpretation, courts can consider striking down the laws as unconstitutional.

Although judges can and sometimes do exercise their authority to temper the costs of bad laws, for several reasons they cannot alone protect against bad laws. First, judges may be directly or indirectly subject to legislative influence. In South Carolina, for example, the legislature appoints state supreme court judges and almost all of those judges are themselves former legislators.[8] The legislature may control judges' appointments, tenure, and salaries. Alternatively, lawmakers can often limit judicial interference by passing clear laws that avoid interpretive and constitutional infirmities.

Second, judges are often not immune to interest-group influence. Elected judges are vulnerable to being voted out by unhappy litigants or their lawyers. Because most voters pay little attention to judicial candidates, the most intensely interested group—trial lawyers—can dominate judicial elections. The problem is especially acute where judicial candidates cannot run on a party slate, or where judicial elections are held on a different date than the general elections, when only the most personally interested participants will vote. Rural state court districts that attract large class actions may be particularly plagued by the dominating electoral influence of local plaintiff class-action lawyers.[9]

Third, interest groups can influence both elected and unelected judges because judges often lack the resources necessary to fully explore the legal issues in the cases before them. When an interest group presents itself in court as a litigant or an amicus favoring a litigant's position, its ability to spend more money defending its assertions can influence both the outcome of the case and how the public perceives it. Also, because judges are even more constrained than legislators in gathering and evaluating the information necessary to produce efficient laws, most judges will defer to legislative statements about the desirability of particular laws.

Spillover Problems and Cross-Border Firms

The risk that legislation creates bad law rises when the law benefits locals at the expense of people and firms located outside the state. Laws often have effects that spill over state borders. For example, a state may decide not to regulate a local polluter in order to retain local jobs or tax revenues so long as these benefits exceed the local harm that the activity causes. If much of the pollution causes harm outside the state, then those costs are often not taken into account through interest-group lobbying. To provide another example, a state might protect local franchisees against termination by franchisors mostly located outside the state even though these protections may impose costs on the franchisors by giving them no effective way to prevent dilution of their brand. Those affected outside the borders may be unable to fight effectively against the proposed law because they have higher costs than in-state groups of being informed about the law or organizing to oppose it.

The spillover problem is especially acute for interstate or international firms that are subject to the potentially burdensome regulation of several states. For example, a lawyer practicing in a Florida office of a New York law firm might be subject to the professional responsibility rules of both New York and Florida though neither state would impose all of those restrictions on lawyers and firms.[10] And an insurance company attempting to operate in both England and the United States might be subject to differing regulations regarding the terms of its insurance contracts.[11] The Internet, mobile telephones, and computer networks let even small firms operate nationally and internationally. Even if each state's bundle of laws is sensible, the laws as applied cumulatively to interstate and international activities can prove unduly burdensome. Expanding interstate and international communication, travel, and business increases both the challenge of and need for sensibly allocating sovereign authority.

Enforcing choice-of-law clauses could partially solve this problem by enabling firms to deal with customers under a single state's laws. Courts are increasingly recognizing the benefits of this approach. For example, in enforcing a clause in a student loan agreement that chose the laws of the lender's state against a student who resided in the forum, a court noted that "[i]t is both rational and reasonable for a lender to operate consistently under the laws of its home state, rather than be forced to operate under 51 different laws."[12] The next section also explores other benefits of party choice.

The Law Market as a Potential Solution

A solution to both imperfect and multiple governing laws is to create a market for law by allowing people to provide in their contracts for the application of a particular state's law to govern their relationship. This section begins to consider some of the general and positive attributes of a market strengthened by the enforcement of choice-of-law clauses.

Note first, however, the difference between the solution that we propose— enabling parties to choose their governing law at the time of contracting—and forum shopping at the time of litigation. If plaintiffs can unilaterally choose the forum (and thereby influence the governing law) after a dispute arises, this is more likely to transfer wealth between the parties than to increase the society's wealth. If the courts have incentives to cater to the interests of plaintiffs or their lawyers in order to attract litigation, this can adversely affect development of the laws and procedures that govern litigation.

For example, Lynn LoPucki documented the competition by federal bankruptcy judges for the most complex cases.[13] Because the bankrupt firms and their lawyers substantially control which bankruptcy court hears the case, some bankruptcy judges have adopted policies that cater to the debtors and their lawyers at creditors' expense. These judges have approved excessively generous attorneys' fees, allowed debtors' managers to stay in control of firms for long periods, and have overlooked other procedures detrimental to debtors' interests. Even if only a few judges compromise their actions to attract cases, those judges obtain a disproportionately large share of the bankruptcy cases. The result is a kind of corruption of the litigation system. By contrast, a forum (or law) selected in a contract between the affected parties is much more likely to reflect the parties' mutual interests, which has the effect of increasing efficiency and therefore wealth. In fact, enforcing these contracts can eliminate the sort of perverse forum competition that LoPucki criticizes.

Our analysis of the market for law begins with the role of party mobility in producing a kind of market for public goods, or government services. We then extend that market concept to consider markets for law, in which people select among given packages of legal rules, and, in turn, these selections also help to shape the laws that states offer. International securities regulation provides an illustration of the market for law in action. This chapter then discusses the benefit to parties of choosing among state law packages of default rules and adds an additional benefit of this law market: the opportunity for experimentation to discover the best laws.

The Tiebout Model

People who lack the ability to directly influence laws sometimes can influence the law applied to them by exiting states with bad laws and moving to states with better ones.[14] The exit option was explored in a famous article by Charles Tiebout.[15] Tiebout argued that public, or government-provided, goods and services, including a jurisdiction's laws, ultimately can reflect residents' preferences. This result holds as long as (1) people can move without costs to places with government packages they prefer; (2) communities offer a variety of packages of public goods and levels of taxation from which people can choose; (3) people know about these differences; and (4) any community can offer these options without affecting other communities.

Unfortunately, few of Tiebout's assumptions hold in the real world. For example, states may impose taxes and tariffs or exit restrictions that impede firms from moving between jurisdictions.[16] Even if people know that a government offers a better package of services, the costs of moving may exceed the benefits; jobs, family, and even inertia tie people to where they live. We offer a partial solution to the problem of costly moves in the next subsection.

The Market for Law

In Tiebout's model, parties choose among a fixed set of public goods packages. In other words, governments decide what services they wish to provide to residents, and people gravitate to those places that provide the services that they desire. Tiebout never explored the fact that people's choices also may affect government-provided services, including laws. Thus, the exit option may not only give people and firms a way to avoid undesirable laws, but also provide a mechanism for pressuring governments to change those laws.

One way to enhance the jurisdictional competition that mobility generates is to enable people to obtain the benefits of desirable laws without actually physically moving from one location to another. Specifically, parties to contracts often can choose their desired law by inserting choice-of-law clauses in their agreements. The clauses provide that the parties' relationship or contract will be governed by a particular state's law.

Enforcing choice-of-law clauses dramatically expands parties' jurisdictional choice. For example, a small business in Delaware, whose corporate law is designed for large corporations, may never be able to persuade the Delaware legislature to enact a law that reflects its needs. But the firm can contract to be governed by the corporate law of North Carolina, which might better reflect the needs of closely held firms. Because of this enhanced choice, contractual choice of law can trigger a competitive process that potentially produces legal improvements even for those people who lack both voice and physical exit options in any single state.

When people contract for the law that will govern their relationship, they choose both the present law and the law that they predict will be in place through the life of their contractual duties. A business therefore must consider the likelihood that a chosen legislature will enact future laws at the behest of interest groups, such as large manufacturers, start-up dot.com companies, or labor organizations. This concern is particularly acute regarding potential laws that would change or abrogate the contracts into which parties already have entered. Firms can assess the risks of undesirable legal change based on the legislature's past conduct, the characteristics of the electorate, and the state's constitutional provisions. For example, Delaware has a long history of stable corporate legislation and a lack of strong antibusiness interest groups, and this legal stability is enhanced by a constitutional provision requiring a supermajority legislative vote to amend its statutes.[17]

The power to exit influences legal systems because it creates powerful local interests that benefit from preventing exit or from attracting newcomers. We refer to these groups as "exit-affected" interest groups. The exit option motivates antiregulatory interest groups that "stand in" for the people and businesses that are directly hurt by a proposed law but are too weak by themselves to prevent its adoption. For example, the next subsection describes the role of exit-affected interest groups in tempering the implementation of the Sarbanes-Oxley Act as applied to foreign firms. Legislators have to balance these groups' demands against those of the interest groups that favor regulation. Mobility therefore provides an indirect voice to outsiders and a stronger voice to insiders who will be burdened by a proposed law.

An apparent problem with exit through choice-of-law clauses is that these clauses can undermine good as well as bad laws. If state regulation is justified, then the states need to be able to bar regulated parties from contracting around the statutes. The problem is ameliorated to some extent by the fact that "choosing law" and "evading law" are not always equivalent. If a person evades a law, she attempts to opt into a state of "lawlessness," where no governmental authority constrains her actions. By choosing law, she instead opts into the laws of another government. The chosen government's laws usually reflect an effort to address the same concerns as those addressed by the government whose laws are avoided. While the two governments might ultimately resolve the issue in different ways, there is no a priori reason to assume that the chosen government's resolution of the problem is any less legitimate than the avoided government's resolution. To help ensure that choice of law is not used to evade law, the competition for law might be subject to the constraint that the parties must be willing to accept entire bundles, or sets, of laws. In other words, the parties would not be able to avoid only the mandatory provision of the law they don't like while accepting the rest of the state's laws.[18]

An Illustration: Securities Regulation

To see how a law market might produce better laws, consider the example of laws regulating the sale and trading of corporate securities. This might seem like an odd example because there is no apparent "market" for such regulation. As discussed more fully in chapter 6, firms are subject to the securities laws of each jurisdiction in which their securities trade, and therefore do not seem to be able to shop separately for law. But securities regulation actually does illustrate how a market for law can develop, as well as the effect such a market can have on law.

The market for law enters the picture with the concept of "cross-listing." Since the mid-1980s, many firms have chosen to trade their shares in markets other than in their home countries, even though this cross-listing can subject the firms to the regulations of *both* their own country and the country where the shares are initially listed. The leading explanation for why the firms do this is that by subjecting themselves to the higher level of regulation in the cross-listing country, the firms in effect "bond" their trustworthiness, thereby enabling them to raise money at a lower price all over the world.[19]

When these firms cross-list, securities professionals, lawyers, and accountants in the cross-listing country earn significant additional fees. These groups therefore have an incentive to press their countries to offer attractive laws. Moreover, securities industry professionals in the home countries of cross-listing firms have an incentive to urge their countries to compete to prevent cross-listing in order to retain more business. The result can be a global competition for high-quality securities regulation.[20]

The cross-listing competition also can constrain overregulation in the cross-listing country. The cross-listing country might increase its regulation to the point that regulatory costs for cross-listing firms exceed the benefits the firms get from bonding their disclosures. While firms based in the cross-listing country may be stuck there in the sense that it is too costly for them to escape local law by moving their operations abroad, cross-listing firms are nevertheless highly mobile in the sense that they can simply decide not to trade in the cross-listing country. Given the local benefits conferred by cross-listing firms, the host country has a strong incentive to refrain from overregulation that drives them away.

This dynamic is illustrated by the effect on the cross-listing market of the U.S. Sarbanes-Oxley Act of 2002 (SOX) and its regulatory aftermath. The SOX dramatically increases the federal regulation of corporate governance by, for example, requiring independent audit committees and requiring disclosures of managers' responsibilities for setting up internal control and financial reporting structures and procedures. The SOX creates particular problems for foreign-based firms listed in the United States because of the inherent differences between the governance law applied to U.S. and non–U.S. firms. Accordingly, for many of these firms, the increased compliance costs under SOX may not be worth the bonding benefits.

Soon after Congress adopted SOX, there was an outcry from non–U.S. firms indicating that it might threaten cross-listings.[21] Moreover, there is significant evidence that the enactment of SOX negatively affected the value of foreign firms subject to U.S. securities laws.[22] These developments spurred loud calls for the revision or elimination of some SOX requirements, particularly by securities professionals. The U.S. Securities and Exchange Commission responded to these concerns by issuing some limited exemptions for non–U.S. firms. For example, the SEC partially exempted foreign firms from the SOX requirement for independent audit committees,[23] which threatened to impose high costs on non–U.S. firms that had different governance structures from their U.S. counterparts.

Despite these exemptions, cross-listing in the United States declined. As summarized by a report by the Committee on Capital Markets Regulation,[24] the U.S. share of funds raised globally dropped from 50 percent in 2000 to 5 percent in 2005. Initial public offerings of foreign firms in the United States dropped over the same period from 37 percent to 10 percent. The United States' share of total equity raised in the top ten countries dropped to 27.9 percent in 2006 from 41 percent in 1995. The United States lost $50 billion in capital raised, indicating a loss of $2.8 billion in U.S. underwriting fees and $3.3 billion a year in trading revenues. A subsequent report by the same committee showed a continued exit from and avoidance of U.S. markets.[25] The decline of the cross-listing industry in the United States, and the widespread perception that this decline was linked to the adoption of SOX, continues to spur calls to roll back SOX, or at least its application to foreign firms.[26]

In general, the history of SOX and cross-listing illustrates several aspects of the law market. First, it shows how even what would seem to be the most mandatory laws must compete in the law market given the increasingly global nature of competition. This competition can increase the level and quality of regulation, as shown by the rise of cross-listing firms. Second, SOX's aftermath indicates that regulated firms may exit in the face of increased regulatory costs. Third, this history shows how the financial impact of exit on interest groups in regulating countries ultimately can cause states to make legal changes that reduce regulatory costs. Although these changes may be provoked by the most mobile firms, they have the potential of reducing costs for all firms, including those that have higher costs of exit.

Contractual Choice of Default Rules

Choice-of-law clauses can be used not only to avoid mandatory laws, but also to choose default rules, or those rules that can be written directly into a contract itself. Rather than incur the costs of drafting individualized rules for a contract, the parties could pick a state's bundle of default rules. When states provide sensible default rules, they end up subsidizing the costs to the parties of drafting their own contracts. When parties can choose their own law, states can specialize in providing off-the-rack default rules specially suited for particular industries. For example, Connecticut historically has provided law particularly well suited for insurance contracts, and Delaware has specialized in the law of corporations and other business associations. A state's investment in lawmaking can therefore benefit not only its residents, but also those from other states and countries.

Off-the-rack rules are particularly important where the parties need not just one simple term but a *set* of default rules, such as the terms of a business association. These rules involve complex tradeoffs between alternative contract devices. For example, business association investors may want either to directly participate in management or to delegate control to others. Each situation calls for a different set of voting rules. Also, delegating control to managers requires rules for ensuring that the managers do not cheat the owners. The parties may want to set up devices for suing the managers, guidelines for monitoring and control by a board of directors, and rules for meetings, voting, transfer of shares, and so forth. These detailed contracts may be very costly to write. Parties therefore might be better off choosing from ready-made sets of terms, particularly in small firms or in small, transitory transactions (i.e., retail sales).

Instead of choosing a state law, contracting parties might agree to be governed by a form that is drafted by a private organization, such as the American Bar Association, or an international lawmaking organization, such as the International Institute for the Unification of Private Law, which created the UNIDROIT contract principles.[27] Also, firms can craft forms for themselves if they can spread the costs over many transactions, such as when a franchisor creates a uniform contract to govern its relationship with many franchisees. However, parties that create their own contract terms may face more uncertainty regarding the interpretation of those terms than parties that choose a state's off-the-rack default or other standard terms.

Experimentation and Discovery

The jurisdictional competition fostered by choice-of-law clauses encourages states and parties to experiment with new legal rules. Experimentation can help legal systems to generate better legal rules. Party choice both enables parties to avoid the results of failed experiments and provides feedback to the states regarding the appeal of the new laws. Consider, for example, the relatively recent development of limited liability companies (LLCs). LLCs provide limited liability to the firm's equity owners without forcing them to incur the extra burden of the corporate tax. Wyoming adopted the first LLC statute in

1976 at the request of one influential firm. When this statute received a tax ruling that firms formed under it could, like partnerships, avoid corporate taxation, then firms formed more LLCs, and states passed additional and more varied LLC statutes. In the end, all states adopted LLC statutes, and the IRS eventually ruled that any closely held firm could choose to be taxed as a partnership. This state experimentation was undoubtedly facilitated by the fact that firms could choose any state they wished in which to incorporate.[28] In addition, a state is more willing to experiment with new laws if its citizens can contract for other laws in the event that the experiment fails. Put differently, experimentation is less risky to undertake with choice-of-law clauses.

Potential Problems with the Law Market

Allowing parties to exit from unfavorable laws can sometimes involve social costs, and when it does, jurisdictional competition can spur a "race to the bottom."[29] This can happen where states or nations compete to attract parties to contracts that impose costs on third parties, or that benefit powerful contract drafters at the expense of weaker contracting parties. The following subsections explore these problems.

Negative Externalities

Contracting parties could choose law that benefits them at the expense of those whose interests are not represented in the negotiation of the contract. Consider, for example, a contract for the production and marketing of child pornography. Suppose that child pornography is illegal in the United States but not in some foreign country. Suppose, to be slightly fanciful, that a group forms its own country, "Seastead," on a gigantic deep sea oil-drilling platform that permits the production and distribution of child pornography.[30] What if the financiers, producers, and marketers who are parties to these contracts made them subject to the law of Seastead? Such contracts clearly are abhorrent and therefore unenforceable in the United States. Surely, the parties should not be able to end-run U.S. law simply by contracting for the law of Seastead.

Third parties need protection only when they lack information or other means to adjust their activities as a consequence of the contract. For example, while a firm's managers choose the state of incorporation, and that law potentially could hurt the corporation's creditors, creditors can protect themselves because they have notice of the debtor's state of incorporation and can therefore price the risks of the incorporation law when setting the interest rate on loans to the corporation.[31] To the extent that parties can protect their interests, the mere fact that choice-of-law clauses affect nonparties to the contract should not justify refusing to enforce the choice-of-law clauses. On the other hand, parties unable to protect themselves may need the protection of the state through the non-enforcement of choice-of-law clauses.

Questionable Party Choice

Sometimes, mandatory rules are designed to protect a contracting party from the other party's superior bargaining power or information. In business-to-business contracts, the parties are typically represented by lawyers and have strong incentives and ability to negotiate the terms of their contract, including the choice-of-law clause. Moreover, in some industries, trade publications cover trends in choice-of-law and forum clauses so parties are relatively well informed about the import of particular choices.[32] In this context, therefore, the parties have the information and the advice they need to negotiate mutually beneficial contracting terms, including choice-of-law clauses. On the other hand, where a company drafts an agreement and offers it to a consumer on a take-it-or-leave-it basis, the consumer may lack both the knowledge and the leverage to ensure that the law chosen protects her interests. In this case, the doctrine of unconscionability may enable a court to throw out unfairly one-sided terms.[33]

Courts and legislators should not necessarily regulate or refuse to enforce all nonnegotiated consumer contracts. The fact that a company offers terms on a take-it-or-leave-it basis does not alone suggest that the company can dictate the terms of a contract. For example, if the company's competitors are in a position to offer consumers better terms, then consumers can shop for the terms they prefer. Thus, the take-it-or-leave-it nature of contract terms may simply reflect that it is not cost efficient for the company to customize the terms of its agreements with each of its customers. Even if the terms are both take-it-or-leave-it and one-sided, market competition can discipline a company's exercise of its rights under a contract. Companies routinely stop short of insisting on their rights under the contract because they want to maintain their reputations for providing effective customer service. They might contract for one-sided terms solely in order to be able to deal with unreasonable customers without incurring the expense of having to litigate "reasonableness."[34] If the company incurs some reputational or other market penalty for unreasonably enforcing one-sided terms, then courts and legislatures may not need to intervene. On the other hand, if the company faces limited competition, there may be some justification for refusing to enforce one-sided terms.

Consider now a slightly different situation, where a company drafts the contract so as to hide an important term or its meaning from the other party. Choice-of-law clauses arguably fall into this category because, even if they are conspicuous, often only the drafter is aware of the legal importance of applying a particular set of laws. Competition may discipline the company's choice of term even in this situation. For example, automobile companies compete on product quality, price, warranties, and available product features, and consumers are aware of and make purchasing decisions based on a comparison of each of these items. On the other hand, consumers are less likely to pay attention to the choice of a bundle of unknown legal rules that would apply only in the unlikely circumstance that the consumer actually ends up litigating with the company. If consumers do not care, firms may not actively compete over the term. In chapter 7, we will discuss in more depth the question of whether markets discipline choice-of-law clauses.

Even this situation is not as bleak for consumers as it might first appear. Consumer groups and consumer-oriented publications can monitor these and other potentially unfair terms as well as the jurisdictions that have consumer-unfriendly laws. Indeed, a relatively small percentage of knowledgeable consumers can effectively discipline terms in a competitive market.[35] Although few consumer groups have focused on choice-of-law clauses, this may just indicate that companies are not using these clauses to hurt consumers. If anything, as discussed above, states may be too inclined to impose excessive regulation on out-of-state companies for the benefit of in-state consumers. If so, firms' use of choice-of-law clauses tempers the costs of consumer protection laws. In any event, any firm that faces competition has an incentive to avoid harm to its reputation by being exposed as tricking consumers.

One might object that the real problem with choice-of-law clauses is that they tend to circumvent state laws intended to redistribute some contract gain from large, wealthy corporations to poorer parties. Contract law, however, is a poor mechanism for achieving redistribution.[36] As long as parties are generally free to contract, regulating some contracting terms will not prevent the stronger party from taking back some of its losses through unregulated terms. For example, if state laws restrict a franchisor's ability to terminate a franchisee, then the protected franchisees can earn more profits by cutting corners and investing less in maintaining the value of the franchised brand. However, eventually, the powerful franchisor can exercise his superior bargaining power to take back the franchisee's extra profits by raising the royalty rates or the payment required for supplies. The state ultimately may accomplish no more than to force the parties to replace a relatively cheap form of contracting profitably with a more expensive contracting scheme.

The important point for present purposes is not that mandatory rules are always wrongheaded, but that courts or legislatures should not necessarily assume that a mandatory rule in one state should prevent enforcement of a clause choosing the law of another state. Suppose, for example, that a buyer from state X, which prohibits the enforcement of class-action waivers, contracts to purchase a product from a seller in state Y, which permits these waivers. Since the two states have come to different determinations regarding the costs and benefits of these provisions, it may not be clear why state X's law rather than that of state Y should dictate the case's outcome. Even where the mandatory law would clearly apply under default choice-of-law rules, the costs of allowing the parties to contract for more permissive law may be small compared to the benefits of using the law market.

On the other hand, parties clearly should not always be able to circumvent mandatory rules with choice-of-law clauses. Any proposed treatment of these terms must acknowledge a role for regulating states to attempt to protect their regulations against the eroding effects of choice of law. We will discuss where lines should be drawn throughout the book and particularly in chapters 7 and 10.

3

Choice-of-Law Principles

This chapter focuses on the legal treatment of choice of law to illustrate one important function of choice-of-law clauses: predictability. Without these clauses, the parties must rely on a morass of legal rules that give them at best vague ideas about what rules apply to their relationships. Parties need to know the governing law prior to the start of litigation. Indeed, the recent trend toward the enforcement of choice-of-law clauses stems in part from a general appreciation for parties' needs for certainty regarding the law that governs their actions.

This chapter describes the choice-of-law theories that scholars have developed and courts have applied since the early twentieth century, with an emphasis on the current choice-of-law rules for contracts. The current system is unsatisfying because it leaves parties with little ability to know at the time of entering into their contract what law will govern their relationships and transactions. Moreover, current choice-of-law rules not only fail to account for the parties' interests, but they also facilitate the passage and maintenance of bad laws. Unfortunately, Congress, the state legislatures, and the Supreme Court have consistently failed to help contracting parties escape from the confusing common-law choice-of-law rules.

At the end of this chapter, we will return to one focus of this book—the enforcement of choice-of-law clauses—to demonstrate that the enforcement of choice-of-law clauses is our best hope for enabling contracting parties to obtain predictability and the best-fitting governing law. Unfortunately, the current state rules governing the enforcement of choice-of-law clauses are insufficiently clear to ensure predictability in governing law. Nevertheless, chapter 4 will argue that, in practice, party mobility can be used to mitigate the current obstacles to the enforcement of choice-of-law clauses.

The Problems of Conflict of Laws

This section briefly describes the law of choice of law, beginning with the principles that courts and scholars have developed for choosing the law that applies to a particular controversy. Over time, courts have resolved choice-of-law issues by using a number of different approaches. These approaches share several problems, however. First, they tend to emphasize lawmakers' abilities to regulate disputes at the expense of determining which laws best suit the parties' needs. Second, many of the approaches apply vague and multifactored standards that give judges broad discretion and undermine the parties' abilities to predict the law that will be applied to their contracts and other activities. Third, states' diverse approaches to dealing with choice-of-law problems further undermine predictability regarding the governing law.

Traditional Rules: Arbitrary and Escapable

In the 1930s, Joseph Beale engineered a comprehensive system for resolving choice-of-law problems. His approach, which was published as the First Restatement of Conflict of Laws, was based partly on his understanding of the rules that courts followed. However, the First Restatement also reflected Beale's own judgment regarding how state powers should be allocated. Beale's approach was based on the prevailing early twentieth-century notion that sovereign powers were territorial in nature: states could control people and events within their borders but had no authority to control people and events in other sovereign territories.[1] Indeed, as discussed below, in Beale's time, these territorial principles were deemed to be embedded in the Constitution.

Beale married territoriality with the idea of "vested rights."[2] Beale believed that only one sovereign should control a particular legal problem. Under

Beale's theory, a right vests (or not) at a particular place and time, and only the law of that place should determine the parties' rights. Specifically, under the First Restatement, rights would vest at the time or place of the last act necessary to create a right or cause of action. Rights in property depended on the *situs*, or location, of the property; compensation for negligence depended on the place of injury; the place of contracting determined the law applicable to the validity of and the basic obligations undertaken in a contract; and the place of performance determined the law applicable to determine the legality and sufficiency of the parties' performance. By putting into operation the vested rights principle, the First Restatement attempted to specify the governing law for all possible legal issues.

The First Restatement rules seemed to provide certainty and predictability because if all courts followed Beale's rules, only one rule could apply to any activity. They also promised to prevent forum shopping by having each state apply the same law to a given set of facts.

While the First Restatement's goals were certainly laudable, its rules do not operate as clearly, simply, and fairly as Beale had hoped.[3] Why, for example, should a negligence case be decided according to the law of the place where plaintiff was injured instead of where defendant acted? And why should some issues in contracts cases be resolved according to the law of the place where the parties contracted, while others are determined according to the law where the performance was to occur? And, how should courts distinguish the two, when, as is often the case, the parties are arguing over whether one of them has breached the contract? Without a theory to justify the First Restatement rules, its results do not seem compelling, and, perhaps worse, courts have lacked guidance when the restatement's rules are ambiguous or silent.

Moreover, the First Restatement fails to yield the uniformity and predictability that it promised because it is riddled with escape hatches. Sometimes, for example, a court might characterize an issue as procedural rather than substantive in order to apply forum law.[4] Additionally, if a claim can be characterized in two ways—as both a tort and a contract, or both a contract and a property dispute, for example—then the courts can manipulate the choice of governing law by manipulating the characterization of the claim.[5] Suppose, for example, that a number of consumers are injured when they purchase and use quintuple-headed razors that scrape the skin off their chins. The consumers file a class action lawsuit against the razor manufacturer, alleging that the razors cause injury when the consumers use them for their intended purposes, and that the company falsely advertised that the razors are safe. If the court decides that this is a negligence claim, then under the First Restatement, the law of the place of injury controls the claims. If the plaintiff-consumers were injured in several different states, then, as discussed below, multiple states' laws will apply. The possibility of multiple applicable laws may prevent plaintiffs from bringing the claims as a class action. If the claims are too small, they might not be pursued at all.

A court could decide that this case presents a fraud rather than a negligence claim because the plaintiffs claim that the company misrepresented the product's features. A First Restatement court would then apply the law of the place where the company engaged in the allegedly fraudulent conduct. If the court instead concludes that this is a breach-of-contract action because the product did not have the promised attributes, it will apply the law of the place of contracting to the suit and the certification decision. If all three characterizations (negligence, fraud, contract) are plausible, then the court can choose whether to apply the law of the place of injury, the place of contracting, or the place where allegedly fraudulent representations were made. The characterization of the lawsuit therefore may determine both the governing law and the viability of the claim. Clearly, the court has significant discretion in this case with no guidance from vested rights theory nor from the actual text of the First Restatement.

The First Restatement contains other devices that enable judges to manipulate which law governs. The most important is the public policy exception: notwithstanding the choice-of-law rules, a court may refuse to apply the law of another state that is contrary to the forum's "strong public policy."[6] The First Restatement provides little guidance as to what the quoted phrase means, so the courts' application of the exception has been inconsistent. Consider, for example, the New York courts' use of the public policy exception. In 1936, a New York court used the public policy exception to refuse to apply a Connecticut law that allowed a wife to sue her husband for driving negligently.[7] Instead, the court applied New York law, which forbade spouses from suing one another for negligence. Just two years later, the same court refused to use the public policy exception to avoid applying the law of Hitler's Germany, which required a firm to dismiss an employee because he was a Jew.[8] Is the law about spouses suing one another really more fundamental than avoiding state-mandated anti-Semitic discrimination?

A final problem with the First Restatement approach is that it leaves no role for the parties to determine the rules that will apply to their dealings. An approach based on the government's prerogatives to legislate within its boundaries obviously is inconsistent with enforcing choice-of-law clauses. Indeed, early First Restatement courts often view choice-of-law clauses as impermissible private legislation.[9]

The First Restatement approach therefore in many respects is not only arbitrary, but it fails even to offer the certainty and predictability of a rules-based system. Conflicts scholars accordingly have proposed alternative approaches to choice of law. New York and California began experimenting with modern choice-of-law approaches, and other states followed. Today, only about ten U.S. states continue to follow the First Restatement rules.[10] Some of the alternatives are discussed in the next section.

From Rules to Standards: Chaos Takes Hold

Given the complexities and perplexities of choice-of-law issues and judges' pressing needs to decide cases expeditiously, it is not surprising that systems to replace the traditional vested rights approach were developed by law professors rather than judges. Unfortunately, these academic theories did not initially focus on the need for efficiency, and they became no more efficient in the courts' hands. Several different vague, standards-based approaches to choice of law operate in state and federal courts today. As a result, chaos reigns.

The first scholar to have his ideas reflected in modern conflicts law was Brainerd Currie. Currie proposed *interest analysis* as a new approach to choice of law in the early 1960s.[11] At a frenzied pace, he wrote a series of articles presenting, illustrating, and defending his approach. Currie's legal legacy is substantial; a majority of U.S. courts today incorporate some form of interest analysis into their choice-of-law methodologies.

Currie sought to correct the seeming arbitrariness of the First Restatement rules. He thought that choice-of-law rules should try to reconcile the political interests of states implicated in resolving particular claims. He believed that many choice-of-law problems involved "false conflicts" in that only one state had a real interest in having its law apply to resolve the dispute. Consider, for example, a case where a California spendthrift fails to repay money borrowed from a California creditor in connection with the spendthrift's business venture in Oregon. California holds spendthrifts liable for breaching their promises to make loan payments, but Oregon does not hold debtors to their promises if liability would imperil the financial stability of their families. Currie would view this as a false conflict because, although Oregon might have an interest in protecting Oregon families, it has no interest in protecting a California family. Only California cares whether a California family or California creditor is entitled to the money owed, so California law obviously should apply.

Currie defined state policies strictly in an effort to get courts to generate predictable results: his state objectives included only desires to (1) compensate plaintiffs; (2) protect defendants; and/or (3) regulate conduct. To illustrate how these policies were assumed to operate, suppose that Texas and Florida have some connection to a tort case and the court must decide which of the two states' laws should apply to resolve the dispute. Suppose further that Texas and Florida laws differ: Florida would impose strict liability on the defendant, whereas Texas would hold defendant liable only if defendant were negligent. Under Currie's approach, the state with the law that favors plaintiff more (here, Florida) is presumed to be attempting to further a policy of compensating plaintiffs while the state with the relatively defendant-favoring law (here, Texas) is presumed to have a policy of protecting defendants from liability. In tort cases, the state with the relatively plaintiff-favoring law (here, Florida) is presumed to be furthering the additional policy of deterring harmful conduct. Texas is interested in applying its law to this dispute only if the defendant is a Texas resident. Florida is interested in applying its law to the dispute if the plaintiff resides in Florida. Florida is also interested in applying its law to the dispute if the accident happened in Florida. Currie assumed that states would have at most these three basic policy concerns, so the parties often could reliably predict the applicable law under his interest analysis.

Judges, however, rendered interest analysis much less predictable, in part because they often attempted to discern the laws' actual policy goals. Currie's approach to defining state interests seemed artificially constrained and therefore as arbitrary as Beale's approach.[12] But courts' efforts to engage in more nuanced inquiry can undermine predictability because a single law serves several possible policy functions. For example, what is the policy goal of a usury law, which prohibits lenders from charging more than a specified maximum interest rate in their loan contracts? Is it protecting creditors, who might never get paid if debtors continue to take out loans at high rates of interest? Is it protecting debtors from loan sharks and unscrupulous creditors? Is it hindering loan sharking by criminal organizations? Other policy goals are also possible.

When courts attempt to discern the actual legislative intent behind a law, other conceptual problems arise.[13] Should courts rely on what the legislature or its drafting committee says, or on the fact that the law was sought by a powerful interest group? If the former, how should the courts treat statements by legislators who might actually dislike the law but who nevertheless voted for it either to appease powerful constituents or to obtain cooperation from the law's supporters for some alternative bill that mattered to the legislator? Should it matter if the reluctant legislator's vote was essential to the passage of the law, especially if that legislator is promoting a narrow interpretation of the statute's language?[14]

The basic problems of determining legislative intent in an intrastate setting are further complicated by the fact that the legislature may have expressed no intent about how the law was to apply to controversies that affect parties in different states. What would legislators care about most in the context of interstate disputes: imposing local policies, preventing forum shopping, or respecting other states' policy judgments?

When no clear intent is evident, some courts simply assume that the legislature intended sensible policy goals. But the result of this reasoning often reflects little more than individual judges' preferred outcomes, which produce arbitrariness, inconsistency, and, thus, unpredictability—precisely what Currie was trying to avoid.

Currie's approach also created systemic biases in courts' choice-of-law decisions which favored *residents, forum law*, and *plaintiffs*.[15] Currie's analysis encourages pro-resident bias by asking courts to assume that states only want to apply their policies to benefit local residents (i.e., that Oregon only wants to protect Oregon spendthrifts).

The bias in favor of forum law emerges from Currie's treatment of "true conflicts" and "unprovided-for" cases. If multiple states wish to apply their laws, then the case presents a "true" rather than a "false" conflict. For example, if an Oregon spendthrift contracts with a California creditor, then a court should presume that California law is intended to protect the California creditor and that Oregon's law is intended to protect the Oregon spendthrift and his family. In these true conflict cases, Currie thought a court should apply forum law consistent with its legislature's wishes.[16] Currie also thought that forum law should apply in unprovided-for cases because then no state has an interest in having its law control the outcome of the case. This might happen when, for example, the spendthrift is a California resident and the lender is an Oregonian. In unprovided-for cases, nothing is gained by deferring to foreign law, and applying local law at least generates valuable precedent for future litigants (a court's interpretation of forum law is binding in future cases, but a court's interpretation of foreign law can be altered by the foreign state's courts). Moreover, judges have more familiarity with local law, so presumably local law enables them to make better decisions with less effort. Unfortunately, these forum-favoring rules compromise uniformity of outcome because the governing law could well turn on where a case is eventually litigated. If the governing law depends on the location of future litigation, parties lack predictability at the time of contracting.

Finally, interest analysis creates a pro-plaintiff bias for choice of law that stems from two sources. First, because interest analysis courts are likely to apply forum law, plaintiffs have an incentive to file suit in the state with the most plaintiff-favoring substantive laws. In contrast, Beale's rules constrain such forum shopping by applying a given state's substantive law without regard to where a case is litigated. Second, courts tended to use interest analysis, at least in its early days, *because* it gave them the flexibility to apply plaintiff-friendly laws.[17]

Academics' attempts to rescue interest analysis and place it on firmer footing have not been successful. For example, William Baxter, a Stanford professor and contemporary of Currie's, thought that conflicts would be better resolved by asking what result states would be likely to reach if they could bargain over choice of law.[18] Baxter assumed that a state would be willing to give up control over cases where its policies were impaired only a little in return for controlling cases where its policies would be significantly impaired if another state's law applied. Baxter's "comparative impairment principle" is followed today in California and used occasionally by courts in other states.

Baxter's approach retains many of the problems of Currie's because it continues to focus exclusively on state policies, and therefore does not address parties' desire for predictability and suitability. Indeed, Baxter's approach is even less predictable than Currie's because it forces courts to determine both states' policies and their relative impairments.

More radically, some scholars have advocated that, instead of adopting interest analysis, courts simply should apply the better law. As early as 1933, prominent Harvard scholar David Cavers argued that courts should strive to do justice in the individual case by applying the more just substantive law.[19] In a 1952 article, two conflicts scholars similarly argued that courts should apply the stronger substantive law when confronting choice-of-law issues.[20] During the 1960s, Robert Leflar argued that courts do and should use five "choice-influencing considerations" for resolving choice-of-law problems, most importantly including the "better" rule of law.[21] Leflar's approach is used by courts in a half dozen states today.

Leflar's focus on the better law theoretically maximizes social welfare because it is designed to confine the reach of poor laws while extending the reach of good laws. Leflar tried to resolve the inevitable conflict of judicial preferences by applying objective factors, such as ignoring outdated and archaic laws and applying majority over minority rules. In the end, though, courts must decide subjectively which law is the better rule. In any event, Leflar concluded that since courts were already applying what they thought was the better rule, the law would be more transparent and predictable if the courts did this openly. However, Leflar's approach is still subject to the criticisms that it encourages judges to act as legislators and that it ignores the parties' superior ability to determine the law that best suits their relationship and obligations. Moreover, the subjectivity inherent in deciding which law is better reinforces the unpredictability inherent in interest analysis.

In short, the modern approaches, while attempting to solve the arbitrariness of the First Restatement approach, virtually eliminated the ex ante predictability of the earlier system and substituted a system that tended to favor plaintiffs, residents, and local law. Moreover, like Beale's system, the modern approaches favored government prerogatives over parties' choices and expectations.

The Second Restatement

The Second Restatement was promulgated in 1971. It still encapsulates the U.S. law of conflict of laws and, in most relevant respects, is similar to the law elsewhere in the world. It manages to stay forever young by saying nothing and everything at once by accommodating all of the judicial approaches to choice of law.[22] Although the Second Restatement provides presumptive rules, which are favored by more traditional judges, courts can ignore those rules any time in favor of a multifactored analysis, which may indicate that a different state's law should apply. The multifactored analysis takes into account virtually every consideration that courts have examined when choosing governing law. As a result, courts can use the Second Restatement to justify any result they want to reach. This is great for courts, but obviously not for people seeking guidance as to what legal rules govern their conduct.

Consider, for example, the Second Restatement approach to choosing the law to govern a contract dispute. If the parties have not included a binding choice-of-law clause in their contract, then the court turns to section 188:

(1) The rights and duties of the parties with respect to an issue in contract are determined by the local law of the state which, with respect to that issue, has the most significant relationship to the transaction and the parties under the principles stated in §6.

(2) In the absence of an effective choice of law by the parties (see §187), the contacts to be taken into account in applying the principles of §6 to determine the law applicable to an issue include:

(a) the place of contracting;

(b) the place of negotiation of the contract;

(c) the place of performance;

(d) the location of the subject matter of the contract; and

(e) the domicile, residence, nationality, place of incorporation and place of business of the parties.

These contacts are to be evaluated according to their relative importance with respect to the particular issue.

(3) If the place of negotiating the contract and the place of performance are in the same state, the local law of this state will usually be applied, except as otherwise provided in §§189–199 and 203.

The locations that these factors indicate may not be clear. Where, for example, is the "place of negotiation" if the parties have met in many places and/or conducted negotiations by telephone, via the Internet, or while traveling interstate? Where is the "subject matter" of an interstate employment contract or agreement regarding intellectual property?[23]

Where multiple locations are relevant, the Second Restatement directs the court to choose the state that has the "most significant relationship" to the transaction and parties. That, in turn, depends on the application of a set of principles listed in Second Restatement, section 6:

(a) the needs of the interstate and international systems;

(b) the relevant policies of the forum;

(c) the relevant policies of other interested states and the relative interests of those states in the determination of the particular issue;

(d) the protection of justified expectations;

(e) the basic policies underlying the particular field of law;

(f) certainty, predictability and uniformity of result; and

(g) ease in the determination and application of the law to be applied.

These factors often suggest that differing possible laws should apply, but the Second Restatement offers no guidance regarding how to prioritize these factors. Although prior approaches to choice of law could generate arbitrary results, it is not clear that a system that attempts to produce the perfectly just result for each individual case is necessarily better if it unduly sacrifices predictability. And, perhaps worse, multifactored approaches to choice of law can significantly increase the costs of litigation, which can have the effect of further advantaging deep-pocketed defendants in their suits with less wealthy plaintiffs.[24]

Can Government Create Sensible Order?

States might create order from this hodgepodge of rules and vague standards if they could somehow coordinate a sensible and predictable approach. There are four possible paths to effective coordination. First, the U.S. Congress could pass statutes to mandate a particular set of choice-of-law rules for the states. Second, the federal courts could generate choice-of-law principles to govern interstate cases. Third, the U.S. Supreme Court could use the U.S. Constitution to police the states' choice-of-law decision making. Fourth, the states could themselves negotiate and then enact uniform choice-of-law statutes. Unfortunately, none of these approaches to achieving sensible order is feasible. Consequently, choice-of-law clauses may not only ensure the application of legal rules that fit the parties' particular circumstances, but they also may be the only route to predictable results. In international cases, where multiple choice-of-law approaches similarly undermine predictability and there are no institutions for creating order, choice-of-law clauses might be even more valuable. We discuss some possible U.S. mechanisms here.

Federal Statutes

Two provisions of the U.S. Constitution give Congress the power to enact legislation that would require state courts to apply particular choice-of-law rules. The Full Faith and Credit Clause empowers Congress to determine the effect that each state must give to the public acts, or laws, of the other states.[25] Congress therefore can tell a state that, in certain cases, it must apply the law of another state. The Commerce Clause empowers Congress to regulate interstate and international commerce.[26] Under this clause, Congress could prevent a state from applying its regulations to interstate activities if the regulation would affect the flow of goods and services across state borders.

Congress, however, rarely exercises these powers. Congressional representatives have little political interest in mediating the choice-of-law decisions that govern matters left to state authority. Even if Congress could summon the will to craft mandatory choice-of-law principles, Congress's principles might well be no sounder than those generated by the states. As we will discuss in chapter 10, however, to attract international trade, Congress conceivably might enact a statute to require the enforcement of choice-of-law clauses.

In response to interest-group pressures, Congress does occasionally pass statutes with particularized choice-of-law principles embedded in them. Consider, for example, the Defense of Marriage Act (DOMA),[27] which catered to conservatives who fear the legalization and proliferation of same-sex marriages in the United States. As we will discuss in chapter 8, Congress merely confirmed in the DOMA the common-law principle that states may decline to recognize foreign marriages that violate their public policy. The move was defensive rather than offensive and does not by itself indicate a willingness on the part of Congress to affirmatively solve state choice-of-law problems.

Another example of Congress mandating choice-of-law rules is contained in the federal banking laws. During the 1970s, inflation rates rose so high that it was becoming impossible to borrow money in some states without running into several state-fixed interest rate ceilings. As we will discuss in chapter 7, Congress responded to the problem with a statute that allowed a bank to charge any interest rate permissible in the state where it was based.[28] Delaware and South Dakota capitalized on this rule by repealing their usury laws, and credit card companies quickly flocked to these states. Today, these companies are legally unconstrained in both the interest rates and the late fees that they charge customers. During the 1980s, South Dakota's tax revenues from credit-card-issuing banks increased ninefold, while Delaware's increased nearly twentyfold.[29] In contrast, North Carolina's deputy commissioner of banks estimated the loss of several thousand jobs as a result of that state's refusal to relax its credit card laws.[30] To preserve the jobs and tax revenues provided by local lenders threatening to leave, other states had to either relax local usury laws or enforce choice-of-law provisions in loan agreements. Congressional choice-of-law rules are in general rare and, like this one, tend to address very specific policy concerns in response to strong interest-group pressures.

If Congress were going to enact a general federal choice-of-law statute, the Class Action Fairness Act of 2005 (CAFA)[31] would have been an ideal opportunity. The CAFA partly responded to the "bootstrapping" of choice of law that occurs when state courts apply local law to multistate class action claims solely because of the class nature of the claims, and then justify certifying the case as a class action on the ground that all of the claims involve similar legal and factual issues.[32] To prevent a single state from monopolizing the legal treatment of these class actions, the CAFA gives the federal courts jurisdiction over large multistate class actions.[33] Although Congress hoped that the federal courts would be less inclined than the state courts to certify nationwide classes through bootstrapping, it stopped short of either specifying a choice-of-law analysis or enabling the federal courts to adopt their own analysis. This failure to resolve the choice-of-law problem is especially striking given that some have justified Congress's actions in the CAFA as a necessary reaction to the Supreme Court's refusal to use the U.S. Constitution to more effectively discipline state courts' personal jurisdiction and choice-of-law decisions.[34] Instead, as discussed in the next section, federal courts sitting in diversity must continue to apply the states' choice-of-law principles.

In sum, Congress has never acted to eliminate the general chaos created by the state choice-of-law systems. Instead, when Congress does act to correct state law problems, it is far more likely to federalize the legal territory than to specify a system of choice-of-law rules.

Federal Courts and Diversity Jurisdiction

The U.S. federal courts can hear suits based on state law (other than the large class actions covered by the CAFA) only if all plaintiffs and all defendants are citizens of different states and the dispute is worth more than $75,000. If the federal courts can exercise this "diversity jurisdiction" over a lawsuit, a defendant has a right to remove the case to federal courts even if the plaintiff originally filed the lawsuit in state court. Thus, federal courts can hear many large interstate disputes.

Federal courts cannot, however, do much to alleviate the mess that states have made of choice of law because of the limits that our federal system imposes on federal courts in diversity cases. Under the so-called *Erie* doctrine, federal courts cannot apply substantive federal law in diversity cases.[35] This rule is designed to prevent forum shopping between state and federal courts by requiring the federal courts to apply the same substantive state law that would be applied if the same case were litigated in state courts. In addition, federal courts sitting in diversity must apply the choice-of-law rules of the state in which the federal court is located.[36] As we will discuss in chapter 4, the federal courts nevertheless have played an important indirect role in addressing the chaos of the choice of law of contracts through their tendency to enforce choice-of-law clauses.

The CAFA could increase the federal role in choice of law. Richard Nagareda argues that the courts in CAFA cases should deviate from state rules at least to the extent of avoiding applying choice-of-law rules in order to bootstrap class certification.[37] Samuel Issacharoff suggests that the federal courts should go even further and craft a distinct federal rule, in these cases selecting the law of the defendant's home state.[38] He argues that *Erie*'s emphasis on uniformity between state and federal courts neglects the important federal role in ensuring predictability through federalization, particularly for mass-produced goods sold in interstate commerce.

Empowering the federal courts to independently choose the governing law raises concerns not only under *Erie*, but also for defining the appropriate judicial role. Professor Issacharoff chose a particular federal choice-of-law rule from among several contenders, including rules based on the place of sale and the plaintiff's domicile,[39] but it is not clear why this rule is better than others. Since this is precisely the sort of policymaking on choice of law that Congress has eschewed, including in the CAFA itself, it is questionable to foist this policymaking onto the federal courts. And, given their general lack of interest in diversity cases, federal courts' approaches would not likely be improvements over those used in the state courts.

The same forces that motivated the CAFA could, however, also spur Congress to enact a federal statute that addresses the enforcement of choice-of-law clauses, and we propose such a statute in chapter 10. Such a statute would enable Congress to enhance predictability and uniformity while avoiding the detailed policymaking involved in fashioning default choice-of-law rules. To be sure, enforcing choice-of-law clauses in the typical class action, which tends to involve consumers or small investors, could prove problematic in the sense that the company chooses the governing laws, but the choice also could make it easier for class actions to be certified.[40] Moreover, our proposal would only apply to contracting parties. Injured nonpurchasers in product liability cases would not be subject to choice-of-law clauses, for example. For many claims, however, federal courts' enforcement of choice-of-law clauses could well help both the courts and the parties.

The Supreme Court and the Constitution

The U.S. Supreme Court could use federal constitutional provisions to help impose a sensible choice-of-law system on the states. Several clauses might be relevant. Although the Full Faith and Credit Clause empowers Congress to decide the respect that states must give to one another's laws,[41] the Supreme Court can take similar action when Congress is silent. Second, the Due Process Clause[42] implicitly guarantees minimal standards of fairness in litigation, including the right to be protected from unfair surprise regarding the applicable laws. The Equal Protection[43] and Privileges and Immunities[44] clauses arguably constrain choice-of-law approaches that discriminate in favor of state residents or against out-of-state residents. Finally, the Commerce Clause[45] in its "negative" form prevents states from usurping the federal role by unreasonably interfering with interstate commerce.

Although these constitutional provisions theoretically could empower the Supreme Court to constrain state chaos in choice of law, in fact state courts have wide latitude to apply the law they prefer in interstate cases. This promotion of federalism is self-defeating, however. If the Court remains unable or unwilling to rescue the states from the chaos of default choice-of-law rules, the only other solution seems to be to remove state decision making entirely by federalizing many areas of the law. We discuss this tradeoff between federal law and state choice of law throughout this book and particularly in chapter 10.

The Court was not always reluctant to police state choice-of-law policies. During the late nineteenth and early twentieth centuries, the Court's opinions showed a commitment to providing predictability to contracting parties. In particular, the Court invoked the Due Process Clause in insurance contract cases to protect parties' expectations by insisting that the law of the place of contracting should apply to determine the parties' obligations. For example, in *New York Life Insurance Co. v. Dodge*,[46] Josiah Dodge had taken out a life insurance policy with New York Life, dealing with this New York company through its Missouri branch office. Dodge later borrowed money from New York Life and secured the loan with the life insurance policy. After Dodge died, his widow attempted to recover the life insurance specified in the policy. The company claimed that, because Dodge never repaid his loan, the policy was no longer valid. The Court required the Missouri court to apply New York law. Because the loan contract was formed in New York rather than Missouri, the company was entitled to rely on the law of New York in lending the money. While Missouri might want to protect its citizens by preventing them from entering into these loan agreements in Missouri, it could not prevent them from entering into loan agreements in New York. Accordingly, Missouri's attempt to strike down the provisions of the loan agreement had the effect of taking the insurance company's property without due process of law. Of course, as Justice Louis Brandeis pointed out in dissent, Dodge had never left Missouri. The Court assumed that the loan contract had been formed in New York only because the contract itself said so—shades of contractual choice of law. In any event, only the law of the state deemed to be the place of contract could control the dispute.

During the 1930s, the Court's focus shifted from mandating the law of the place of contract to ensuring that the set of possible regulating states did not become unreasonably large. In *Home Insurance Co. v. Dick*,[47] for example, the Court rejected a Texas court's effort to regulate a contract even though one of the parties was a Texas resident. Dick owned a tug that was destroyed in Mexico. He had taken over an insurance policy from the tug's previous owner, who was a Mexican citizen, and the policy was issued by a Mexican insurer. The policy insured its owner against loss only in Mexican waters. Before the tug was destroyed, Dick was living in Mexico. The Court held that the Texas court lacked authority to apply its own law to the contract because nothing related to the contract was ever done or required to be done in Texas. The Court's reasoning suggests, however, that if the contract were formed in Texas but to be performed in Mexico, then either law could apply.

In *John Hancock Mutual Life Ins. Co. v. Yates*,[48] Harmon Yates entered into a contract for life insurance in New York, where he and his wife resided. When Yates died in New York, the insurance company refused to pay the proceeds of the contract because his policy application contained false statements about his medical condition. Yates's widow moved to Georgia, where she sued the insurance company. Georgia law required an insurance company to pay the promised proceeds from a life insurance policy in this situation if the applicant was at least verbally honest with the insurance agent. The Supreme Court reversed a judgment based on the application of Georgia law because Georgia's connection occurred only after the parties' rights accrued.

Shortly after this case, the Supreme Court decided *Erie Railroad v. Tompkins*, which held that federal courts sitting in diversity had to apply state law in resolving the parties' substantive rights. Although *Erie* did not preclude the Court from policing state choice-of-law decisions under the federal Constitution, in effect *Erie* ushered in an era of federal courts' deference to state law, including state choice-of-law rules. This left the field open to the anything-goes conflicts rules under the modern choice-of-law approaches.

A glimmer of this new deference was evident in *Watson v. Employers Liability Assurance Corp.*,[49] where plaintiff sued in her home state of Louisiana for damages she suffered from using a hair-waving product that she bought in Louisiana. The product had been manufactured by the Toni Company, a subsidiary of the Gillette Safety Razor Company. Toni and Gillette had bought an insurance policy that would protect them from liability, so Watson sued the insurance company directly. The policy had been negotiated and issued in Massachusetts (Gillette's headquarters) and delivered in Massachusetts and Illinois (Toni's headquarters). The contract attempted to preclude direct claims against the insurance company. However, under Louisiana law, these clauses were not enforceable against consumers because they were not parties to the insurance contract and thus not bound by its terms. The Court held that the insurer was not unfairly surprised to find that Louisiana law was applied to the contract because the policy covered liability for injuries to customers and the insurance company knew that Toni's products were sold in Louisiana. Louisiana also had a legitimate interest in ensuring that its residents receive compensation and that its medical creditors be promptly paid. Although Massachusetts might also have had an interest in enforcing contracts made within its borders, that interest did not outweigh Louisiana's and, in any event, the Constitution allowed more than one state to apply its law.

Ten years later, the Court made clear that *Watson* did not rest on the happenstance that the plaintiff was not a party to the contract. In *Clay v. Sun Insurance Office, Ltd.*,[50] Clay bought an insurance policy to cover the loss of personal property when he lived in Illinois, and then moved to Florida, where he suffered a loss to the property. The insurance company, a British company licensed to conduct business in both Illinois and Florida, denied Clay's claim for compensation on the ground that Clay failed to file the claim within one year of the loss as required by the contract. A Florida court refused to enforce this term because Florida law does not permit parties to agree to limit their abilities to sue one another to a period that is shorter than five years. The Supreme Court affirmed, noting that the application of Florida law would not unfairly surprise the insurer under the Due Process Clause: the policy stated that it was covering the loss of Clay's property wherever it was located, and the company knew that Clay had moved to Florida and would presumably take insured property there. So, in contrast to the decisions in the early part of the twentieth century, nothing in the Due Process Clause today requires that courts apply the law of the place of contracting.

A similar evolution from relatively strict Court supervision of choice of law to a much more laissez-faire approach is apparent in the Court's treatment of the Full Faith and Credit Clause. The clause requires in part that each state give full faith and credit to the "public acts" of every other state.[51] Justice Robert H. Jackson described the clause as protecting against the "disintegrating influence of provincialism."[52] Under this approach, a state must respect the laws of other states at least to the extent of having a principled basis for refusing to follow the law in a particular case.[53]

The Court's early view of Full Faith and Credit is illustrated in a series of cases involving fraternal benefit associations. These cases involved members who joined the organizations through local lodges and agreed to pay periodic assessments to the national organizations. The organizations agreed to make payments to the member's family when the member died, and in that respect they functioned as nonprofit insurers. When a member or one of his beneficiaries made claims against one of the organizations, the Court consistently determined that the member's rights must be determined according to the law of the place of formation of the organization rather than the law of the place where the contract between the member and the organization was created. Because members paid assessments into a common fund, the Court deemed it important to the success of the organization that the members have uniform rights to the proceeds of the fund.[54]

The fraternal benefit cases stand in curious contrast to the Court's failure to give constitutional status to the place of incorporation more generally, as will be discussed in chapter 6. Moreover, the Court has specifically rejected the argument that a contractual choice-of-law provision in a non-fraternal-benefit insurance case should be enforced as necessary to apply a uniform law to all policyholders.[55] The Court rationalized the distinction between fraternal benefit associations and other cases by saying that membership is "something more than a contract, it is entering into a complex and abiding relation,"[56] and that a fraternal benefit association is a creature of state law.[57] But obviously, fraternal benefit associations share these characteristics with corporations and other business associations. Moreover, even if the case for enforcing a single rule seems compelling in some instances, in others applying different rules to different contracts would not seriously compromise an organization's ability to function nationally.[58] Thus, in one case, four of the nine justices questioned the distinction between fraternal insurance associations and other reciprocal, cooperative, and mutual insurers.[59] Eventually, courts became free under the Full Faith and Credit Clause to apply forum law any time this furthered a legitimate state interest, thus easily accommodating the modern approaches to choice of law discussed above.

In *Allstate Insurance Co. v. Hague*,[60] the Court merged its Full Faith and Credit and Due Process analyses, holding that a similar test would be applied under both clauses.[61] Moreover, the Court indicated that, under these clauses, a state could apply local law as long as it had an interest that made applying local law neither arbitrary nor fundamentally unfair. *Hague* held that Minnesota could apply its own law to an insurance contract even though the policy was issued and the insured resided in Wisconsin and the accident occurred in Wisconsin. Because the decedent worked in Minnesota, his widow became a Minnesota resident after the accident, and the insurer was doing business in

Minnesota, there was "no element of unfair surprise or frustration of legitimate expectations as a result of Minnesota's choice of its law."[62]

Four years later, the Court did strike down a forum court's application of local law under this test. In *Phillips Petroleum Co. v. Shutts*,[63] the Court held that a Kansas court could not apply its law to land leases with no connection to Kansas. The Kansas court had, in effect, used choice of law to bootstrap itself into position to hear a class action involving the leases. The Kansas court "solved" the choice-of-law problem, which otherwise might have impeded class certification, by holding that the application of local law was justified in order to simplify the aggregate litigation of royalty claims involving plaintiffs and land throughout the United States. The Supreme Court reasoned in part that, for many of the claims, the parties could not have anticipated that Kansas's law would control when they executed the leases.[64] *Shutts* is the only case since the 1980s where the Court has overturned a choice-of-law decision on constitutional grounds.

The Commerce Clause is the final remaining realistic basis for constitutional limits on choice of law.[65] The Court has sometimes cited the need for national uniformity in striking down state regulations under the Commerce Clause, especially when one state attempts to pass regulations that would force businesses everywhere to comply. For example, the Court has invalidated state regulation of the length of interstate trains[66] and trucks,[67] and an Illinois law requiring a contoured mudguard instead of the straight mudguard permitted in 45 states and required in at least 1.[68] The Illinois mudguard law could, in effect, have forced all trucks to comply because of the costs of changing flaps when driving through Illinois.

The question of how far this uniformity concern constrains choice of law will be discussed in chapter 6, which explores the corporate internal affairs doctrine. If Illinois cannot require trucks to take off their straight mudguards when they enter the state, can it, for example, require firms to revise their tender offers when they are soliciting Illinois shareholders of a firm incorporated outside of Illinois? Indeed, the Court struck down just such a law in *Edgar v. MITE*.[69]

State Cooperation

Conflicts scholars have suggested that states should cooperate with one another to diminish the chaos in choice of law. Lea Brilmayer, for example, thinks that the American Law Institute should draft a Third Restatement of Conflict of Laws, which could be used as a device for returning states to sensible choice-of-law principles.[70] Larry Kramer wants the National Conference of Commissioners on Uniform State Laws (NCCUSL) to promulgate a uniform choice-of-law provision that could be shopped to state legislatures.[71] Kramer thinks that states are reasonably likely to adopt NCCUSL provisions because each state sends delegates to NCCUSL. Thus, any proposed statute that NCCUSL produces presumably would already have taken into account competing state interests. So far, however, there has been no movement toward interstate agreement. We will discuss the uniform lawmaking process, its limitations with respect to dealing with choice of law, and the consequent need for federal law on this issue in chapter 10.

Some uniform laws contain choice-of-law principles that govern the specific substantive law topic addressed. For example, the Uniform Commercial Code provides choice-of-law provisions for secured transactions and for contracts for the sale of goods (discussed below), the Uniform Child Custody Jurisdiction Act allocates state authority over child custody determinations, and the Uniform Probate Code attempts to determine which state law controls the validity of a will. Successful uniform laws can create uniform choice-of-law treatment for a particular topic. But, of course, if the states actually reach consensus regarding the substantive content of a uniform law, then the choice-of-law provision embedded in that law becomes unnecessary. Conversely, as we will discuss in chapter 10, the enforcement of choice-of-law clauses eliminates the need for uniform laws in the first place.

Enforcing Party Choice

To recap our discussion, the common-law treatment of choice of law has created chaos for parties who wish to better assess their legal rights, obligations, and risks. The federal government shows no sign of easing the problem. Because federal courts hearing state claims must apply state conflicts rules, federal courts can only make a marginal difference. When state chaos motivates federal action, Congress typically replaces state substantive law with federal substantive law. It appears that Congress therefore cannot be bothered to solve the problem. Furthermore, the U.S. Supreme Court has abandoned its efforts to sensibly allocate lawmaking authority across the states.

This leaves the enforcement of choice-of-law clauses as the sole avenue for clarifying choice of law. Since the late twentieth century, the enforcement of choice-of-law clauses has grown dramatically. Section 187 of the Second Restatement, which is widely applied throughout the United States, takes the law selected in the contract as the starting point for the choice-of-law analysis. Under section 187(1), the parties can choose any law they wish to govern interpretation of the contract. This makes sense, since the parties could have written these default rules directly into their contracts.

Section 187(2) provides that parties can choose their governing law even as applied to mandatory rules, which are those rules that the parties are not permitted to contract around directly. If, for example, a state requires that all contracts for the sale of goods include minimum warranties, but the parties choose the law of a state with no required warranties, the parties' contract might legally eliminate all warranties as part of the sale. The enforcement of choice-of-law clauses that have the effect of circumventing mandatory rules is subject to two exceptions, which are provided in section 187(2). First, state mandatory rules trump the choice-of-law clause where the parties chose the law of a state that "has no substantial relationship to the parties or the transaction and there is no other reasonable basis for the parties' choice." Second, even if the chosen state has a "substantial relationship" with the parties or contract, a court may refuse to enforce the clause if the chosen law is "contrary to a fundamental policy of a state which has a materially greater interest than the chosen state in the determination of the particular issue" and that state would be selected under the Second Restatement choice-of-law principles. These provisions are explained below.

The Uniform Commercial Code, which has been widely adopted by the states, applies to the sale of goods and some other commercial transactions. Because the UCC is enacted in each state as a statute which is controlling in that state's courts, the UCC provision replaces the Second Restatement when choice-of-law clauses appear in contracts governed by the UCC. The UCC has long provided for the enforcement of a clause specifying the law of any state that "bears a reasonable relation" to the transaction.[72] However, this portion of the UCC was revised in 2001, and the states are gradually adopting the new provisions.[73] The revised UCC provides that, in nonconsumer transactions, the parties can contract for the application of any law, even the law of a state unrelated to the contract, so long as the choice is not contrary to a fundamental policy of the state or country whose law would govern without the clause.[74] But in transactions involving a consumer, the UCC retains the reasonable relationship requirement. Moreover, a choice-of-law clause can never work to deprive the consumer of the protection of a law in a state in which either the consumer principally resides or the contract is made and the goods delivered.[75] Unfortunately for its drafters, the states that are adopting UCC revisions are routinely choosing not to adopt this amended choice-of-law provision.

A half dozen states have passed their own choice-of-law statutes that do not reflect the same concerns for connection and public policies. Statutes in California, Delaware, Florida, Illinois, New York, and Texas provide for the enforcement of choice-of-law clauses in high-value contracts without regard to the public policies of other states, as long as the parties have chosen local law.[76] Delaware's provision applies to contracts worth more than $100,000, Texas's provision contains a dollar threshold of $1 million, and the other states' statutes cover contracts in excess of $250,000. As the dollar value of the contract rises, so does the likelihood that the parties are either themselves sophisticated or are represented by lawyers who will appreciate the consequences of a particular choice-of-law clause. Thus, there is less need to subject these choices to a vague public policy exception. Florida and Illinois deny the automatic enforcement of choice-of-law clauses in household and labor contracts, and Texas precludes automatic enforcement in agreements involving the transfer of real property, the construction or repair of real property, marriage or adoption (at least as regards their validity), and rights under a will. All but Texas and Florida have eliminated their connection requirements for large-value contracts. Indeed, the Delaware statute specifically states that a choice-of-law clause that chooses Delaware law is to be enforced even if the clause is the sole connection that the transaction has with Delaware.

Oregon and Louisiana also have enacted comprehensive statutory choice-of-law rules for contracts.[77] Oregon enforces choice-of-law clauses as applied to "contractual rights and duties" if the parties' choice is "express or clearly demonstrated from the terms" in non-standard-form contracts or, in standard form contracts, "express and conspicuous." However, the act requires that Oregon law, not contrary law chosen by the parties, will apply to some contracts, including Oregon-connected construction, employment, and consumer contracts. In addition, the contractual choice will not be honored where it would contravene requirements or prohibitions at the place of performance or "established fundamental policy embodied in the law that would otherwise govern." A policy is fundamental if it "reflects objectives or gives effect to essential public or societal institutions beyond the allocation of rights and obligations of parties to a contract at issue." According to the Louisiana law, the parties can choose their governing law "except to the extent that [the] law contravenes the public policy of the state whose law would otherwise be applicable."

In summary, most of the U.S. provisions to regulate contractual choice of law share the following elements:

(1) Non-enforcement where the parties or transaction are not reasonably related to the chosen jurisdiction. Except for Louisiana, the main exceptions to the reasonable or substantial relationship requirement are the amended UCC and state statutory provisions, which apply to big transactions involving presumably sophisticated parties. And the amended UCC provision is being rejected in state legislatures, in part because of its attempt to eliminate the connection requirement.[78]

(2) Non-enforcement where the chosen rule conflicts with the fundamental policies of a closely related jurisdiction or the forum. These policies are typically reflected in mandatory rules that would otherwise apply. Laws that cannot be circumvented even with choice-of-law clauses might be called super-mandatory laws.

For present purposes, we are less interested in the details of the case-by-case enforcement of choice-of-law clauses than we are in understanding the general mechanisms of the law market. Accordingly, we will try to get a general sense of the rules applied under the most litigated contractual choice-of-law rule, Second Restatement, section 187(2). The subsections below focus on that section's reasonable relationship requirement and the fundamental policy limitation.

Throughout this discussion, it is important to keep in mind that the general "black-letter" rules do not give a complete picture of how and when courts enforce choice-of-law clauses. The rules indicate when courts have discretion regarding whether to enforce, but they do not themselves provide effective limitations on that discretion. As we will discuss in chapter 4, powerful practical and political forces promote the enforcement of contractual choice, and the enforcement of these clauses may be broader than might appear from the black-letter rules.

To complete this discussion, it is worth noting that Europe has adopted a regulation for contractual obligations that generally provides for the enforcement of choice-of-law clauses,[79] with the main exception that the parties' choice is subject to "overriding mandatory provisions" that might render the performance of the contract "unlawful."[80] The Rome I Convention, a uniform law that binds European countries, provides that "effect may be given to the mandatory rules of the law of another country with which the situation has a close connection, if and insofar as, under the law of the latter country, those rules must be applied whatever the law applicable to the contract."[81] The convention defines "mandatory rules" as "provisions which cannot be derogated from by agreement."[82] In contrast, the more recent Rome I Regulation states that "'overriding mandatory provisions' should be distinguished from the expression 'provisions which cannot be derogated from by agreement' and should be construed more restrictively."[83] The use of the word "unlawful" in the Rome I Regulation suggests that choice of law is unenforceable only when the performance is prohibited by provisions of public law, rather than, for example, merely because of a disparity in bargaining position.

The Rome I Regulation thus appears to give greater deference to the parties' choice-of-law clause than do U.S. rules, both in the more limited definition of super-mandatory rules and in dispensing with a general requirement of a connection between the parties or transaction and the designated state. The comparison of the U.S. situation with the convention indicates that Europe is moving toward greater enforcement of contractual choice of law by means of a "federal" choice-of-law rule. It remains to be seen, however, whether the application of these European rules on contractual choice differs from the enforcement of contractual choice of law under the seemingly less permissive U.S. rules.[84]

Substantial Relationship Requirement

As discussed above, the Second Restatement, section 187(2), provides that the choice-of-law clause is not enforced where the chosen law "has no substantial relationship to the parties or the transaction and there is no other reasonable basis for the parties' choice." The important question is why the enforcement of a choice-of-law clause should hinge on any relationship with the chosen state. The typical justification for the connection requirement is that validating a contract "under the law of a state that can have only an officious and meddlesome interest in affecting the result is to exalt certainty and predictability over all other social purposes including the cogent reasons any state must find before it can rationally interdict a bargain freely struck."[85]

This reasoning rests on two faulty assumptions. First, it assumes that a state that lacks a *connection* with the parties or transaction has no *interest* in them. To be sure, states may be motivated to compete for business in the law market to attract investments and residents. But attracting investments is not the states' *only* motivation for competing in the law market. Some states may want to simply attract litigation to their courts by holding themselves out as willing to enforce contracts. A connection requirement could frustrate this state interest.

Second, and more important for present purposes, the above defense of the substantial relationship requirement assumes that the only interests that should be considered are the legislative goals of the regulating jurisdiction. This reflects a distrust of states that seek to aggressively compete for law business, like Delaware in the corporate, trusts, and credit card contexts. These competitors are viewed as upsetting the apple cart of a sort of regulatory "cartel" that divides legislative power according to territorial reach. However, the law market and the choice-of-law clauses that fuel it also implicate the interests of private parties in avoiding inefficient regulation. As will be discussed in chapter 4, these laws can be ameliorated by permitting exit and by activating interest groups that are affected by exit. Also, limiting parties' legal options to connected states may deny them the advantages of other laws that are best suited to their needs. If a company wants a single law to apply to all similar contracts, it can choose the law where it is located but probably not other laws. In effect, a connection requirement forces parties to bundle all of their regulatory environments even if they would prefer to choose different laws for different transactions or activities.

Even if courts do not require a connection with the *designated* state, they probably should at least take into account the parties' connections with the *regulating* state. Excessive or otherwise inefficient regulation discourages parties from making local investments or otherwise establishing connections that might justify applying the state's law. To ensure the application of high-quality laws, courts should take into account state policies against enforcement *only* when these states have material connections with the parties or transaction. As noted in the next section, this is in fact what the Second Restatement provides.

Moreover, the Second Restatement does not actually *require* a substantial relationship with the law chosen; another "reasonable basis" for the choice may suffice. Comment f says that if parties are

> contracting in countries whose legal systems are strange to them as well as relatively immature, the parties should be able to choose a law on the ground that they know it well and that it is sufficiently developed. For only in this way can they be sure of knowing accurately the extent of their rights and duties under the contract. So parties to a

contract for the transportation of goods by sea between two countries with relatively undeveloped legal systems should be permitted to submit their contract to some well-known and highly elaborated commercial law.

The Reporter's Note cites the famous English case of *Vita Food Products, Inc. v. Unus Shipping Co.*,[86] which enforced the contractual choice of otherwise unrelated English law in a contract for shipment of goods from Newfoundland to New York. A "reasonable" basis for that choice clearly included the parties' convenience in being able to rely on a trustworthy set of laws and to avoid potential home court bias favoring either side.[87]

Once a reasonable basis suffices, any choice agreed on, short of facts supporting unconscionability, should be deemed to be reasonable.[88] The choice-of-law clause is the only way the parties can "be sure of knowing accurately the extent of their rights and duties under the contract." While support for this reasonable basis test is not universal, many of the cases that have refused to enforce the choice of unconnected law actually seem better explained as enforcing the strong policy of a closely connected jurisdiction.[89]

We will return to the connection requirement in chapter 4 in our discussion of states' incentives for enforcing contractual choice of law.

Super-Mandatory Laws

Most rules on contractual choice of law preclude the selection of a law that is contrary to an interested state's "fundamental policy." In general, these rules carve out a category of super-mandatory rules that trump attempts to contract around them by choosing alternative law. Under the Second Restatement, the trumping state must be one that (1) would be selected under the default choice-of-law rules in section 188; *and* (2) "has a materially greater interest than the chosen state in the determination of the particular issue."[90] Thus, a court determining whether the contractual choice is subject to a super-mandatory rule must consider both the nature of the policy involved (i.e., whether it is "fundamental") and the level of that state's interest in having its policy control in the case.

What is a "fundamental" policy? That's anyone's guess. Comment g to Second Restatement, section 187, warns that "[n]o detailed statement can be made of the situations where a 'fundamental' policy of the state of the otherwise applicable law will be found to exist." But it does note that "fundamental" means "substantial," but not necessarily *so* substantial as to rise to the level of "strong" that is required in order to refuse to recognize a foreign cause of action.

Some courts will invoke the public policy exception to strike clauses in the following contracts: franchise and distributorship agreements, noncompetition provisions in employment contracts, loan interest rates, and insurance contracts.[91] To be sure, some courts will enforce clauses in these contracts. But differences often can be explained either by differences in the language of the mandatory laws or similarities between the chosen and avoided laws. For example, in the franchise regulation context, the court in *Tele-Save Merchandising Co. v. Consumers Distr. Co.*[92] applied the contractually selected New Jersey law rather than Ohio law because Ohio's fundamental policy to protect franchisees against wrongful termination would not be thwarted. In that case, New Jersey allowed common-law remedies, so much of Ohio's policy would be respected. In contrast, the court in *Wright Moore Corp. v. Ricoh Corp.*[93] applied Indiana franchise law rather than the contractually selected New York law because Indiana had a strong public policy in favor of regulating franchises that application of the New York law would thwart. And in *Bush v. National School Studios*,[94] Wisconsin included in its Fair Dealership Law statutory language declaring the law to be fundamental policy and providing that the statute's effect could not be varied by contract. Naturally, the choice-of-law clause was deemed to be inoperative.

Consider also noncompetition clauses in employment contracts, which are contract clauses that provide that the employee agrees not to work for a competitor after leaving the firm. In *Application Group, Inc. v. Hunter Group, Inc.*,[95] a California state court applied California law to protect a local employer that had raided an employee of a Maryland firm despite the facts that the former employer was in Maryland, Maryland law had been chosen, and the employee remained in Maryland after being hired away. Under Maryland law, noncompetition clauses are enforceable so long as they are reasonable in geographic scope and duration, but under California law these clauses are not enforceable because they constrain competition and limit employees' future earning potential. The court held that California's anti-noncompetition policy trumps the parties' choice of law when the new employment involves the performance of "services for California-based customers" even if the employee has no contact with California other than being hired by a company that is based there. The court reasoned:

In this day and age—with the advent of computer technology and the concomitant ability of many types of employees in many industries to work from their homes, or to "telecommute" to work from anywhere a telephone link reaches—an employee need not reside in the same city, county, or state in which the employer can be said to physically reside. California employers in such sectors of the economy have a strong and legitimate interest in having broad freedom to choose from a much larger, indeed a "national," applicant pool in order to maximize the quality of the product or services they provide, as well as the reach of their "market."

In other words, the court let California employers compete for employees nationwide irrespective of the costs incurred by non-California employers when their noncompetition agreements are abrogated.

Thus, states can still rely on courts to protect some of their mandatory regulations from evasion through contractual choice of law. In some cases, state regulations are important and deserving of protection. In others, the non-enforcement of choice-of-law clauses does little more than preserve hills of chaos and parochialism from the eroding influence of the law market. It may be difficult to decide when states should be able to impose their super-mandatory rules on contracts that affect their citizens. For example, in *Application Group*, California might be unable to protect its policy against noncompetition clauses if firms from other states could raid California firms but the latter could not retaliate.

Perhaps the most we can do is to protect states' policymaking role while enhancing predictability. To this end, in chapter 10, we propose a federal statute that would force states to enforce choice-of-law clauses *unless* state legislatures clearly specify which of their rules are super-mandatory. But before doing that, it is necessary to consider some of the mechanics of the law market in chapters 4 and 5 and then focus on some actual and potential law markets in chapters 6–9.

4

The Creation of a Law Market

This chapter discusses the essential elements of a law market. By *law market*, we refer to ways that governing laws can be chosen by people and firms rather than mandated by states. This choice is created by the mobility of at least some people, firms, and assets and the incentives of at least some states to compete for people, firms, and their assets by creating desired laws.

How can law markets persist despite states' incentives to squelch them in order to protect their regulation? Chapter 2 proposed the law market as a way to ameliorate the problem of special-interest legislation. Specifically, one way to avoid regulations designed to transfer wealth from group A to group B is for members of group A to opt out of the wealth-transferring law by choosing the law of another state. Knowing this, however, group B should lobby the legislature to prevent group A from avoiding those laws, including through choice-of-law clauses. Alternatively, judges influenced by group B might interpret mandatory rules in statutes to also prevent evasion through choice of law. Indeed, judges often independently prefer to apply forum law both because it is more familiar to them and because they help to shape its content through interpretation.

Judicial attitudes toward these clauses have changed dramatically in recent decades, so that now the clauses are routinely enforced. This chapter discusses the trend toward the enforcement of contractual choice of law. The enforcement of choice-of-law clauses has significantly fueled a market for law. "Market," in this instance, does not refer to any particular set of idealized conditions of exchange, but rather simply to buyers demanding a commodity (law) and sellers being willing to provide it for a benefit. We contrast this sort of exchange with the view that law is decreed by government and forced on parties subject to its jurisdiction. Both the traditional and modern approaches to choice of law facilitate this view of law as absolute decree by focusing on the allocation of sovereign authority to the exclusion of party preferences. This chapter tells a very different story of how choice-of-law rules can enable the parties to decide which law applies to their dispute.

Governments cannot control everyone everywhere. Physical mobility allows a person or firm to choose a single state whose laws would apply to all of her or its activities. States compete for mobile parties and their assets by attempting to provide the laws that they want. This chapter shows how parties' fundamental ability to choose among these bundles generates a willingness on the part of states to enforce choice-of-law clauses, which in turn facilitates an even more valuable market in laws to govern particular relationships and disputes.

We first discuss the buyer side of the market. In a sense, parties "shopping" for law have created their own market by using several mechanisms for avoiding costly regulation. In particular, contracting parties have broad discretion to determine where and how their disputes will be resolved. They can also affect the enforcement of choice-of-law clauses by deciding in which state to establish the contacts that matter for enforcement.

On the seller side of the development of the law market, party shopping creates incentives on the part of some interest groups to push for laws that favor contracting, and therefore to resist interest groups that favor regulation. The law market thus adds a new dimension to the standard story of interest groups contending over regulation. The contest involves not only the groups directly affected by the regulation, but also exit-affected interest groups, which have a stake in the parties' decisions whether to locate, invest, or litigate in the state. Finally, this chapter begins to demonstrate the law market at work through evidence of the output of these market interactions, including judicial decisions regarding contract clauses.

The Buyers' Side: Mobility and Choice

This section shows how people and firms can circumvent government regulation by strategically locating themselves, their assets, and the adjudication of their disputes.

Avoiding Personal Jurisdiction

Parties often can evade a state's law by preventing its courts from obtaining personal jurisdiction over them. *Personal jurisdiction* refers to the power of a particular court to force a party to defend itself in that state. If a state cannot compel you to enter its courts, then those courts cannot enter judgments that affect either your behavior or your assets. Avoiding a state's courts does not guarantee that a party will avoid a state's law, since another state's courts might apply that law. However, once a party defeats a state's personal jurisdiction, it is unlikely that other states will feel compelled to apply the avoided state's law. To avoid personal jurisdiction in a state, one must avoid creating contacts there. As discussed in chapter 3, lack of contact with a state typically also defeats any justification for applying that state's law.

Personal jurisdiction is limited in the United States by the Due Process Clauses contained in the Fifth and Fourteenth amendments to the U.S. Constitution. The Due Process Clauses allow courts to assert jurisdiction only over parties who have had "minimum contacts" with the state.[1] A party establishes minimum contacts when she directs action toward the forum in a way that makes it fair to require her to defend a lawsuit involving the action in that state.[2] A court also may assert "general" jurisdiction over a defendant who has extensive local contacts, such as someone residing in a jurisdiction or maintaining a principal place of business there, even if the cause of action did not arise out of or relate to the contacts with the state.[3]

These rules enable people and firms to circumvent state laws they do not like by avoiding contacts with those states. For example, a car rental company seeking to avoid the laws of New Jersey could refuse to set up rental offices in the state and could prohibit renters from taking its vehicles there. Insurers can stop doing business in states whose insurance regulations reduce profits.[4] Employment data indicate not only that franchisors reduce their activities in states with the most stringent franchise regulations, but also that the reductions are greater where the states prohibit evasion through choice-of-law and choice-of-forum clauses.[5] Exit therefore can thwart (though not completely neutralize) states' attempts to block the operation of the law market.

Physical movement is, to be sure, a costly way for parties to control the application of a state's laws. But if the costs of complying with bad law are high enough, the benefits of the move may outweigh the costs, particularly given the pervasiveness of business regulations. Moreover, moving is becoming cheaper with the rise of computers, the Internet, express delivery service, and other technological innovations. Modern businesses rely less on bricks-and-mortar buildings and instead increasingly focus on geographically independent or mobile assets, such as intellectual property and human capital. Reduced trade barriers let firms find trade and investment opportunities anywhere in the world. Firms therefore may be willing to incur the costs of avoiding a state if the state's regulations impose higher costs. They also may be willing to move to a state if that state's overall legal environment, including its general policy of enforcing contracts, provides benefits across the range of the firm's activities.

The discipline that mobility exerts on state politicians depends on the benefits that states can offer firms to offset bad laws. The more desirable a location is because of its nonlaw attributes, such as its labor pool, its extensive consumer market, or its plentiful natural resources, the more it can get away with harsh regulations promoted by local interest groups. We would therefore expect large and rich states like California to be less responsive to the law market than small states like Delaware. In short, physical mobility works to enhance, but not to guarantee, the enforcement of choice-of-law clauses.

Avoiding and Choosing Laws

As an alternative to avoiding contacts with a state, parties might avoid undesirable laws by contracting for the more desired laws of another state. As discussed in chapter 3, section 187 of the Second Restatement provides that the parties' contractual choice of law is enforced *except* to give effect to the fundamental public policy of a state with a materially greater interest in the determination of the issue if that state would be selected under default choice-of-law rules. This rule lets a party avoid the application of a disfavored law not only by preventing the state from asserting personal jurisdiction, but also by manipulating contacts toward states with favorable regulations or policies favoring the enforcement of contractual choice of law and away from states with unfavorable policies or choice-of-law rules. For example, a firm can boost the chances that a state's law will apply to its transactions by establishing a home office or major activities in the state and then contracting for application of that state's law.

Choosing Where to Sue

A plaintiff can control the governing law to some extent by choosing where to sue. As discussed in chapter 3, courts have both strong incentives and substantial freedom to apply local law. Moreover, even if some other court would apply the preferred law, the judges in the preferred state are more likely than those elsewhere to attend to the nuances of its law and to appreciate the underlying policy considerations.

Plaintiff's choice is limited, however. Recall that the plaintiff can sue only where the state can assert personal jurisdiction over the defendant. Moreover, a potential defendant can sometimes choose the court by preempting plaintiff's lawsuit; specifically, defendant can initiate its own lawsuit by suing for a "declaratory judgment" that asks the court to declare that the contract is valid.

Within the United States, contracting parties are often also able to choose between federal and state courts. Federal courts can exercise jurisdiction over state law contract disputes if the parties have more than $75,000 in dispute and there is diversity of citizenship.[6] *Diversity of citizenship* requires either that the parties be from different states or that one of the parties be a foreign citizen or foreign state.[7] A corporation is deemed to be a citizen of the state in which it is incorporated as well as of the state where it has its principal place of business.[8] Importantly for present purposes, if the plaintiff sues in a state court, the defendant has an automatic right to remove the case to federal court as long as the diversity jurisdiction requirements are satisfied and the plaintiff has not sued the defendant in its home state.[9]

Suing in federal court might seem to accomplish little in terms of shopping for law because a federal court exercising diversity jurisdiction must apply the choice-of-law principles of the state in which the federal court is located,[10] including the rules on enforcing choice-of-law clauses. However, we have seen that these rules give courts significant leeway in deciding whether to enforce choice-of-law clauses. Judges' incentives therefore matter, and federal judges have less reason to enforce local state legislators' regulatory deals since these legislators do not control their tenure or salary. Moreover, federal judges get less benefit from applying local state law because they are typically not experts in that law and are not able to craft binding precedent by applying it. One might therefore predict that federal courts would be more inclined than state courts to enforce choice-of-law clauses.

The cases discussed at the end of this chapter support this predicted difference: federal courts hear the vast majority of cases involving the enforcement of choice-of-law clauses, and they enforce these decisions at a much greater rate than do state courts.[11] Perhaps these differences reflect the fact that, because of the $75,000 minimum amount for federal diversity jurisdiction, federal courts do not hear many consumer cases, in which courts may be most dubious about enforcing contractual choice. On the other hand, as we will see below, the leading non-enforcement categories in both federal and state court—franchise agreements and noncompetition clauses in employment agreements—are likely to involve more than the jurisdictional amount.[12]

Choice-of-Court Clauses

Choosing where to sue at the time of litigation is an imperfect mechanism for controlling the forum. The defendant may find itself at the mercy of the plaintiff's unilateral decision about where to sue. A party's ability to sue in or remove to federal court also is limited by the rules governing diversity jurisdiction. Although defendants can initiate declaratory judgment actions, this strategy is only effective to counter plaintiff's forum shopping if defendant's court reaches judgment before plaintiff's court. In either case, parties choose the forum unilaterally.

As an alternative to this unilateral choice, contracting parties might mutually agree to insert a choice-of-court clause in their agreement which designates the state or federal court where their future disputes will be litigated.[13] The designated court should be one that is likely to apply the law that the parties prefer. In general, a court is more inclined to apply the parties' choice of law if the parties choose local law. Thus, parties commonly use choice-of-law and choice-of-court clauses that both designate the same state.

Choice-of-court clauses serve other purposes. First, choice-of-court clauses operate as waivers of each party's right to assert that the chosen court lacks personal jurisdiction over her. Choice-of-court clauses also ensure that the case will be heard in a convenient forum, or in a court that offers fast, expert adjudication. Also, parties may prefer particular procedural rules, such as limited or more expansive discovery, rights (or not) to jury trials, time limitations for filing suit, and increased ability to compel third-party witnesses to testify. The choice of court can make a significant difference in the outcome of a dispute even apart from the law applied. For example, a study of 3 million U.S. federal cases filed over a 13-year period indicated that the plaintiff win rate dropped from 58 to 29 percent for cases that were transferred from plaintiff's to defendant's chosen forum, despite the fact that federal rules ensure application of the same law after a case is transferred.[14]

Do choice-of-court clauses actually work to ensure the application of a particular law? What if a party ignores the clause and sues in a court that is disinclined to enforce the choice-of-law clause? If so, would that court not also be hostile to the choice-of-court clause? Indeed, some scholars have argued that courts should not enforce choice-of-court clauses because they are used as a way to manipulate the governing law.[15]

Choice-of-court clauses are potentially effective because courts' incentives to enforce them differ from those that apply to choice-of-law clauses. In deciding whether to enforce a choice-of-law clause, a judge must weigh the policies of the competing laws, and must account for any decision that thwarts local policies. Moreover, foreign law is costly to ascertain and provides no precedent for future cases. Applying foreign law is considered so costly that, in these cases, some judges use the *forum non conveniens* doctrine to dismiss the case on grounds that hearing it would be unduly inconvenient. Indeed, courts have been known to dismiss these cases even when a court-selection clause indicates that the parties agreed to that court's exclusive jurisdiction. By contrast, enforcing a choice-of-court clause requires neither understanding nor analyzing another state's law. Especially when dockets are crowded (and they typically are), judges might dismiss or transfer a case to the chosen forum without examining the underlying merits.

For present purposes, we focus on the role that choice-of-court clauses play in enhancing the buyers' side of the law market. Only a few states refuse to enforce these clauses,[16] though as we discuss in chapter 7, courts in some states are more reluctant to enforce the clauses in consumer cases. Enforcement has been significantly spurred by Supreme Court decisions applying federal law, particularly including admiralty law. A leading case was the 1972 decision in *M/S Bremen v. Zapata Off-Shore Co.*,[17] enforcing a choice-of-court clause in a commercial admiralty case. In *Bremen*, a German company contracted to tow a Texas company's oil rig from the Gulf of Mexico to the Adriatic Sea. The Court noted that the rig "was to traverse the waters of many jurisdictions" and the parties "sought to provide for a neutral forum for the resolution of any disputes arising during the tow. Manifestly much uncertainty and possibly great inconvenience to both parties could arise if a suit could be maintained in any jurisdiction in which an accident might occur or if jurisdiction were left to any place where the *Bremen* or *Unterweser* might happen to be found." The Court also concluded that the clause "was a vital part of the agreement" and that the "consequences of the forum clause [figured] prominently in [the parties'] calculations."[18]

Although later cases could have limited *Bremen* to its compelling commercial facts, less than 20 years later, the Court made clear that its pro-choice stance would extend beyond the sophisticated commercial context.[19] In

Carnival Cruise Lines, Inc. v. Shute,[20] it enforced such a clause buried in the fine print of a consumer's passenger cruise line ticket.

Judicial enforcement of choice-of-court clauses was itself spurred by the general operation of the law market. Through the 1950s, the courts and commentators quite generally agreed that enforcing these clauses would amount to an illegal "ouster" of a court's jurisdiction.[21] Yet now, the states quite routinely enforce these clauses. This almost complete turnabout occurred because commercial parties discovered an alternative way of avoiding undesired U.S. courts. As discussed in the next chapter, the parties could agree to arbitrate their disputes, thanks to the Federal Arbitration Act, enacted in 1925.

Choice-of-court clauses often work even in the few places where state courts will not enforce them. If the plaintiff sues in a state court that is hostile to the clauses, the defendant often can remove the case to the local federal court under the federal diversity statute. Once there, the defendant can use the forum-selection clause as part of the basis for having the case transferred to the selected federal court.[22] Even if the local state law (which arguably should be applied under the *Klaxon* case discussed in chapter 3) would not recognize enforcement of the clause, the Supreme Court held in *Stewart Org., Inc. v. Ricoh Corp.*[23] that federal law—including the liberal federal policy on court-selection clauses—applies in deciding the transfer motion.

The federal courts have been receptive to court-selection clauses in part for the same reason they were willing to enforce choice-of-law clauses: they owe no allegiance to local state legislatures. But the federal courts also seem more sensitive to competition from foreign countries' courts. Thus, the *Bremen* Court reasoned:

> The expansion of American business and industry will hardly be
> encouraged if, notwithstanding solemn contracts, we insist on a
> parochial concept that all disputes must be resolved under our
> laws and in our courts.... [I]n an era of expanding world trade and
> commerce, the absolute aspects of the doctrine of [non-enforcement
> of choice-of-court clauses] have little place and would be a heavy
> hand indeed on the future development of international commercial
> dealings by Americans. We cannot have trade and commerce in world
> markets and international waters exclusively on our terms, governed by
> our laws, and resolved in our courts.[24]

The use and enforcement of choice-of-court clauses may increase, particularly in international commercial agreements, if the United States ratifies the

Hague Convention on Choice of Court Agreements. Article 5(1) of the convention provides that "[t]he court or courts of a Contracting State designated in an exclusive choice of court agreement shall have jurisdiction to decide a dispute to which the agreement applies, unless the agreement is null and void under the law of that State."[25] The ratification of this convention might spur the United States to adopt a general federal law on the enforcement of choice-of-court clauses. Adoption by many nations would further enhance the law market.[26]

The enforcement of choice-of-court clauses, particularly since the mid-1970s, may have played a significant role in spurring the enforcement of choice-of-law clauses because it has enabled parties to funnel their disputes into courts that are more likely to enforce contractual choice of law. Parties now widely use choice-of-court clauses as an adjunct to choice-of-law clauses. An empirical study of merger and acquisition agreements filed with the Securities and Exchange Commission, for example, found that once parties choose a particular law to govern their transaction, they are likely to also provide that disputes should be resolved in the courts of the same state.[27] Chapter 5 discusses the important role that arbitration has played in motivating courts to enforce both choice-of-law and choice-of-court clauses. In general, both options for contractually choosing the adjudicator have been fueled by party and asset mobility and have, in turn, been important in enhancing the buyers' side of the law market.

The Sellers' Side: Lawmakers' Incentives

Buyers can choose their governing laws only if there exists a law market with a corresponding sellers' side, that is, a political mechanism that causes governments to legislate in response to movements in and out of a state. Sellers' incentives are obvious in the business world: if people stop buying a product, profits decline, the stock goes down, the selling firm cannot raise money, and in order to survive it must replace the responsible agents. But states are not like businesses. Politicians are responsible to an electorate whose concerns are more complex than those of a firm's shareholders. Politicians will care about the buyers' side of the law market only if exit-affected interest groups act as a sort of feedback mechanism to turn parties' choice of location, or "exit," into "voice," or political action.

When a state's laws drive people and firms away and when that exit is undesirable, states can address the problem either by changing their substantive laws or by allowing contractual choice of law. Without contractual choice of law, the law market would consist of the standard Tiebout mechanism of citizens and firms physically moving among jurisdictions with relatively static laws. We now discuss the mechanisms that cause states to, in effect, allow other states to sell their laws separately from the rest of their bundle of attributes. In general, we show how the buyers' side of the law market, including both physical exit and choice of adjudicator, operates in conjunction with standard interest-group politics to give states incentives to enforce choice-of-law clauses even if these clauses erode their regulatory authority.

Responding to Physical Mobility

How might states gravitate toward accommodating laws? Most states prefer to attract the employment opportunities and tax revenues that accompany firms' choice of physical location. More generally, any regulation that attracts or repels businesses also contributes or detracts from the state's overall economic environment and thereby potentially affects the welfare of all participants in this environment. Some businesses pay taxes that exceed the costs of the services they consume, particularly if the state can offer a generally favorable business environment. Businesses also employ workers of all types and buy goods and services from other businesses in the state.

On the other hand, not all groups affected by a reduction of in-state business will successfully resist bad laws. Recall, for example, that franchise termination laws can cause a reduction in new franchises in some states that could reduce local job opportunities.[28] In that example, low-wage employees do not have as much political clout as existing franchisees; members of the latter group each benefit directly from franchise regulation, and their common professional interests give them other reasons to form into a tightly coordinated group. However, any influence that the exit-based interest groups can exert would be in addition to, or in combination with, the influence of the groups directly burdened by the regulation: here, the franchisors. Thus, if franchisors and existing franchisees are closely matched in political strength, the political scales might tip to franchisors if they are joined by, or can make arguments on behalf of, exit-affected interest groups.

Lawyers

One particularly important exit-affected interest group is lawyers. Lawyers clearly stand to gain or lose legal business on account of the laws of the states in which they are licensed to practice. The more parties that are attracted to a state, its laws, and its courts, the more potential clients are available to the lawyers licensed in that state. Moreover, lawyers have significant advantages over other interest groups, such as taxpayers or low-wage workers, in promoting the law market. Lawyers obviously have lower lobbying costs than most groups because they don't need highly paid outside experts to make their legal case. They also have ready-made organizations—bar associations—through which they can coordinate their political activities. And lawyers have an incentive to invest personal time in the law market. Participating in law reform helps lawyers to acquire an aura of professionalism and enhances their reputations for expertise in particular areas of the law. Lawyers can gain similar benefits by writing forms, manuals, treatises, continuing legal education materials, and other material to explain new laws.

Although lawyers have special advantages in promoting law, it may not be obvious why they would promote the law of any particular state. After all, lawyers have general legal expertise that permits them to advise on the law of any state. But lawyers have a special incentive to develop the law of the state where they are licensed to practice because of the interaction between lawyer-licensing laws and choice-of-law rules.[29]

To begin with, *state licensing laws* give lawyers exclusive rights to practice in the courts of the state and to advise clients who are based in the state. Because it is costly to be licensed in a particular state, lawyers tend to be licensed only in the state where they reside and maybe one or two others. Lawyers therefore have an incentive to attract clients and cases to the states and the courts where they are licensed.

Choice-of-law rules, in turn, are one reason that lawyers can attract clients and cases by improving the law in their state of license. As we saw in chapter 3, judges tend to apply forum state law. Also, as discussed in chapter 3 and more fully below, the application of a particular law under default choice-of-law rules and the enforcement of a choice-of-law clause may depend partly on the parties' contacts with the relevant jurisdiction. Parties therefore have an incentive to establish connections with states whose laws favor them over the range of their likely transactions.

Contrast this involvement of lawyers in the law market with plaintiffs' lawyers in litigation-friendly locales who seek local and state laws favorable to plaintiffs suing national firms with class actions. In the class-action cases, the plaintiff can sometimes unilaterally choose the law by choosing where to sue. By contrast, the law selected by a choice-of-law clause must appeal to *both* contracting parties. Thus, lawyers interested in attracting choice-of-law business will favor different types of laws than those solely interested in attracting plaintiffs, or defendants, to the state.

To be sure, even lawyers involved in the law market may not always promote the best laws for society. These lawyers too may want rules that encourage more litigation, or more lawyers' work in litigation.[30] Parties disadvantaged by lawyers' self-serving rules might respond by seeking out less lawyer-friendly states. But when the state has particular attractions for contracting parties, as Delaware does for corporate law and New York for commercial law, lawyers can exploit this competitive advantage for their own gain. In other words, lawyers can distort the law for their own benefit up to the point that this drives parties to other states. If so, then lawyer-friendly rules can be viewed as the product of lawyer groups capturing some of the gains that dominant states earn in the law market.

Lawyer-friendly rules arguably could persist even when a state's laws are *not* generally attractive, because parties sometimes follow their lawyer's self-serving advice in choosing law for their contracts. Thus, one study of choice-of-law clauses in corporate agreements shows evidence that parties' choices of law in merger agreements are correlated with where their attorneys are located.[31] On the other hand, it is not clear how lawyers can systematically exercise this perverse influence. The firms that use choice-of-law clauses in merger agreements are likely to be relatively large and sophisticated and advised by their own in-house legal departments, which have no stake in a particular state's law. Their outside law firms usually have offices in many jurisdictions and therefore are not tied to any single state. Indeed, these multijurisdictional firms may compete with smaller firms partly on their ability to practice national law. This suggests that self-interested lawyers' advice may not be a big factor in choice of law. Instead, firms may hire lawyers in the state after having chosen that law on their own.

Lawyers advise clients in many different situations, not all of which fit the model of parties negotiating contracts that contain choice-of-law clauses. For example, courts use local law in marriage, divorce, and estate administration, and yet people often do not shop for law in the sense of selecting out-of-state law or deciding where to live based on these legal rules. But while competition in the market for this law appears thin, a market of sorts often lurks in the background. Some people do physically move in order to take advantage of or to avoid legal rules in any situation where the law matters. For example, people choose where to retire and may at that point care a lot about estate law, state investment taxes, or both. States no doubt use law along with other attractions to compete for retirees and their investments. Chapter 9 discusses the significant state competition for investments that is evident in the elimination of the rule against perpetuities and the rise of perpetual trusts. As we discuss in chapter 8, people may travel far to marry and to divorce if constrained at home. Lawyers have reason to care about this movement because it can directly affect their business. And lawyers often know better than other interest groups exactly what changes in the law will attract or repel potential clients.

Why Choice of Law?

The analysis so far shows why a competition for laws might develop, but not why the competition would take a particular form. If, for example, a state is concerned about franchisors leaving to escape its franchise regulations, it could simply repeal the regulating statutes or allow firms to waive them rather than enforcing choice-of-law or -court clauses. It is not clear why states do not simply repeal, since enforcing choice-of-law clauses inevitably weakens mandatory rules. Waiver or repeal might induce local investments but would not necessarily facilitate a market specifically for laws.

A choice-of-law market might develop for several reasons. First, choice-of-law clauses enable states to engage in legal "price discrimination." Pro-regulatory interest groups likely prefer regulations that bind the maximum number of firms. Accordingly, state legislatures may exempt only the firms that are most likely to make location decisions on account of the state's law. Maintaining mandatory provisions but enforcing choice-of-law clauses is particularly useful for national or international firms that must in any event operate under the laws of various states. Because of their national or international scope, they may be represented by lawyers expert in many states' laws. These firms face lower costs of shopping for law and moving operations than do firms that are based primarily within a single state. Thus, the state could offer national or international firms the ability to contract for another state's law, while still being able to apply its laws to locally based and other firms that do not care enough about the law to contract for it. As discussed below, this price discrimination is enhanced by the connection requirement for enforcing choice-of-law clauses.

Second, legislators providing for the enforcement of contractual choice may garner support from business groups that not only want to avoid oppressive laws, but also want to choose laws that are superior in some other way. Delaware corporate law, New York commercial law, and Connecticut insurance law are all examples of laws that appeal to a broad range of businesses across the United States. In each case, a state has invested in a sophisticated, highly functional body of laws and accompanying legal precedents. Similarly, U.S. securities laws may appeal to foreign firms by enabling them to bind themselves to higher standards of disclosure, as discussed in chapter 2. The law market therefore is based on lawmakers' incentives both to avoid imposing laws that *repel* firms and to craft laws that *attract* people and firms. By enabling parties to reach out to more desired laws, a state can retain local residents and investments without creating its own costly sophisticated legal infrastructure.

Third, the enforcement of choice-of-law clauses may follow from the enforcement of choice-of-court clauses. As we will discuss in chapter 5, once courts enforce arbitration clauses, they have little reason to refuse to enforce choice-of-court clauses. Both arbitrators and courts in the state whose law is chosen are inclined to enforce choice-of-law clauses. Courts in other states may follow these precedents. In this way, rules favoring the enforcement of choice-of-law clauses are often created passively by courts rather than actively by legislatures (though legislatures may have the last word by specifically prohibiting the enforcement of choice-of-law clauses).

Parties' Relationship with the Chosen State

As discussed in chapter 3, the rules for enforcing choice-of-law clauses typically require some connection between the chosen law and the parties or transaction. Increasingly, however, statutes are eliminating the connection requirement, at least for large commercial and other business-to-business transactions. A connection requirement appears problematic for the law market because it limits the state laws for which particular parties can contract. However, by balancing the functioning of the law market against states' interests in regulating, a connection requirement can contribute to the development of an efficient market for law.

First, making another state's law available only to firms that have connections with that state gives firms that are connected with many states an opportunity to exit local law, which may not be available to local firms. By contrast, eliminating the connection requirement would permit both interstate and purely local firms to exit. This focus on interstate firms gives choice to the firms that need it most. Because national firms may have less voice in a state's political process than do locally based firms, they are more vulnerable to costly legislation.

Second, a connection requirement makes it more likely that a single state's law will apply as a bundle to a number of a firm's activities. A firm can have its home office or main factories, for example, in only one place. Requiring a choice among bundles of state laws, in turn, encourages state lawmakers to think in terms of attracting firms to their legal *systems* instead of to *particular laws*. This encourages lawmakers to decide which issues are most appropriate for mandatory regulation.

Third, a connection requirement permits states to share the law market rather than creating a potential winner-take-all outcome. Firms' headquarters and operations are located throughout the country based on numerous state characteristics other than the applicable law. Thus, with a connection requirement, each state competes for only a subset of the total contracts. By contrast, without a connection requirement, a single state may be able to use its favorable law and courts to dominate the market irrespective of other local amenities, as Delaware has for corporate law.[32] This sharing outcome promotes reciprocity among all states. Under a winner-take-all regime, states might have an incentive to reject the enforcement of choice-of-law contracts.

Fourth, requiring the parties to establish a connection with the designated state as the price of getting the advantages of the state's law gives states an incentive to compete to supply good law. Local investments, employment, and revenues benefit exit-affected interest groups in the state and therefore give them reason to lobby for attractive laws and for enforcing choice-of-law clauses. This particularly matters to lawyers who, as discussed above, are important to the operation of the law market. A lawyer's license entitles her to represent locally based clients as against lawyers licensed elsewhere. Lawyers who specialize in transactional business rather than litigation therefore might favor a connection requirement because it encourages clients to move to the state in order to take advantage of its law.

Some state choice-of-law rules, as discussed in chapter 3, eliminate connection requirements for the enforcement of choice-of-law clauses. How do these rules fit with the above analysis of the connection requirement? To begin with, these states actively compete for law business by developing a clear and sophisticated body of commercial law. Lawyers in these states hope to attract nationwide litigation by maintaining a sophisticated judiciary and bar. These lawyers have no reason to limit their potential business by requiring parties to have a connection with the state.

Keep in mind also that states eliminating connection requirements do not control whether *other* states will honor the choice of unconnected law. If a contracting party sues in a state different from the one with the choice-of-law statute, the parties' connection with the *enacting* state may matter to whether the forum enforces the parties' choice. This ironically may encourage firms to establish connections with the states that adopt the choice-of-law statutes even if those states do not themselves require a local connection.

Alternatively, the connection requirement may encourage firms to use the laws of their home states rather than those of a state that is actively competing for law business. If a company prefers, say, Arizona's general environment, it might be content to use Arizona rather than Delaware law, but only if the alternative entails having to physically move to Delaware. Most important, if the firm uses the home state's law, it would have a reason to use the home state's lawyers. This would give lawyers an incentive to develop their state's law.

On the other hand, recall that under the Second Restatement a state can enforce the clause without a substantial connection so long as there is another reasonable basis for the choice.[33] This indicates that even states that are not actively competing for law business have an incentive to facilitate a competition for law. One possible explanation is that, for high-value contracts and particularly favorable state laws, some firms would avoid the non-enforcing forum altogether rather than being forced to move to, say, New York, in order to get the advantage of New York commercial law. Another is that these statutes involve contracts between sophisticated parties that are likely represented by lawyers, where states have relatively little interest in enforcing mandatory rules.

In short, three factors seem relevant to whether states will enforce contractual choice of law without requiring a connection between the parties and the designated state. First, actively competing states, particularly their lawyers, may conclude that eliminating the connection requirement will attract litigation business that is more valuable to the state than the investments the state could attract with a connection requirement. Second, the freedom to choose a state's law without moving there must be so important to the parties that they are willing to avoid states whose courts will impose a connection requirement as the price of applying the designated law. Third, where the non–actively competing state has little interest in regulating the transaction, it will be inclined to enforce the choice even without a connection, even if there is little risk that parties will avoid states that impose a connection requirement.

In some cases, however, a state's regulation might be important enough so that the state is willing to withstand exit threats. We now turn to that subject.

Super-Mandatory Rules

Although the potential for firm exit will put pressure on states with excessive regulations, the political balance in many states nevertheless may continue to favor protecting at least some types of regulation—what we refer to as "super-mandatory rules"—from the eroding effects of the law market. For example, states have enacted a wide range of employment, insurance, and franchise regulations, and these states continue to resist erosion by the law market by imposing super-mandatory rules on the contracting parties. In these situations, the interest groups that favor regulation have been able to muster the strength to defeat not only the antiregulatory pro-industry groups, but also the exit-affected interest groups.

Some of these super-mandatory rules can be troublesome. National firms continue to be subject to multiple states' local regulations, forcing them to comply with a bundle of rules that no one state would impose on local businesses. To avoid these sometimes significant costs, national firms may decide to lobby for federal laws that displace state regulations. As we will see throughout this book, there is a continual tension between federal law and the choice-of-law market as mechanisms for enabling national firms to avoid the costs of 51 sets of state regulations. Increased enforcement of choice-of-law clauses can be viewed as a way to preserve state autonomy vis-à-vis the federal government. This helps add to the pressures placed on these states to nevertheless enforce choice-of-law clauses.

Evidence of the Law Market

The existence of a law market depends, first, on parties' willingness to contract for the law of a particular state, and second, on courts' and legislatures' willingness to enforce those contracts. This section provides evidence of these law market components within the United States.

Parties' Choices of Law

Contracting parties widely use choice-of-law clauses. The most extensive evidence is available from the University of Missouri's Contracting and Organizations Research Institute (CORI) database of contracts entered into by publicly traded companies and collected on the Securities and Exchange Commission's EDGAR (electronic data gathering and retrieval) system.[34] A search conducted on the system's 89,097 contracts found 49,383 contracts with choice-of-law clauses.[35] Of these, Delaware (14,098) and New York (16,643) were each chosen in nearly a third of the total clauses, with California (5,485), Texas (2,787), and Illinois (1,548) also drawing significant numbers. This indicates that there is a market for *law* separate from a jurisdictional competition to attract firms' investments or business establishments. That conclusion is strengthened by the dominance of the choice of Delaware law overall for many different types of contracts, despite the fact that only a small number of firms have significant contacts with Delaware other than as a state of incorporation. A study by Theodore Eisenberg and Geoffrey Miller of choice-of-law clauses in merger and acquisition contracts[36] confirms the existence of a national market for law dominated by Delaware and New York. Eisenberg and Miller found that of 412 total contracts specifying the governing law, 132 chose Delaware law, while 70 chose the second-place state, New York.

One might suppose that Delaware's role as a source of law has something to do with its dominance as a state of incorporation, discussed in chapter 6. But that is not the case. The fact that a firm chooses Delaware corporate law does not itself motivate the firm to choose Delaware law for other contracts. We will see in chapter 6 that incorporation in a state does not necessarily provide a connection that validates the contractual choice of that state's noncorporate law. Indeed, Eisenberg and Miller found a "flow away" from Delaware as many Delaware corporations choose non-Delaware law for other contracts.[37] Also, Delaware has been in the forefront regarding law reform as applied to many subject areas outside of corporate law. The data indicate that Delaware has been actively competing in the general law market, rather than merely relying on its role as the leading corporate-law state.

Another indication of the market for law is that the top states chosen in the CORI database (California, Delaware, Illinois, New York, and Texas) are also those with choice-of-law statutes that explicitly make enforceable choice-of-law clauses that choose these states' laws.[38] This is no coincidence: the adoption of these statutes, confirming the enforcement of contractual choice of law, indicates that these states are announcing their willingness to compete in the law market.

Enforcement of Contractual Choice of Law

Chapter 3 discussed the general rules applicable to enforcing contractual choice of law, particularly the principles embedded in the Second Restatement. These general rules do not tell the whole story about the extent to which the courts actually are enforcing contractual choice of law. Instead, they are mere guidelines that the courts are applying in reaching their decisions.

In an extensive survey, Ribstein examined about 700 cases decided prior to 2003 where the court considered whether to apply the law chosen in the contract.[39] A second review of cases decided prior to mid-2006 confirms these results. The later review focused on cases citing the Second Restatement provision governing the enforcement of choice-of-law clauses (section 187).[40] That study included more cases that likely considered the policies embodied in the Second Restatement provision: contacts between the party and the relevant jurisdiction, and enforcing the mandatory laws of a related state. In general, these studies provide evidence that choice-of-law clauses are broadly enforced, and they support many of the theoretical points about the mechanisms of the law market made in this chapter.

Here is a summary of some of the findings:

1. In the first survey, courts enforced choice-of-law clauses in over 80 percent (459 of 565) of the cases in which the court opined on the validity of the clause. In most of these cases, the court enforced the contract's selection of the law of a state other than the forum.[41] In the second survey, the enforcement percentage was around 78 percent.

2. The first survey shows that party use and court treatment of choice-of-law clauses are increasing over time. Of the 697 cases involving choice-of-law clauses that were decided from the 1920s, only 100 of these cases were decided before 1985.

3. In both surveys, many of the cases in which choice-of-law clauses were not enforced fall into two specific categories: noncompetition clauses in employment agreements and franchise agreements. The facts that nonenforcement is both relatively rare and confined to a few specific categories suggest that courts broadly enforce contractual choice except where strong local interest groups support the regulation that the choice-of-law clause would avoid.

4. Most of the cases were decided by federal courts: 529 out of 697 in the first survey, 194 out of 289 in the second. As discussed earlier, although federal courts must apply the same rules to determine the enforceability of choice-of-law clauses that the local state court would, all courts have significant discretion due to the generally vague rules that are applied to choice-of-law clauses. With that discretion, state courts have stronger incentives than federal courts to protect forum legislation from evasion through contractual choice. As a

result, we would expect to see the party seeking enforcement trying to get the case into federal court. Consistent with this theory, the first survey found that 88 percent of the federal cases that opined on validity enforced the clauses, as opposed to only 75 percent of the state cases. In the second survey, the percentages were 80 percent enforced in federal court, 72 percent in state court.

5. The law chosen in the litigated cases tends to reflect the data on actual choice-of-law clauses. In the first survey, the major states are New York, with 129 cases, or more than 18 percent of the total, and then Illinois (58), California (49), and Texas (45). In the second survey, the same states are important, but a couple of others also emerge as significant: California (22), Delaware (12), Illinois (20), Massachusetts (13), New York (56), Pennsylvania (20), and Texas (16). The surprise here is Delaware, which is the chosen state in a much lower percentage of the litigated cases than in the actual contracts in the CORI database. Two possible inferences can be drawn from this discrepancy. First, perhaps parties go to court less frequently with Delaware choice-of-law clauses than with clauses choosing other laws. One possible speculation is that Delaware law is more predictable, so parties have less to gain by going to court. A second competing inference is that the data on firms' choices in the large contracts contained in the CORI database differ in significant ways from choices in the broader universe of contracts. Put differently, the strong presence in Delaware of exit-affected interest groups tied to publicly traded firms also might translate into competition for other types of laws that in the aggregate fit those publicly traded companies better than they fit other parties.

6. Consistent with the analysis above, courts rarely enforce choice-of-law clauses when enforcement is contested unless there is some connection between the parties or the transaction and the state chosen in the clause. Of the 590 cases in the database where the clauses were enforced, 429 opinions noted that one or both of the parties *resided* in the designated state. In 143 cases, the opinion did not clearly identify contacts with the designated state, usually because the parties did not contest enforcement of the choice-of-law clause. Only 18 cases clearly did not involve any parties that resided in the designated state, and in most of these, the designated state had significant contacts with the transaction. Thus, although there is a general trend in state statutes toward eliminating the connection requirement, so far overall, connections with the selected state still seem to matter to enforcement.

5

Arbitration and the Law Market

Chapter 4 described mechanisms that parties can use to avoid undesired law: physical exit as well as contract clauses, including arbitration, choice-of-court, and choice-of-law clauses. Sometimes these mechanisms are used defensively simply to evade laws and regulations. For example, physical exit from California could enable a party to avoid California law, although the exit alone does not determine which law will replace California's. Parties also use these mechanisms, alone or in combination, to affirmatively choose the law that best suits the parties' activities. The choice-of-law clause is a tool that enables the parties to make an affirmative choice of governing law.

This chapter more extensively describes the role of arbitration in the law market. By *arbitration*, we refer here to any private dispute resolution process that affected parties choose and by whose decision they agree to be bound. The parties may decide to arbitrate after a dispute arises[1] or when they form their relationship. We discuss arbitration as a mechanism for enabling the parties either to defensively avoid undesirable law or to affirmatively choose the law that will govern the parties' relationship. Thus, we focus on arbitration mandated by the parties' predispute contracts. State and international competition for favorable arbitration laws powerfully illustrates how the threat of physical exit (or, conversely, the carrot of interstate and international trade and investment opportunities) profoundly influences the shape of a state's laws.

As described in this chapter, nations routinely require their courts, with limited exception, to enforce arbitration clauses in contracts and to enforce the arbitrator's ultimate award. Once judges had to enforce both arbitration provisions and arbitration awards, their attitudes toward choice-of-court and choice-of-law clauses changed dramatically. Judges no longer had the same freedom to refuse to enforce these clauses because parties could avoid court altogether and go to arbitration. This expansion of the law market in turn increased competitive pressures on arbitration: once parties could use choice-of-court and -law clauses to affirmatively choose their law, private arbitration associations have an incentive to work even harder to attract cases by precommitting to apply the parties' chosen law. State courts and legislatures also have competed to meet parties' demands for more effective and efficient court dispute resolution.

Finally, a more detailed description of the development of the role of arbitration in the law market provides essential background for the discussion of current controversies surrounding the use of arbitration clauses in consumer contracts, an issue explored in chapter 7.

Despite state efforts to improve the courts, some contracting parties still prefer to resolve their disputes through arbitration. This chapter details some reasons that contracting parties might prefer arbitration. The ability to avoid or choose governing law turns out to be just one of many positive features of arbitration that help to explain the strength of the demand side of the market for arbitration. We then describe how states' competing for increasingly mobile trade and industry has provided for the strong enforcement of arbitration provisions and awards. Importantly, competition to enforce arbitration now extends not only to matters that parties traditionally could control through private ordering, but even to the subjects of public regulation. This rich competition for arbitration, in turn, has forced courts to rethink their stance toward enforcing choice-of-law and -court clauses.

The Demand for Arbitration

Arbitration laws across the world have made arbitration very appealing to many contracting parties. Since the mid-1980s, arbitration has emerged as an important dispute resolution tool for international commerce. Some commentators estimate that 80–90 percent of international commercial contracts have arbitration provisions,[2] while the number of arbitration requests filed with international arbitration associations has grown considerably since the mid-1990s.[3] The demand for arbitration is not, however, universal. One study shows that the percentage of large commercial contracts opting for arbitration varied significantly by form of contract, with the highest proportion being only 37 percent.[4] Commercial contracts involve heterogeneous sets of interests and concerns, resulting in differing preferences for courts and arbitration. This section describes some of the considerations that influence parties' preferences for arbitration.

Contracting parties have significant freedom to choose between one or more court systems and arbitration. If the parties agree to resolve their disputes with binding arbitration, nations with significant international trade and investment activity commonly will enforce the arbitration clause and the subsequent arbitration award.[5] If the parties opt for arbitration, they can choose both the arbitral organization through which the dispute will be handled and the location where the arbitration proceedings will occur. Arbitral organizations use many different mechanisms to choose arbitrators and resolve disputes.

These organizations and individual arbitrators increasingly also let the parties customize the arbitration. The location of the arbitration specified in the contract need be no more than a legal fiction in the sense that all arbitration proceedings actually might occur somewhere else. By designating the place of arbitration, the parties may just want to choose the courts that can review an arbitrator's award and assist in facilitating the arbitration or the law that governs arbitrability, arbitration procedures, and possibly the legal issues in the arbitration.[6] In general, therefore, arbitration's flexibility stems in part from competition in the markets for courts and law as well as for arbitration services.[7]

Many factors contribute to a choice between and among arbitration and court options. In general, contracting parties seek to minimize their costs both of resolving their disputes and of ensuring compliance with contract terms.[8] Though arbitration clauses may sometimes harm a contracting party or third parties, usually arbitration agreements appear to provide significant efficiency advantages.

Choosing Governing Law

Most courts and arbitrators apply the law chosen by the parties. Indeed, the American Arbitration Association specifically requires its arbitrators to respect the law chosen by the parties.[9] Arbitration associations are particularly likely to encourage their arbitrators to apply this chosen law because the association desires future arbitration business. In contrast, because courts are routinely clogged, and judges are paid a constant salary and are typically subject to political discipline, they may have stronger incentives than arbitrators to enforce local law.[10] Arbitrators therefore are more likely than judges to focus on the terms of the parties' contract, and their decisions are less likely to turn on the public policy or regulatory concerns of states whose law is not chosen. Moreover, arbitrators' respect for the parties' chosen law is difficult for the courts to undo because any court in a nation that has acceded to the New York Convention (which governs the use of arbitration in international contracts) must enforce arbitration awards except in limited circumstances. Legal and factual errors are not generally grounds for vacating arbitration awards.[11]

On the other hand, parties that primarily want a law applied in a particular manner might instead prefer to have their disputes heard in the courts whose law is chosen. Even if enforced, a choice-of-law clause does not guarantee that an arbitrator will apply the chosen state's law exactly as that state would apply it. This problem is particularly acute where the legal rule is identical in each state, but the interpretation of the rule varies across states.[12] In contrast, although arbitrators are at least willing to apply the law chosen by the parties, their preference for the contract language and perhaps their relative lack of expertise regarding formal legal principles suggests that arbitration might be a poor choice for parties that are depending upon the nuances of their chosen law.

Availability of Private Law

Trade associations may develop private law to govern their members' contractual relationships. Some also establish their own arbitration system in which they require their members to resolve disputes. Diamond merchants, for example, have created their own system of private governance which utilizes both arbitration and reputational sanctions.[13] Because historically the industry has been characterized by culturally homogeneous traders who engage in repeat dealings, the traders have been able to rely on a private law system characterized by informal rules of equity. The grain and feed sales industry also has gravitated to private law principles applied by private arbitrators.[14]

Courts sometimes are similarly willing to resolve disputes according to private law. In international commercial contracts, the parties can have their dispute resolved according to the UNIDROIT principles, which are not binding law in any particular country.[15] Indeed, much of contract law in the United States consists of default rules that the parties can rewrite in their contract. For example, the Convention on Contracts for the International Sale of Goods (CISG) indicates that all of its rules are default rules.[16] In principle, then, many courts will allow the parties to incorporate a set of private law rules into their agreement.

To the extent that court attitudes toward applying private law rules vary across nations, however, the parties might prefer that their disputes be resolved by someone who has prior experience applying the private law rules to other contracts in their industry. The grain and feed association and diamond bourse arrangements illustrate that industry arbitration might best enable the parties to opt for the reliable application of private law principles. Thus, just as courts are experts in applying local state law, arbitrators who are experts in industry customs, trade usage, and private law principles often have a relative advantage in applying private law.

Soft versus Hard Law

Parties sometimes prefer arbitration as a means to better tailor their preferences for the application of either hard or soft legal principles. When courts litigate contract disputes, they vary in the extent to which the "hard law" of contract language and formal legal rules dominate their determination about contracting parties' obligations.

Some courts are eager to account for the "soft law" of trade usage, customs, industry norms, and the parties' past dealings and course of performance. These considerations are legal in the sense that they end up being used to craft rules of conduct for the parties to the contract. Because customs and norms are vague, fluid, and subject to nuanced contextual interpretations, the parties may not be able to reliably predict their legal obligations before trial. On the other hand, legal rights determined according to the customs and norms of the industry are more likely to fit the parties' environment than will rigid, all-purpose legal principles.

Other courts rely more heavily on the hard law of formal legal rules and contract language provided by the parties. Hard law principles might not fit the parties' relationship perfectly, but they enable parties to more easily ascertain their obligations than when courts rely on soft law.

Courts typically resolve disputes according to a compromise hybrid of hard and soft law. The compromise results because courts often attempt to fashion a single body of contract doctrine to govern many types of contracting relationships. These one-size-fits-all rules are too flexible for some parties but too rigid for others. Parties seeking the application of either extremely rigid rules of interpretation or extremely flexible or equitable rules of interpretation often need to opt for arbitration rather than a court resolution of their disputes.

An example of the use of hard law in arbitration is the grain and feed sales industry, where the parties use arbitration to ensure that their disputes are resolved according to formal rules of interpretation.[17] These formal rules consist of private rules that the industry has developed to deal with common issues that arise in the sale and transportation of grain and feed. Lisa Bernstein argues that the trade association members prefer formal, rigid principles because their disputes typically arise after their relationship has soured. Parties that find themselves in a mutually beneficial relationship are likely to treat one another's needs and desires flexibly. Their relationship therefore might differ significantly from the document they signed. When the relationship becomes contentious, the parties might turn to arbitration to ensure that the court applies the principles stated in their contract and in industry rules. In other words, the parties really have two contracts: an implicit agreement in effect while the relationship is cooperative, and an explicit agreement that governs the resolution of disputes that they can no longer resolve peacefully and privately. The industry members opt for industry arbitration because U.S. courts generally lack an appreciation for this distinction and will attempt to enforce the contract as it has evolved rather than as it was written.

Contracting practices vary across societies. Phillip McConnaughay describes the contracting practices used by many East Asian parties, which often prefer soft law.[18] While Western contracting parties typically believe that the contract contains much of the parties' agreement, East Asian parties are more likely to see the contract as the parties' efforts to describe only the beginning of an evolving relationship. These contracting parties would prefer that their disputes be resolved with little reference to the written contract and much more reference to the course of the parties' performance as well as principles of fairness and equity. While U.S. courts may use far more soft law tools than the feed and grain association members prefer, they use too few for contracting parties with non-Western preferences. Because many arbitration associations specialize in the informal resolution of disputes using generalized or equitable principles, these non-Western parties might choose informal arbitration over relatively hard-law-minded judges.

The type of contractual relationship often influences the parties' preference for hard versus soft legal principles. In a long-term employment contract, for example, employment terms are complex and change over time, so formalistic, generally applicable legal rules are unlikely to serve them well. Instead, the parties might prefer to resolve their disputes according to soft law, including the customs and norms that apply to employment relationships in the particular industry. This consideration may lead some contracting parties to use arbitration. Thus, empirical surveys have found that 37–41 percent of high-value employment contracts contained agreements to arbitrate disputes.[19] Collective bargaining agreements between employers and labor unions also frequently provide for arbitration of employment disputes.[20] Even if the parties are confident that a court will incorporate a reasonable amount of soft law in resolving the dispute, they might not trust the court to accurately determine industry customs and norms. When parties opt for private arbitration, they can choose arbitrators who will utilize soft law principles in a more desirable or more reliable manner than will the courts.

Expert versus Generalist Decision Makers

Most judges lack expertise in sophisticated commercial affairs. They are therefore prone to misinterpret the parties' intent in using particular contract language and to fail to appreciate the value of particular contract terms to the parties. If parties prefer an expert decision maker, they might add an arbitration clause to their contract that requires disputes to be resolved by someone who has expertise or experience in the industry.[21] For example, a survey of franchise contracts indicates that some arbitration provisions require that the arbitrator have experience in franchising law, some require experience in franchise arbitration, and some require experience in either the franchise industry or the particular line of business in which the franchise was engaged.[22]

The parties may opt for courts when the advantages of judicial decision making are more important than arbitrators' industry-specific expertise. For example, the parties to bank debt contracts continue to opt overwhelmingly to use courts to resolve their disputes. The banks presumably are confident that they can write the parties' obligations in the form of clear, express, and easily understandable terms and therefore have little need for experts.[23] Any risks of mistakes made by generalist judges may be offset by other advantages of court litigation, such as the availability of effective remedies. Similar considerations influence the employment contracts of corporate chief executive officers, which often opt for arbitration but reserve claims involving the non-competition clauses for courts.[24] These clauses are designed to prevent the employee from sharing trade secrets and other valuable confidential information with a competitor. To protect this information, the company must have a mechanism for preventing the employee from working for the competitor. Because the employee may share this information at the very beginning of employment, the first employer needs to preserve its right to go to court to obtain a speedy preliminary injunction. Also, 86 percent of franchise contracts gathered for a particular study provided that trademark disputes would not go to arbitration.[25] Arbitrators are not likely to have more expertise than judges in deciding trademark cases, and courts rely on a well-developed body of precedents in making their decisions.[26]

Some states are developing courts that can compete with arbitrators to provide expert decision making. State competition for sophisticated commercial cases has caused several states, including New York, Pennsylvania, Massachusetts, Maryland, Colorado, Florida, North Carolina, Nevada, and Oklahoma, to establish specialized business courts to resolve disputes that arise in commercial contracts.[27]

Avoiding Bias

Arbitration can enable a foreign party to avoid a court's perceived bias in favor of local parties.[28] Arbitration enables the parties to choose a neutral decision maker without necessarily forcing both parties to travel to a remote location. Arbitration is rapidly growing as a mechanism by which to resolve disputes involving international trade and investment, where local bias may be particularly acute. The caseload of the American Arbitration Association, which is now chosen in more than 10 percent of international contracts utilizing arbitration, more than tripled from 1993 to 2003.[29]

The choice between courts and arbitrators might take account of other forms of decision-maker bias that at least one party might prefer. Some courts are made up of conservative judges, or liberal juries, for example, who are likely to interpret governing substantive procedural rules or factual disputes in favor of one of the parties. On the other hand, arbitration may present an even more serious bias problem because repeat players, such as employers and merchants, often fare better in arbitration than do their single-dispute counterparts, including employees and consumers. Commentators have noted a number of benign explanations for these outcomes.[30] But can an arbitrator in a consumer case be neutral if she is aware that the company both takes the lead in choosing her and may be required to pay her fee? We explore this issue in chapter 7.

Application of Preferred Procedures

Arbitration is important as a mechanism for choosing procedural rules, such as limited or more expansive discovery, rights (or not) to jury trials, time limitations for filing suit, or differing abilities to compel third-party witnesses to testify.[31] By separating the parties' choice of forum from their choice of law, the parties may pick favorable substantive law from one state and favorable procedures from another state. Choosing the forum can make a significant difference in the outcome of a dispute. For example, a study of 3 million U.S. federal cases filed over a 13-year period indicated that the plaintiff win rate dropped from 58 to 29 percent for cases that were transferred from plaintiff's to defendant's chosen forum.[32] Because federal rules of procedure provide that the substantive law applied remains the same after a case is transferred, all that should have changed was the choice of judge and jury pool and subtle differences in procedural rules. Yet, the forum still significantly affected case outcomes.

Arbitration enables the parties to more precisely choose their preferred bundle of procedures than does a choice-of-court clause. Arbitration historically has been considered to be a much less formal and therefore cheaper mechanism for resolving disputes than are courts. For example, many arbitrators do not hold pretrial proceedings, entertain pretrial motions, keep transcripts of the proceedings, or issue written opinions with their awards.[33] Perhaps most important to some parties, arbitration does not usually entail substantial discovery.

More recently, however, much arbitration has begun to look more like formal court proceedings. According to the rules of some arbitration associations, routine discovery, motion practices, and written opinions with findings of fact and conclusions of law are becoming commonplace.[34] Indeed, a survey of contracting parties indicated that arbitration is no longer perceived as a relatively cheap mechanism for dispute resolution.[35] To some extent, this is because the bar association is attempting to ensure that lawyers enjoy a slice of any arbitration business that comes into the state. For example, California and Ohio do not permit individuals to represent parties in arbitration unless the individual is either licensed to practice in that state or teams up with a lawyer licensed to practice locally.[36] Although lawyers' participation adds formality and cost, it also motivates lawyers to retain and enhance arbitration.

Despite the increased formality of arbitration, parties that value quick and inexpensive dispute resolution can get it by opting for arbitration while contracting around particular burdensome procedures. Many associations' procedures are merely default rules that the parties can contract around. Thus, contracting parties often remain free to choose a particular arbitration association for access to neutral, expert, and professional arbitrators while replacing the association's undesirable procedural rules with rules that better fit their needs.[37] They can also get simple and speedy dispute resolution by threatening to fire an arbitrator who insists on using a cumbersome process.[38]

States now recognize arbitration's procedural advantages and are attempting to compete by providing courts that can resolve disputes quickly. For example, Virginia provides a "rocket docket" court, and New York's business court provides streamlined proceedings that have cut in half the average time from filing to final resolution.[39] But even with these improvements in state courts, arbitration still gives parties more scope to choose the exact bundle of procedures they prefer.

Limiting Remedies

Arbitration clauses can better enable the parties to limit or to specify the amount of damages recoverable in the event of breach.[40] For example, some arbitration associations will not let their arbitrators award punitive damages unless the contract specifically provides that they can be awarded, while others permit their arbitrators to consider whether punitive damages are appropriate, at least in the absence of a contract clause prohibiting them.[41] In contrast, courts are less likely to honor contract clauses regarding damages. Courts may not allow parties to contract for specific performance,[42] and they may strike down damage limitations they deem to be unconscionable.

Similarly, parties sometimes attempt to limit available remedies by choosing a forum that effectively eliminates consumer claims by requiring consumers to litigate in remote fora or to submit to arbitration without the possibility of class actions.[43] These topics are explored further in chapter 7.

Some companies are taking arbitration clauses out of their contracts in response to courts' insistence on affording consumers a right to class-wide arbitration. In particular, companies fear arbitral determinations that are so adverse that they could bankrupt the company. For these "bet the company" disputes, companies sometimes prefer litigation in court, both because they can better forecast the court's outcome and because there is a greater ability to appeal the court's determination.[44] Thus, contracting parties may not always welcome the ease of enforcement of arbitration awards.

Convenient Forum

The parties might choose a forum—whether court or arbitration—because it is located close to one or both of the parties, likely witnesses, and evidence. Arbitration associations may have a slight competitive edge in this regard because, unlike courts, they often can open branch offices in a number of countries or states in order to attract more parties to use their services. Moreover, arbitrators can travel to the parties to conduct local proceedings. Arbitration proceedings typically remain unregulated by the states where they are located.[45]

Ease of Enforcement of Judgment or Award

Within the United States, a judgment rendered in one state's courts virtually always must be given effect (including enforcement) in all other states' courts.[46] With respect to enforcing orders to perform acts or to pay money, courts therefore seem preferable to arbitration. But this may not always be the case. First, under the Federal Arbitration Act (FAA), in most cases, courts are also required to enforce arbitration awards.[47]

Second, arbitration awards may be even more enforceable than court judgments in international cases. No federal law obliges a U.S. court to enforce judgments rendered by courts outside the United States. Indeed, no global international treaty effectively constrains courts to enforce judgments rendered in other countries' courts. In contrast, many countries (138 at last count) have signed the New York Arbitration Convention, which narrowly confines the circumstances under which the members' courts can refuse to enforce an arbitration award. Indeed, in an effort to attract foreign trade and investment, most of the countries that have joined the New York Convention interpret their arbitration award enforcement obligations broadly.[48] Moreover, all member nations must enforce written arbitration agreements at least as they apply to arbitrable disputes. If the parties' assets are located in a country that is a member of the New York Convention, the parties can choose to arbitrate in any other member country while relying on the enforceability of both the arbitration provision and any resulting award. The ease of enforcement of arbitration awards has much to do with the prevalence of arbitration provisions in international commercial contracts.

The courts may catch up with arbitration in this regard. The Hague Convention was drafted in an effort to provide for international enforcement of at least those court judgments that contain choice-of-court agreements.[49] The United States has pushed hard for the Hague Convention because many foreign courts do not consistently enforce U.S. court judgments.[50] If this effort is successful, international contracting parties will have a more meaningful choice between courts and arbitration.

Summary

Arbitration has many potential advantages over courts. It is not always preferable, as when the parties have specific needs for the procedures and respect for precedents that only courts can provide. But arbitration's many advantages—including its opportunities to customize procedures and applicable law and to use industry experts as adjudicators—make it an effective dispute resolution mechanism. We explain below more directly how arbitration can contribute to the operation of the law market.

Law Market Pressures toward Arbitration: Private Law

This section ties arbitration to the rest of the law market by describing the role of jurisdictional competition in providing contracting parties with reliable enforcement of their arbitration clauses and arbitration awards, at least as to issues traditionally subject to private contract law.

Transnational investment and trade opportunities expanded dramatically during the late nineteenth and twentieth centuries. Billions of dollars of cross-border business is now transacted daily. During this period of rapid expansion, nations were forced to recognize that their domestic economic welfare hinged on their ability to attract both cross-border business and local investment. Economists and business analysts have extensively explored many of the factors that influence investment decisions, such as the quality of human capital, the availability and abundance of natural resources, the health of a nation's capital markets, the stability of a government, and its commitment to the rule of law. One important factor often overlooked by the academics, but not by policymakers or the businesses they seek to attract, is the availability of a neutral, reliable, and effective dispute-resolution mechanism.

Consider the problem from the perspective of the parties to a joint venture. An American company wants to partner with a German company to produce cell phones in China for eventual sale in Australia. Though the joint venture contract between the American and German companies would probably look more like a book than a single-page document, it would necessarily leave many terms unspecified. The joint venture likely will change over time as the business of the joint venture takes shape. What happens when the parties cannot agree, for example, about their respective responsibilities to commit sufficient resources to ensure the success of the joint venture? How will they distribute the assets and liabilities on termination? What happens if one of the parties refuses to perform as required in the document? Business executives must think about how to handle business failure as well as success. Even if the executives are irrationally optimistic that their joint venture will proceed smoothly, their lawyers will surely nudge them to think about what will happen if the relationship sours. Sophisticated parties often negotiate very carefully the contract's dispute resolution provisions.

Special challenges confront the parties to international business and commercial contracts. For example, each may worry that the other's courts will be biased in favor of local companies and against foreign companies, and they may be concerned about the costs of attempting to litigate with foreign lawyers, researching foreign legal precedents, and managing dispute resolution in a foreign language. The American company might worry about the socialist strain in German law, and the German company might fear the extensive discovery and possible punitive damage jury awards that can occur in American courts.

Even if a neutral court is available to resolve potential disputes, the prevailing party ultimately might have difficulty enforcing that court's judgment. For example, an American company may trust the neutrality of the German courts to resolve disputes but not be able to enforce the German court's judgment in China, where the joint venture assets are located. Uncertainty regarding the enforcement of the parties' legal rights might prevent the joint venture from forming.

Now, consider the problem from the perspective of states and nations attempting to attract these international commercial opportunities. Nations can do little to change their natural resources, and it takes time and significant government effort to alter the country's human capital and its reputation for providing stable capital markets or neutral courts. But a quick and surprisingly cheap way for states to attract international commercial opportunities is to (1) permit the parties to choose private arbitration to resolve their disputes; (2) commit the courts of the states to the enforcement of the arbitration clauses (by referring all of the parties' lawsuits to arbitration); and (3) commit the courts to the recognition and enforcement of the arbitrator's awards. A country that takes these steps stands to attract business that brings with it cash, employment opportunities, and tax revenues.

When a state enables the parties to choose private arbitration, it helps to facilitate a market for the provision of arbitration services. Many arbitration associations now compete worldwide for the business of resolving international commercial disputes.[51] Parties that desire arbitration are able to choose the arbitration association in their contract. Because the arbitrators' fees are paid by the parties, the associations seek to ensure that the parties are satisfied with the services that they receive. Although no arbitrator can please both parties to a dispute, an arbitration association can increase the likelihood that contracting parties will choose it by earning a reputation for hiring arbitrators who enforce the parties' contracts and who render decisions that accord with the spirit of their agreements. When the parties form their contract and choose their arbitration association, they often cannot predict which party will end up needing the help of an arbitrator to enforce its rights. But each wants assurance that the arbitrator will respect the rights it has negotiated.

The genius of this form of competition deserves emphasis. To attract international commerce, a country need not start by providing business-friendly laws, courts, juries, or regulations. It can gain substantial economic opportunity from simply privatizing the parties' dispute resolution mechanism. In a sense, countries grant these international parties the right to privatize their own law. In the process, states may relax mandatory rules in favor of enforcing the parties' contracts. But because evading local law through arbitration is subtle and indirect, states may be willing to pay this price to reap their share of economic gain.

Jurisdictional competition for facilitating arbitration began in the late nineteenth century and has intensified in recent decades. For example, England made arbitration clauses enforceable by statute in 1886, and thereby popularized the use of the London Court of Arbitration.[52] Thirty years later, the New York Chamber of Commerce, which also provided arbitration services, lamented its competitive disadvantage relative to the London Court and lobbied the New York state legislature to provide a similar statute.[53] In 1920, New York became the first U.S. state to enforce arbitration clauses, with New Jersey following New York's lead in 1923.[54] Without the cooperation of the federal and other state courts, however, these statutes provided little assurance to the parties because one party could avoid arbitration simply by filing suit elsewhere or removing a diversity case to federal court.

At least partly to boost interstate enforcement of arbitration awards, New York commercial arbitration interests, including lawyers, lobbied Congress for a federal arbitration statute.[55] Congress passed the basic provisions of what is now the Federal Arbitration Act in 1925. The act binds both state and federal courts to enforce arbitration provisions in contracts.[56]

For much of the twentieth century, disputes that primarily involved private law were routinely referred to arbitration when the contract provided an arbitration clause. International competition forced American courts to release their grip on private contract law in order to provide contracting parties with an alternative to the formal court system. When U.S. courts expanded the recognition and enforcement of arbitration agreements and awards, the United States was positioned to compete more effectively for international commerce.

Other nations also began to provide pro-arbitration laws to attract international commerce, and, in 1958, 24 nations signed the New York Convention on Arbitration. The convention strengthened the enforcement of arbitration clauses in several nations and enabled nations to coordinate and harmonize their laws to promote the enforcement of arbitration awards. Although prior to the convention several nations provided for the enforcement of locally rendered arbitration awards, some of these nations were reluctant to enforce foreign arbitration awards without some assurance that their own arbitration awards would be reciprocally enforced. Merely bilateral reciprocity treaties were not enough for contracting parties, because contracts can designate the place of arbitration but often not the place of enforcement of the arbitration award. To the extent that the award takes the form of a money judgment (and it typically does), the prevailing party will seek to enforce the award wherever it can locate the losing party's liquid assets. Since money and other types of assets can be moved, the prevailing party might not know until the award is issued where it will need to be enforced. Worse, to defeat enforcement of the award, the losing party might be tempted to move its liquid assets to a state that has not entered into a bilateral agreement with the award-rendering state. International commercial interests therefore needed a broadly multinational treaty. Once the convention was in place, countries that wished to attract transnational commercial opportunities could signal their commitment to provide a hospitable environment by joining the convention. Today, more than 130 nations are members, representing virtually all of the developed world and many developing countries that are important players in international commerce.[57]

The convention requires signatory nations to enforce written agreements to arbitrate disputes[58] and to refrain from imposing substantially more onerous conditions on the recognition or enforcement of foreign arbitral awards than are imposed on the recognition or enforcement of domestic arbitral awards.[59] Nations must enforce arbitration awards that involve international business contracts pursuant to the agreement with limited exceptions. Unlike the standard rules on enforcing contractual choice of law (discussed in chapter 3), the enforcement of arbitration clauses and awards under the convention does not depend on a connection between the parties or transaction and the designated state. Enforcement may be restricted by the law of the state where the losing party's assets are located, the arbitration location, or the location designated in the choice-of-law clause. However, the contract can control most of these locations. Most important, the convention specifies the permissible grounds for refusing to enforce an arbitrator's award. It does not permit courts to review arbitration awards for mere legal error, which further secures the enforceability of the arbitrator's award.

Countries often obligate themselves to comply with a treaty but later attempt to interpret those treaty obligations narrowly. This has resulted in some treaties setting up international tribunals to determine whether states are complying with their international obligations. The New York Convention operates very differently, however, due to the powerful jurisdictional competition that drove the creation of the treaty negotiations. In an effort to obtain or maintain their competitive advantage, many nations, including the United States, have interpreted their convention obligations broadly.[60] Indeed, some states have enabled parties to end-run most or all court review of arbitration awards, at least those that are rendered locally. In England, for example, if neither party is a British resident or national, then the parties can preclude judicial review of the arbitration award except for matters of arbitrator misconduct. Under both Swiss and Belgian law, if the parties reside outside of the country, then they can contract to exclude court review entirely.[61]

As state policies on judicial review of arbitration awards indicate, states compete to attract the arbitration proceedings as well as the commercial contracts that arbitration facilitates. Industry experts, existing arbitration associations, and other potential arbitrators all benefit from laws that make it easier and more appealing for contracting parties to arbitrate in their jurisdictions. Although one might think that lawyers would oppose the facilitation of local arbitration on the grounds that arbitration substitutes for litigation, which keeps lawyers lucratively employed, local arbitration actually can increase the demand for lawyer services. But while nonlawyers typically serve as arbitrators in trade industry arbitration, in many other types of arbitration, trained lawyers are increasingly used as arbitrators.[62] Moreover, lawyer representation is increasing in arbitration. For example, lawyer representation in American Arbitration Association tribunals rose from 36 percent in 1928 to 91 percent by 1947,[63] and the representation rates have remained high ever since. With lawyers routinely representing the parties and often rendering the decisions, demand for their services continues to increase. This encourages lawyers to lobby in state legislatures for arbitration-friendly laws. Lawyers and other arbitration beneficiaries have been very successful in helping to ensure that the United States is perceived as a hospitable location for arbitration proceedings, and the choice of the United States as a site for arbitration and the choice of American arbitrators have both grown substantially in recent years.[64]

On the other hand, various interest groups may try to limit the enforcement of arbitration clauses. For example, a federal law prohibits the enforcement of predispute mandatory arbitration clauses in franchise contracts between automobile manufacturers and dealers,[65] and a bill introduced in the U.S. Senate would ban enforcement of the same clauses in livestock and poultry contracts.[66] As discussed further in chapter 7, as of this writing there is currently a bill pending in Congress that would retroactively strike predispute arbitration clauses from all consumer and franchise contracts.[67] These examples illustrate the tension between law market forces and the pro-regulatory interest groups whose power the law market threatens.

Arbitration and Public Law

Arbitration is not just about choosing a quick, neutral way to resolve purely private disputes. It also can be a mechanism for evading a nation's regulations.[68] This evasion is a subtle by-product of international commercial competition rather than a consequence of formal international agreements or arbitration association rules. The New York Convention, for example, leaves nations free to determine which types of claims are arbitrable. Moreover, although arbitration association rules often obligate the arbitrator to uphold the parties' contract, they stop short of stating outright that the arbitrators will ignore otherwise controlling mandatory laws. Although courts might be expected to preserve their jurisdiction to decide matters of public policy by narrowly interpreting the scope of arbitration, there is a tension between these incentives and the pressures of competition for international commerce. And when the courts, including the U.S. Supreme Court, respond to these international pressures by enforcing arbitration agreements, their rulings tend to apply equally to domestic contracts.[69] Once international parties get the benefits of arbitration, the courts have little reason to hamper the ability of domestic parties, which might be competing with the international parties in world markets, to obtain the same benefits.[70]

The U.S. Supreme Court clearly has broadly interpreted arbitration under the FAA, which embodies U.S. convention obligations in its chapter 2. For example, one might suppose that a court would have to determine the validity of the contract itself as a prerequisite to enforcing an arbitration clause embedded in that contract. However, the U.S. Supreme Court has held that, because the parties have indicated in their agreement that they wish their disputes to be resolved by an arbitrator, the arbitrator must determine in the first instance whether the contract is valid.[71] Indeed, requiring judicial determination of contract validity would sacrifice the benefits of arbitration, including avoiding biased courts and obtaining quick and inexpensive dispute resolution. The United States is therefore one of at least 71 nations that recognize some form of "separability" doctrine, which views an arbitration clause as an agreement that exists separately from the underlying agreement.[72] Though Congress has proposed abrogating the separability doctrine in the United States,[73] a blanket repeal of the separability doctrine is unlikely, given the law market forces pushing states to maximize parties' abilities to choose arbitration. Finally, in order to preserve these benefits of arbitration, the Supreme Court has decided that the FAA prevents states from requiring administrative review of regulated contracts as a prerequisite to arbitration.[74]

More generally, the U.S. Supreme Court has, since the 1970s, steadfastly refused to allow the courts to preserve their jurisdiction to decide matters of public policy when the parties have opted for arbitration. Instead, the Court has found an increasing number of public and quasi-public law claims related to the contract to be arbitrable, including antitrust,[75] securities fraud,[76] antiracketeering,[77] and civil rights and employment discrimination[78] claims. The Court and federal appellate courts have admonished state and lower federal courts against attempting to impose local notions of justice on international transactions. The Court has reasoned that we can no longer insist on conducting world trade according to our norms and our laws, with disputes resolved in our courts.[79] In other words, if the United States acts like a bully and attempts to interfere with the goals of international businesses, these firms can decide to play ball somewhere else. The threat of physical exit therefore influences the balance between arbitration and courts.

Several features of arbitration facilitate a disregard of public law. First, the parties typically maintain control over the choice of arbitrator, and nothing requires parties to choose an arbitrator who is trained in law, much less in the particular law of the regulating state. Second, even a trained lawyer is much more likely to concern herself as arbitrator with the specific terms of the contract than with state public policy for the simple reason that she presumably wants to serve as an arbitrator in future cases. Third, the arbitrator's ability to ignore regulatory law is enhanced in international cases, where it is often unclear which nation's regulations should apply even if they were given serious consideration. To the extent that a credible case can be made that a particular nation's regulations are inapplicable, the arbitrator can further justify her decision to focus on the contract instead of national laws. Fourth, recall that arbitration decisions are not reviewed for simple legal error in U.S. courts.[80]

Although courts may be tempted to enforce their local regulations, jurisdictional competition remains a powerful counterforce. In an effort to gain a competitive advantage, some nations have let the parties reduce judicial review of arbitration awards even further than already provided by international convention. If an arbitration award can be enforced in one of these states, parties can circumvent other nations' limitations on enforcement. Moreover, the U.S. cases illustrate that jurisdictional competition constrains nations' courts from liberally invoking the public policy exception found in the New York Convention.[81] In short, arbitration has played a critical role in facilitating the law market.

Arbitration's Role in Promoting Other Law Market Clauses

Arbitration's role in promoting the law market extends beyond its use as a mechanism for avoiding unwanted laws. Once courts had to refer cases to private arbitration and generally enforce the resulting arbitration awards, their attitudes toward choice-of-court and choice-of-law clauses were bound to change. In the United States, for example, courts historically were hostile to choice-of-court clauses as private efforts to oust the courts of jurisdiction.[82] Courts similarly struck down choice-of-law clauses as private efforts to legislate the law that would govern activities.[83] Since the mid-1980s, however, courts' attitudes toward these clauses have changed radically. This shift is partly due to the same competitive pressures that produced the worldwide facilitation of international commercial arbitration. Nations wish to be seen as desirable places to locate transnational commercial activities, and allowing parties to choose their courts and their governing law is faster and cheaper than reforming domestic laws and court systems.

At least in the United States, the process of change was different for choice-of-court and choice-of-law provisions than it was for arbitration. For arbitration clauses, the branches of the federal government worked together to force state courts to enable parties to opt for arbitration. Congress passed and modified the FAA, the executive branch helped to negotiate U.S. eventual accession to the New York Convention,[84] and the Supreme Court has interpreted the federal arbitration laws broadly. All of this suggests a federal concern that state courts were reluctant to loosen their grip on commercial cases. In contrast, while the enforcement of choice-of-court and choice-of-law clauses grew at about the same time, they evolved without the coercive efforts of the federal government. But these seemingly disparate trends likely were actually related to each other in the sense that the enforcement of choice-of-law and choice-of-forum clauses largely responded to the growing threat that arbitration posed for the courts.

Consider the choices facing the state courts. Prior to the passage, amendment, and enforcement of the arbitration laws, state courts had a monopoly on cases filed in them as long as basic jurisdictional requirements were satisfied and no other court had already rendered a judgment. Because choice-of-court and choice-of-law clauses threatened the courts' power, judges not surprisingly were hostile to them. Though enforcing these provisions could further the cause of international commerce, no one state can much influence the availability of international commercial opportunities. If a New Hampshire judge agrees to enforce choice-of-court provisions while the Massachusetts courts remain hostile to them, this has only a trivial effect on international commerce for the nation as a whole. For example, a party seeking to avoid U.S. courts altogether might find itself ensnared in the grasp of a Massachusetts judge, so the fact that the New Hampshire judge will enforce a choice-of-court clause provides incomplete comfort to the foreign entity. Similar problems might have plagued the enforcement of choice-of-law provisions. What good does it do New Hampshire to enforce a choice-of-law clause that chooses Massachusetts law if the Massachusetts court would not provide the same courtesy to clauses choosing New Hampshire law? The economy as a whole might be better off if all states enforced choice-of-court and choice-of-law clauses, but no one state has much incentive to provide for enforcement unilaterally.

The calculus changes for the courts once they have to enforce arbitration clauses and arbitral awards. Now, a party seeking to avoid the grasp of U.S. courts can do so with an arbitration clause. Indeed, as mentioned in the previous section, the arbitration clause typically enables the party to avoid not only the U.S. courts but also the laws of the United States and its states. In this new environment, states' costs of enforcing choice-of-court clauses fall considerably. Courts historically disliked choice-of-court clauses because they tended to oust the courts of jurisdiction. But arbitration enabled just this result and thereby diminished the threat represented by choice-of-court clauses. At least choice-of-court clauses enable courts as an institution to maintain their influence as lawmakers and dispute resolvers.

State courts' concerns for sister state courts' actions also change in the face of arbitration. Without arbitration, a judge in New Hampshire might worry that Boston judges would apply different procedural rules and substantive laws and that the case's outcome therefore might differ from the one that the New Hampshire courts prefer. With arbitration, the parties can opt for dispute resolution using a drastically different set of procedural rules and substantive laws. Indeed, the procedural rules and "legal" principles used in arbitration can be entirely private, reflecting the law and policy of no single state. The procedural rules and substantive laws of the foreign courts therefore may seem preferable to arbitration. If litigation occurs in the courts of another state, then at least some public policy concerns or considerations of public justice could influence the outcome of the case. The choice-of-court clause avoids the threat of complete lawlessness.

Over the past decade, the United States has spearheaded the negotiation and conclusion of an international convention to enhance the enforcement of choice-of-court clauses. Some parties that might otherwise prefer to have their disputes resolved in courts nevertheless choose arbitration because of the relative ease of obtaining transnational enforcement of arbitration awards under the New York Convention. Parties to international commercial contracts hope similarly to ease the enforcement of court awards. The United

States led the formation of the Hague Convention on Choice of Court Agreements in the hope of reducing foreign courts' hostility to the product of U.S.–style litigation. The convention requires signatory states to enforce awards rendered by courts chosen by the parties in their contract clauses and denies effect to judgments rendered by courts in contravention of a choice-of-court clause. Moreover, courts can strike down choice-of-court clauses only according to the law of the state chosen in the choice-of-court clause.[85] No state has signed the convention, which was concluded in June 2005. Ratification by the United States, the world's leading commercial nation, likely would spur international acceptance of the convention.

Arbitration similarly influences the enforcement of choice-of-law clauses. Arbitration enables the private legislation that once concerned courts in the context of choice-of-law clauses. In some senses, arbitration clauses are worse than choice-of-law clauses, because arbitrators can apply purely private law principles, and they can end up applying no law at all. When the parties instead use a choice-of-law clause, they are at least choosing the law of some state. In any event, choice-of-law clauses do not remove the courts' remaining authority, given the parties' ability to completely circumvent the states' substantive law with private arbitration.

These effects of arbitration further enhance the effects of choice-of-court clauses on the enforcement of choice-of-law clauses. State courts can compete for cases by routinely enforcing both choice-of-court and arbitration clauses. Parties are more likely to choose a state's courts for the litigation of future disputes if they have a reputation for honoring the parties' choice of governing law. In order to exercise any jurisdiction over the parties' disputes, then, courts might have to loosen their grip on determining the governing law of the parties. And, as is by now obvious, once the parties can choose their law, the law market can firmly take hold.

To even further enhance party autonomy, courts have quite generally applied the separability doctrine to both choice-of-court and choice-of-law clauses.[86] Thus, a party cannot effectively strike an arbitration, choice-of-court, or choice-of-law clause on the grounds that the contract itself is invalid. The separability doctrine therefore helps to strengthen the law market's power to facilitate these clauses.

6

The Corporate Law Market

Scholars have long studied the state competition for corporate law as a distinct phenomenon. The basic idea is that because U.S. companies can choose to incorporate in any state, states end up competing with one another for the provision of corporate laws. Indeed, Roberta Romano has characterized corporate law as a "product" that states sell and firms buy.[1]

The corporate law market is driven by a special choice-of-law rule known as the "internal affairs doctrine" (IAD), which is what enables corporations to organize under the law of any state regardless of where they are physically located.[2] Moreover, there is no public policy exception to the IAD. By contrast, as discussed in chapter 3, the rules applicable to many other contracts, summarized in the Restatement (Second) of Conflicts, section 187, condition the enforcement of choice-of-law clauses both on the presence of a substantial connection between the chosen law and the parties or transaction and on the regulatory interest of the state with the mandatory rule. Under the internal affairs doctrine, the law of the place of incorporation governs the relationships among the officers, directors, and shareholders of the corporation. The law market thus enables states to compete to supply this corporate law as distinct from other laws and amenities, including the general economic climate of the state.

Why a special rule for corporations? After all, a corporation is basically a set of contracts among and between many parties, including creditors, shareholders, employees, and directors.[3] Although the IAD governs the law applied to the relationships between the corporation and its officers, directors, and shareholders, a different rule governs the other corporate relationships. Why not apply the same choice-of-law rules to all of these contracts? Indeed, why not apply the same rule to all contracts, corporate as well as noncorporate? We often hear two answers. First, corporations began as recipients of special privileges and concessions from the state.[4] Scholars and courts therefore have accepted that corporations are "creatures" of the incorporating state.[5] It seems to follow that only the creating state's law should apply to the internal affairs of the corporation. Second, there are obvious practical reasons for ensuring that only one lawmaking body can determine a firm's basic governance and financial rights. It would be a logistical nightmare if California and Delaware required different methods of voting for directors in the same corporation.[6]

It is not really so clear why there should be different rules for contracts within and outside the scope of internal affairs. Firms that sell insurance, franchises, or anything on the Internet have similar difficulties in customizing contracts for buyers in different states. Yet these firms cope with imperfectly enforced choice-of-law clauses. Additionally, as discussed in chapter 7, contractual choice of law does not currently work for all of the legal rules applied to mass-produced consumer products. In any event, the need for a single rule does not alone justify enabling the firm to choose its own corporate governance law because the single rule could be that of the corporation's base of operations. This alternative rule would facilitate a very different market for corporate law, but it would not be unworkable.

Nor can the history of the IAD alone explain its continued survival. Once corporations began to travel from their states of incorporation, other states in which they established headquarters or transacted business could have decided to apply their own local laws. In any event, corporations long ago broke from their origins as concessions or franchises and have been treated more like ordinary contracts.[7] And the historical explanation for the IAD completely disappears when one considers that courts have applied something like the IAD to partnerships and other business associations that traditionally have *not* been regarded as state creations. If the IAD can be applied to what is essentially a contract among individual members or partners of an unincorporated business association, why not to other long-term business contracts?

This chapter revisits our understanding of the market for corporate law. We will show that the corporate law market is simply a part of the broader market for law that we are identifying in this book. As we have shown, the law market exists because parties to most contractual relationships have a strong incentive to contract for the law applicable to those relationships. States enforce these contracts despite the fact that they have the effect of eroding connected states' regulatory power. States cede this regulatory authority in order to attract, or at least to avoid repelling, mobile firms. In short, the IAD did not spring only from forces unique to corporations, but also from these general law market forces.

This law market analysis has important implications for corporate law. The traditional approach to the IAD suggests that the IAD is constitutionally mandated. This would sharply contrast with the lax constitutional supervision of other choice-of-law rules (discussed in chapter 3). However, our analysis indicates that the choice-of-law treatment of corporations does not require a special relationship between state governments and corporations, and the IAD therefore does not justify special constitutional protection.

We will first discuss the demand for and supply of corporate law. We then contrast enforcement of the IAD with enforcement of other party choices of law. The chapter continues with a demonstration that the corporate law market is more multifaceted than most scholars recognize and discusses how that market responds to supply and demand forces. We conclude with an exploration of the legal implications of our analysis.

The Demand for Corporate Law

The IAD seems to have sprung full-blown from the corporation's origin as a creature of state law. But when those creatures roamed to other states to conduct their business, it is not clear why those states were willing to apply the creating state's law to matters of corporate governance—particularly since this effectively meant that the new state's legislators would have to give up their control of corporate rights and privileges. Lawmakers' benefits from the incorporation process, including attracting local investments, employment, and tax revenues, obviously would not be worth much if corporations could buy charters from any state but conduct their business in other states. The explanation for the IAD lies in the same forces that underlie the market for other types of law.

The increasing mobility of the corporation in the latter part of the nineteenth century was an important factor in the evolution of the IAD. The railroad and telegraph, mass advertising, and assembly line production made possible nationwide firms.[8] These firms could choose their incorporating state based on a state's law and legal environment independently of the firm's reliance on particular resources and markets.

Until the 1890s, states competed for corporations' investments rather than specifically to supply corporate law, since corporations had to incorporate in states with which they had significant contacts.[9] One way that states competed was through "general incorporation" statutes, which let any firm form a corporation without getting special permission from the state.[10] But a state had to be willing to incorporate "tramp" firms that had no local connections in order to create today's corporate law market.

Legal changes were provoked by firms' increasing need for legal flexibility. For example, state rules requiring shares to be priced at their initial sale price, or "par," even as the market price rose or fell, significantly constrained corporate finance in modern capital markets. Firms could and probably did lobby their home states to ease these restrictions, but clearly found it easier to choose another state's law without having to physically move there.

New Jersey saw a market opportunity. In the 1890s, the state started "charter mongering," that is, using a flexible corporate law to attract incorporations by out-of-state firms that maintained no more than a virtual presence in New Jersey.[11] A key move was to permit holding companies, which accommodated John D. Rockefeller's effort to create the first large integrated corporate enterprise.[12] When the Ohio Supreme Court ruled in 1892 that the trust agreement binding Standard Oil of Ohio was an illegal attempt to monopolize the petroleum business, Standard Oil simply dissolved the trust and integrated its business holdings by forming a New Jersey holding company.[13] Other firms that desired consolidation followed suit. New Jersey also offered firms the ability to use company stock to buy property and gave directors leeway in valuing this property.[14] New Jersey law quickly captured the interest of a broad range of firms.

For New Jersey to succeed, however, other states had to apply New Jersey law to New Jersey corporations. Why did they cooperate? The explanation ultimately rests at least partly on demand-side factors, which should be familiar from chapter 4. Without broader recognition of New Jersey law, corporations might have decided to sell their stock and locate their factories and other corporate assets only in states that applied the IAD.[15] To be sure, these moves could impose significant costs on firms, particularly if firms had to forgo conducting business with customers, suppliers, or shareholders in noncooperating states. But at the same time, corporations benefited significantly from the flexible rules that New Jersey offered. And they also had strong reasons to want a single corporate law to apply to their internal affairs.

At any rate, the corporate law market soon got its first test. Woodrow Wilson, at the time the governor of New Jersey, responded in 1913 to reformers' protests against New Jersey's monopoly-friendly law by convincing the legislature to amend its corporate law to restrict holding companies and to add strict antitrust provisions. Delaware promptly took over its neighbor's corporate law business by enabling tramp firms to incorporate and reincorporate in Delaware as a mechanism for avoiding these New Jersey law reforms. By the time New Jersey came to its senses and tried to recapture its business by reversing its regulations, it was too late: Delaware was already entrenched and gave the corporations no reason to reverse their new choices.[16]

The Supply Side

We saw in chapter 4 that the demand side of the law market can spark competition for the supply of law. Exit and entry by firms seeking to avoid regulation creates costs and benefits for other interest groups in the state. These exit-affected interest groups combine with the groups that are directly burdened by the regulation to promote contractual choice of law even if the antiregulatory groups could not alone either defeat the regulation or provide for the enforcement of party choice.

We can readily understand the supply side of the corporate law market, given the IAD. The standard explanation of corporate law competition asserts that states compete to obtain local incorporation fees.[17] Delaware's franchise tax, which is imposed on all firms that incorporate in Delaware, is as high as $150,000 per firm. In the aggregate, these franchise fees represent a significant percentage of the budget of this small state.[18] The franchise fee story seems to disconnect the IAD from the rest of the law market, since franchise fees do not explain the enforcement of other types of contractual choice of law.

The franchise tax does, in fact, go a long way toward explaining Delaware's dominance of the market for publicly held firms. Because Delaware is so small, it uniquely relies on this tax. This reliance serves as a sort of "bond" to commit Delaware to continue to supply high-quality corporate law. Delaware is unlikely to make New Jersey's mistake and neglect its corporate law business in favor of reform-minded interest groups.

The franchise tax cannot, however, be the only thing driving the corporate law market. It cannot fully explain even Delaware's production of high-quality corporate law. Of course, Delaware's taxpayers like not having to bear the state's tax burden, and so their legislators appreciate the franchise tax as well. But firms will not pay these taxes unless they get the sort of benefits that Delaware can provide. Even state legislators who care about franchise tax revenues may not have enough time, energy, and expertise to provide a state-of-the-art corporate law and corporate infrastructure. Perhaps more important, the franchise tax cannot explain the conduct of states other than Delaware. Delaware is one of only a couple of states that charge a fee based on the size of the corporation (most important, according to the number of shares) and for which franchise taxes provide enough profit to motivate the state to compete.[19] Where franchise fees are a tiny part of the budget, taxpayers probably care little about attracting incorporations.

In addition to the franchise tax, and consistent with the general law market, lawyers are an important driver of active corporate law market competition. For example, a lawyer named James B. Dill was almost single-handedly responsible for promoting New Jersey's corporate law.[20] Delaware lawyers similarly have played an important role in developing Delaware's corporate law.[21] The Delaware corporate bar drafts the corporate laws for the legislature, which passes the lawyers' recommendations verbatim.[22] In return, lawyers reap the significant benefits of a thriving corporate practice: Delaware lawyers' income is 50 percent higher than lawyers in comparable states.[23] Lawyers also actively participate in developing corporate law outside of Delaware.[24]

One might wonder why lawyers have a special incentive to develop the law of their state. After all, any lawyer could develop an expertise in Delaware law whether or not the lawyer is licensed in Delaware. Part of the answer, similar to the general law market discussed in chapter 4, is that only lawyers licensed in a state may practice regularly in its courts. Delaware's courts, in fact, are a big reason that firms choose Delaware incorporation.[25] Parties to cases in Delaware courts must hire Delaware lawyers to at least act as local counsel in litigation, and Delaware lawyers' inside knowledge of Delaware procedure and judging could be expected to give them an edge in drafting agreements that Delaware judges will interpret. Delaware lawyers therefore have an incentive to write laws that will attract corporations, and their litigation, to Delaware.

More important, although franchise taxes help us to understand how the market for law has developed *under* the IAD, it does not explain the development of the IAD *itself*. In particular, why do states that are not actively competing for out-of-state corporations respect the IAD? If lawyers outside Delaware want to encourage firms to incorporate locally, why do they not insist on a rule that requires these firms to do so as the price of operating in their states? After all, this would make lawyers' expertise in their states' local corporate law all the more valuable and enable more states to reap the franchise tax bounty.

Chapter 4 argued that, in the general law market, exit-affected interest groups can pressure states to enforce contractual choice of law in order to encourage firms to maintain and enhance connections with their states. The same forces contribute to the enforcement of the IAD in noncompeting states. If firms avoid non-enforcing states, lawyers, for example, may lose potential clients and litigation business.

States also have incentives to protect the IAD because it entitles their own corporate governance rules, as applied to their own local firms, to respect in other states. Courts understand that their decisions denying recognition of the IAD could be used against their own state's corporations transacting business elsewhere. Moreover, a state's attempt to regulate the internal governance of firms that are nearly purely foreign might be unconstitutional under the Commerce Clause even under the vague constraints discussed in chapter 3.[26]

To be sure, none of these pressures prevents states from imposing their laws on locally based firms. But ignoring the IAD as applied to local firms could deter firms from making significant local investments, which might trigger a local political backlash against the regulation. That may explain why only large and rich states like New York and California have attempted such a move.[27] These states have a captive market that local interest groups can exploit, in part, by lobbying to apply local corporate law to foreign corporations that conduct business in the state.

Limits on Enforcement

The IAD at first glance seems strikingly different from the rules governing choice-of-law clauses generally. In contrast to these general rules, the IAD is enforced without any requirement of a connection between the corporation and the state of incorporation and without a "fundamental policy" exception. Here, we show that the differences between the IAD and the general rules governing choice-of-law clauses are actually not as great as they seem and can be explained by general law market demand and supply forces.

Fundamental Policy Exception: The IAD as Optical Illusion

As we have seen, under general choice-of-law rules, courts make exceptions to the enforcement of choice-of-law clauses for certain fundamental policies strongly favored by pro-regulatory interest groups. Yet the courts do not recognize such an exception for the IAD. This seems odd in light of the controversies perennially raging in Congress and the press about corporate governance, including the corporate scandals that drew so much attention at the turn of the twenty-first century, as well as concerns about executive compensation, shareholder voting, fraud, and the protection of nonshareholder stakeholders, such as powerful labor groups. Shareholder interests alone are probably too diffuse to block such regulation even if it reduced shareholder wealth.[28] So why is there no fundamental policy exception to the IAD?

The absence of such an exception is not at all surprising for Delaware. The corporate leader is small enough that its incorporation fees really matter to its fiscal health. In addition, Delaware lacks the interest groups that might agitate for enforcing local public policies against foreign corporations.

But what about other states that are called on to apply the IAD to Delaware corporations doing business locally? There are at least two possible explanations for the absence of a fundamental policy exception to the IAD. First, there is only weak pressure for such super-mandatory rules in connection with corporate governance. Shareholders do not need these rules because they can protect themselves through voting provisions in corporate charters. Even if dispersed shareholders might need protection from strong managers, they are too diffuse to be politically effective. Creditors have no voting power within the firm and need protection from owners' manipulation of corporate assets. But banks and other large creditors could insist on contractual protection, while small trade creditors are no more able than shareholders to coordinate politically. Tort creditors, such as accident victims, were initially weak. By the time trial lawyers became a potent force in speaking for them, corporate features were well established, accounting and disclosure technology provided significant protection for creditors,[29] and trial lawyers had plenty of corporate assets to go after.

A second explanation for the lack of fundamental policy exceptions is that pressure for legal protections has been channeled outside the IAD. The IAD is a sort of optical illusion: it looks absolute only because its focus has been limited to the area in which it can comfortably operate absolutely. For example, creditors' rights are subject to choice-of-law principles that apply to contracts generally. The IAD only covers creditor protection rules that affect *shareholders'* financial rights, including shareholders' personal liability for corporate harms, obligations to commit their capital to the firm, and restrictions on distributions to owners that increase the risk that the firm will not be able to pay its debts. Unlike shareholders, creditors have no voting rights, so the firm has significantly less need for a single firm-wide rule for them.[30]

Shareholders need disclosure and fraud protection, which also lie outside the IAD. States' securities, or "blue sky," statutes specify disclosure rules for securities transactions and apply to transactions occurring in the investor's home state.[31] Here, too, the firm has less need for a single set of firm-wide rules.[32] Moreover, in the early twentieth century, strong interest groups, including well-organized regional securities firms and local banks that feared the big New York investment banks, asserted their will on behalf of shareholders.[33] So, even if firm-wide rules are desirable, state interest groups have prevented their evolution.

Ethics rules for professional firms also lie outside the IAD. In general, ethics rules regulate the conduct of individual professionals based on where they practice and are not really part of "corporate" law. Some of these rules, such as those specifying the members' vicarious liability for the firm's debts, have at least as much impact on the firm's governance as the rules that are subject to the IAD.[34] For example, a publicly held corporation may not practice law in the United States, and accountants and other professionals may not co-own a law firm. The persistence of these rules is readily attributable to professional groups that want to restrict competition from nonprofessionals.[35] Because professional groups are among the most powerful and cohesive interest groups, they would be formidable opponents of enforcing contractual choice of law.

Federal law is an important part of this story. In general, as discussed in chapter 4, when super-mandatory state laws threaten to subject national firms to numerous state regulators, business groups may lobby for a single federal law to regulate the area and to preempt inconsistent state laws. For example, federal securities laws have provided a federal disclosure regime that has mostly supplanted the blue sky laws mentioned above. Thus, federal law is part of the optical illusion of the IAD: it provides another way to move contentious issues, such as bankruptcy, securities, antitrust, and other laws that otherwise might trigger exceptions to the IAD, outside the scope of that rule.[36]

The ever-present possibility of federal preemption can serve to protect the law market. Early in the corporate law market's history, before the IAD was thoroughly entrenched, the federal government seriously considered the federal chartering of corporations.[37] The states and pro-regulatory interest groups need to wonder whether aggressive state conflict, which brings disorder into the corporate law market, could trigger such a drastic federal reaction. Interest groups acting at the state level must constantly balance the benefits they derive from enacting particular regulation against the possibility of losing their clout altogether. In this sense, state law operates in the shadow of federal law.[38]

These exceptions to the IAD show that corporate governance, if broadly construed to include matters that are technically outside the IAD, actually is subject to the same antichoice pressures that affect other types of contracts. The success of contractual choice depends on the same factors that matter elsewhere in the law market, including the benefits of contractual choice, the costs and benefits of exit, and the role of federal law in mitigating the costs imposed by multiple state regulators. The only difference is that, in the corporate context, the exceptions have developed outside the IAD, thereby preserving the apparent absoluteness of the doctrine.

Connection Requirement

It is easy to see why Delaware is willing to apply its corporate law to firms lacking local connections. Delaware's incorporation business confers significant benefits on the state's taxpayers whether or not the corporations have made local investments. Even apart from the franchise fee, Delaware lawyers would want to attract both litigation and its associated transactional work to the state.

But why do courts *outside* of Delaware also apply the IAD even to firms that lack a connection with the incorporating state? Again, we might refer to the market for high-value commercial transactions. Consider the Hobson's choice that a connection requirement would impose on a firm that strongly valued Delaware corporate law: either incorporate under the significantly inferior home state's law, or move to Delaware. The firm might well move, if not to Delaware, at least to a state that tolerates its choice of Delaware law. In fact, states are unlikely to impose this choice because they have little to gain from insisting on a connection requirement. As mentioned earlier, the IAD does not cover most important policy questions concerning corporate governance.

In sum, the factors that lead to the erosion of connection requirements, discussed in chapter 4, are present in the corporate law market. Because firms that choose Delaware law are choosing both the law and the courts of Delaware, Delaware lawyers are inclined to lobby the Delaware legislature to recognize tramp firms. In addition, the noncompeting states respect the law of the state of incorporation without imposing a connection requirement because they do not care enough about regulating corporate governance to risk forcing firms that highly value Delaware law to avoid their borders.

The Structure of the Corporate Law Market

So far, we have focused on the traditionally emphasized market for corporations whose stock is traded publicly on stock exchanges. Here, we broaden the analysis to other types of firms operating in the corporate law market. These variations confirm that the corporate law market is not a unique phenomenon, but rather is best analyzed in terms of the overall market for law. The different characteristics of the markets for publicly held firms, closely held firms, publicly held unincorporated firms, and European firms all can be explained by applying the same general supply and demand forces to different sets of legal needs.

Publicly Held Corporations

The Delaware-dominated state market for publicly held corporations is shaped by the nature of these firms. In dynamic capital markets, corporate law needs to change over time. But because amending a public corporation's charter is costly and cumbersome, it may be hard for corporations to change their internal affairs contracts to efficiently reflect changing economic or general market circumstances that a firm might face over its long life. Firms, therefore, must trust state courts and legislatures to make necessary changes.[39] And publicly held firms need to subscribe to a common standard law to better enable the securities markets to accurately price their shares. Finally, all firms take the risk that the incorporating state's politicians will pull a move like New Jersey did, that is, suddenly decide that they want to use the state's corporate law to regulate corporate misconduct.

Delaware is uniquely suited to respond to these needs. The many Delaware corporations produce cases and common practices, and those practices help to clarify contract terms over time.[40] Delaware offers a legal infrastructure consisting of the country's most expert corporate court and bar. And most large corporations subscribe to the Delaware "standard" of corporate law. A would-be competitor would have to make a large investment to try to compete with Delaware. Meanwhile, Delaware could quickly respond to any other state's attempt to actively compete with it.[41] As a result, public corporations are willing to pay Delaware enough in franchise taxes to give it an incentive to maintain a substantial infrastructure and to post a "bond" to secure the future direction of its law.[42]

Given these significant advantages of corporate law, is there *any* realistic competition in this market? Apparently, yes. Corporate law innovations have spread through the states in the same way that innovations in competitive markets have been shown to spread,[43] and states earn franchise revenues in proportion to their willingness to respond to changes in the market with innovative legislation.[44] States are motivated to compete because, as discussed above, their lawyers have strong incentives to keep corporations at home, and thereby increase the value of their expertise, rather than sending them off to Delaware lawyers.

Another factor at work in this broader state competition is that the firm's place of incorporation can influence its governing law regarding issues that fall outside of the IAD. For example, there is evidence that, when Delaware corporations do not choose Delaware law for their merger contracts, they most often choose the place where at least one of the businesses is located.[45] This may be because linking the firm's physical location with the designated law makes it more likely that courts will enforce the choice-of-law clause. Recall from our discussion of the Second Restatement, section 187, that a state's public policy can thwart the parties' choice of law only if the trumping state is the state with the most significant relationship to the parties and the transaction. If a firm prefers its home state law and would like it to apply to its non-IAD contracts, then incorporating at home rather than in Delaware adds contacts to the home state that can help to ensure that no other state has a more significant relationship. The place of incorporation can help to bolster the enforcement of choice-of-law clauses choosing that law in otherwise close cases.

For example, in *Nedlloyd Lines B. V. v. Superior Ct.*,[46] a California court enforced the choice-of-law clause designating Hong Kong law in an international multiparty shareholders' agreement. The agreement had created a joint venture shipping firm that was incorporated in Hong Kong but primarily located in California. Because the shareholders were located in several jurisdictions and the joint venture engaged in worldwide shipping, no state clearly stood out as the one with the most significant relationship to this shareholders' agreement. In the end, the place of incorporation, coupled with the location of some of the shareholders, was enough for the court to determine that no other state replaced Hong Kong as the state with the most significant relationship. Even if the state of incorporation is a minor factor in determining the state with the most significant relationship, firms that use choice-of-law clauses in repeated transactions might nevertheless wish to maximize the likelihood of success over the range of cases.

Closely Held Business Associations

The IAD applies to closely held as well as publicly held corporations. It traditionally was linked to the corporate form and therefore did not traditionally apply to unincorporated firms.[47] But choice-of-law clauses are now enforced so commonly in general partnerships that the rule closely resembles the IAD.[48] The IAD is explicitly applied to limited liability partnership-type entities, such as the LLC.[49] Thus, the IAD applies to all closely held business associations, corporate as well as noncorporate.

Despite the application of the same choice-of-law rule, the law market forces play out differently for these entities than they do for publicly held corporations. Closely held firms face many fewer internal affairs lawsuits over their lives than do publicly held firms—usually no more than one, when the relationship falls apart. They therefore derive much less benefit from a sophisticated set of corporate statutes and cases. Closely held firms also do not need to subscribe to a common standard because their shares are not publicly traded. It follows that closely held firms would be less willing than publicly held firms to incur the costs of operating outside their formation state, which include paying a foreign firm fee, particularly since these fees are likely to be higher per dollar invested in the closely held firm than they are for publicly held firms.[50] Unlike closely held firms, which often operate within a single state, publicly held firms are more likely to have to operate as foreign firms in some states whether or not they incorporate in their home state, and they therefore are relatively less burdened by the costs of shopping for law.[51]

Despite these constraints, there is some competition for the law of closely held firms, as well as for the law of LLCs, which can be closely or publicly held. To begin with, about half of larger closely held corporations (those with more than 1,000 employees) incorporate outside their principal place of business (the majority in Delaware), and apparently they are most likely to do so if their home state has a low-quality judiciary, a high propensity to pierce the veil for creditors, or a high level of minority shareholder protection.[52]

There is also evidence that states have actively competed to supply the law of closely held *unincorporated* firms, and that this competition has led to efficient legal rules.[53] Moreover, while there is no dominant state for closely held firms, Florida has emerged as a clear leader for LLCs, with Delaware next but far behind Florida, and several states bunched not far behind Delaware.[54] Delaware formations may include many publicly held unincorporated firms, and therefore Delaware law may be specially suited for them. But the Florida formations are somewhat of a mystery.

Florida's success in attracting LLC formations may be a by-product of its success in attracting investments. Florida has an active real estate market, fueled by retirement, tourism, and a large homestead exemption for sheltering debt from bankruptcy;[55] thriving small service businesses in the real estate, tourist, and retirement industries; an estate planning industry generated by Florida's large retirement community; and a large population of Latin American immigrants. The Florida bar has used the LLC form to exploit these advantages in a number of ways, including by making it tax friendly, reducing fees, and crafting the statute to fit estate planning and asset protection needs.[56] As a result, formations of Florida LLCs increased from 1,892 formations to 130,558, or 6900 percent, from 1996 to 2005, a period during which formations of for-profit Florida corporations increased from 104,173 to 168,182, or 62 percent.[57]

Florida therefore might be competing simultaneously in a chartering market for closely held firms and in a state market for investments. Florida is probably drawing investments even from firms that are organized elsewhere. At the same time, its competition for investments might have motivated it also to try to attract business formations, since it could expect that people and assets that were already based in Florida would be inclined to form into firms there. The Florida evidence therefore indicates that there may be no clear separation between the unbundled market for corporate law alone and the bundled market for law that generally appeals to businesses and others.

Publicly Held Unincorporated Firms

The market for publicly held corporations discussed above is in many ways similar to that of publicly held unincorporated firms. Therefore, it is not surprising that Delaware dominates the market for publicly held, or "master," limited partnerships.[58] But Delaware does not dominate the market for all types of publicly held unincorporated firms. Massachusetts closely competes with Delaware for statutory business trusts.[59] Most mutual funds are either Massachusetts business trusts or Maryland corporations, although Delaware statutory trusts are rapidly catching up.[60] Maryland has nearly all of the market for real estate investment trusts (REITs) and has always led in providing a statutory vehicle for these instruments.[61] Maryland has no franchise tax and offers takeover protection, shareholder restrictions, director powers, and other provisions that are specially tailored to REITs.[62]

Why do other states compete with Delaware more successfully for some publicly held unincorporated firms than for publicly held corporations? The answer may be that the governing state law is a smaller formation factor for these other types of firms. Rather, their terms are heavily governed by federal law, including the Investment Company Act of 1940[63] for mutual funds formed as statutory business trusts and the REIT provisions of the Internal Revenue Code.[64] In these niches, Delaware's unique lawmaking advantages and bond are less important, and Delaware is not able to command the significant premiums that it gets for corporations. Indeed, as just noted, Maryland attracts REIT business in part by having no franchise tax. Again, the underlying supply and demand forces in the market for law account for the structure of the market.

European Firms

European countries apply the "real seat" choice-of-law rule, under which corporate governance is subject to the law of the firm's headquarters. However, as in the United States, increased firm mobility provoked by liberal trade rules within the European Union put pressure on this choice-of-law rule. The big break came in 1999 with the *Centros* case,[65] in which the European Court of Justice held that Denmark could not bar a UK corporation from opening a "branch" in Denmark merely because the corporation had never done business in the United Kingdom. The court relied on the "right of establishment" in what is now article 48 of the Treaty of Rome, which provides that companies formed in accordance with member state law shall "be treated in the same way as natural persons who are nationals of Member States." This protection was available even if the company that was incorporated in the United Kingdom simply wanted to obtain more favorable law. In later cases, the same court held that Germany could not deny a Dutch corporation the right to sue,[66] and that the Netherlands could not impose local regulations on a locally based company that had incorporated elsewhere solely in order to avoid these regulations.[67] In general, these cases have clarified that the EU Constitution protects full-fledged Delaware-type charter competition for tramp, or in European parlance, "brass plate" corporations.[68]

So now there is the possibility of full-fledged U.S.–style charter competition in Europe. This seems to be happening, with the United Kingdom attracting companies based elsewhere in Europe. However, the United Kingdom leads tramp incorporations not because of its law or courts, but simply because UK corporation law has lower minimum capitalization requirements and simpler procedures.[69] Other European countries are responding in kind by revising their minimum capitalization requirements and simplifying incorporation requirements.[70] The UK tramp firms are not the big Fortune 500–type companies in which Delaware specializes, but smaller companies for which incorporation costs are significant. These firms arguably do not need corporate law as much as they need cheap recognition. Thus, Europe is arguably not yet a market for law in the same sense as the U.S. corporate law market.

Three aspects of the European corporate law market differentiate it from that of the United States. First, differences in laws, languages, and customs among EU countries make it difficult for a firm to operate in one country while litigating in another country or under another country's law.[71] Second, countries are more complex political environments than states like Delaware, and therefore are more likely to compromise shareholder and manager objectives with those of other interest groups. In particular, labor's participation on corporate boards, or "codetermination," remains a contentious issue in some European countries. Third, franchise fees are unlikely to drive a Delaware-type competition in Europe. The EU limits a country's gains from chartering fees and taxes,[72] and in any event, a European country probably could not earn enough fees to have the sort of incentive that Delaware gets from the combination of its small size and dominant position in the competition.[73]

Competition like that in the United States might, however, eventually break out in Europe, with England probably playing Delaware's role.[74] The United Kingdom has an edge because it has delegated much of its securities law to responsive private lawmaking by the London Stock Exchange. More-over, Europe has an advanced common law system, sophisticated courts, and a "charmed circle" of leading international UK law firms. As in the United States, lawyers rather than franchise fees may play a leading role in the corporate competition.

Again, the basic supply and demand forces of the law market are playing out in the corporate sphere, this time under different legal and cultural conditions from those in the United States.

Securities Regulation

As discussed above, securities regulation has been moved to the federal sphere, outside the reach of U.S. states' jurisdictional competition. Indeed, throughout the world, securities are traded in each country according to that country's law.[75] This means that firms cannot easily shed the regulations of their home states. Some would like this restriction on competition to change. For example, Roberta Romano has argued forcefully for allowing jurisdictional choice as to securities law, comparable to the IAD for corporate law.[76] However, even if one agrees with her policy arguments, it is still not clear how states or countries can be brought to disregard strong local political support for securities regulation, particularly given that these rules have resisted the embrace of the IAD.

There are various potential mechanisms for introducing party choice of securities regulation. One may be through the cross-listing market for securities, which we introduced in chapter 2. By cross-listing in other countries, firms can opt into higher disclosure requirements, which can have the effect of increasing the value of the firm's shares. It is conceivable that this limited choice of law might pave the way for full-fledged choice. Host countries have an incentive to avoid regulation that would drive away cross-listing firms, while home countries have an incentive to increase the quality of their rules and enforcement in order to encourage firms to stay home. The cross-listing market therefore may be an example of how jurisdictional competition can break out even where the initial rules are not conducive to it—just as U.S. states ultimately came to apply the IAD to tramp corporations.

Another mechanism for introducing party choice of securities laws is through the enforcement of choice-of-law clauses. In a series of cases, U.S. courts allowed Lloyd's of London to contract for English courts and law in transactions involving U.S. investors that otherwise might have been subject to U.S. securities laws.[77]

In general, the usual law market forces could work for securities regulation,[78] just as U.S. states ultimately came to apply the IAD to tramp corporations. The regulation and non-enforcement of contractual choice of law create an incentive to leave, and exit activates local industries that depend on the exiting firms. This, in turn, pressures politicians to enable party choice.

Implications

Analyzing the market for corporate law as an aspect of the general market for law, subject to the same general supply and demand considerations as the markets for other types of law, has broad legal implications.

Constitutional Protection of the IAD

The Supreme Court has not spoken definitively on whether the courts in the United States are constitutionally compelled to apply the IAD. This issue therefore remains in the realm of policy and conjecture. What does our analysis have to say about it?

Recall from chapter 3 that three constitutional provisions are relevant. The Full Faith and Credit Clause empowers Congress to decide the respect that each state must give to another's laws.[79] The Due Process Clause[80] implicitly guarantees minimal standards of fairness in litigation, including the right to be protected from unfair surprise regarding the governing law. The Commerce Clause[81] empowers Congress to regulate interstate commerce and in its "negative" form prevents states from usurping the federal role by enacting regulations that unreasonably interfere with interstate commerce.[82]

Most relevant Full Faith and Credit Clause cases involve members of fraternal benefit associations who paid periodic assessments to a national organization that agreed to pay death benefits to the member's family. As discussed in chapter 3, the Court consistently has held that the member's rights must be determined according to the organization's formation state law, noting the importance of the members having uniform rights to the proceeds of the fund. These firms were more like insurance cooperatives than business associations, however. Closer to the corporation context, the Court held that New Jersey could not prevent a New York bank from suing its New Jersey shareholders under New York law, reasoning that "the act of becoming a member (of a corporation) is something more than a contract, it is entering into a complex and abiding relation, and as marriage looks to domicile, membership looks to and must be governed by the law of the State granting the incorporation."[83]

This case addressed whether New Jersey could thwart an assessment by a New York official, which the court held was a type of decree directly governed by the Full Faith and Credit Clause. This leaves open the question of whether a New Jersey court would have been required to enter a judgment consistent with New York law if there had been no prior court order equivalent in New York.

Whatever the constitutional support for the IAD before the mid-1930s, this support is much weaker now with the decline in the importance of the Full Faith and Credit Clause for state choice-of-law policies. As discussed in chapter 3, *Allstate Insurance Co. v. Hague*[84] and *Phillips Petroleum Co. v. Shutts*[85] merge Full Faith and Credit with Due Process Clause considerations, and, in general, constitutional scrutiny of choice of law has declined markedly. Indeed, the Court has struck down the application of forum state law under these clauses in only one case since the late 1970s. In *Shutts*, the Court refused to allow a Kansas court to apply forum state law in a nationwide class action, reasoning that because some of the leases had nothing to do with the state of Kansas, the parties did not expect the forum's law to control when they executed the leases.[86] These cases indicate that parties should anticipate at the time of the transaction that the law of any state with a connection to that transaction might apply. If a court attempts to apply wholly unrelated law to that transaction, as Kansas did in *Shutts*, then the Court may strike down that choice. Although the cases protect the parties from courts' arbitrary choices of law, they would not compel the enforcement of choice-of-law clauses. A constitutionally mandated IAD is similarly unlikely.

The Commerce Clause provides an alternative constitutional basis for the IAD. Because the clause most clearly prevents only overt discrimination against interstate commerce,[87] one might think that it clearly would not prevent a state from applying the same law to a foreign corporation that it applies to its own firms. But the Court also has used the clause to protect against a state's imposing costs on parties in other states by effectively regulating interstate commerce. For example, as discussed in chapter 3, the Court has struck down a law that required a type of mudguard that differed from the type permitted in many other states. Forcing trucks to change mudguards at the state line unreasonably hindered interstate commerce. Closer to the IAD, in *Edgar v. MITE Corp.*,[88] a plurality of the Court applied this principle to invalidate an Illinois law that regulated national tender offers to shareholders residing in Illinois.[89] By contrast, *CTS Corp. v. Dynamics Corp. of America*[90] held that the Commerce Clause supported the application of the IAD to allow Indiana to regulate a tender offer for control of an Indiana corporation.

These cases seem to suggest that the Commerce Clause permits only the state of incorporation to regulate corporate governance. The Supreme Court of Delaware—the state that has the most to gain from the IAD—thinks that the IAD is therefore constitutionally protected.[91] California disagrees: its courts upheld the constitutionality of its "outreach" statute regulating the internal governance of firms with significant California contacts.[92] California asserts that its law controls a number of internal governance issues if a foreign company conducts at least half of its business in California and California residents hold at least 50 percent of the company's voting securities.[93]

California has the better argument. The Court has never held that the Commerce Clause precludes a state from regulating the internal governance of a firm incorporated under another state's law. Violations of the IAD often can but do not necessarily involve the sort of insuperable multiple-regulation problem that demands Commerce Clause attention. As a California court noted in applying the California statute to a Utah corporation, given the significant presence in California that was necessary to trigger the statute, it is unlikely that more than one such state law would apply to a given corporation.[94] So, while the Commerce Clause *might* bar *some* corporate statutes that force firms to comply with multiple states' laws, this does not elevate the IAD to special constitutional status.

Although the U.S. Constitution probably does not forbid a state from regulating the internal governance of a firm that is incorporated elsewhere, it may confer some extra regulatory power on the incorporating state. In *CTS Corp. v. Dynamics Corp. of America*, the Court reasoned that "no principle of corporation law and practice is more firmly established than a State's authority to regulate domestic corporations, including the authority to define the voting rights of shareholders."[95]

This "authority" in *CTS* allowed the incorporating state to regulate the governance of firms based in other states, consistent with the Commerce Clause, and to preserve a state *corporate* law provision notwithstanding a potentially preemptive federal law, under the Supremacy Clause. Conversely, the Court has held that state *securities* actions were preempted by a federal law, stressing "[t]he magnitude of the federal interest in protecting the integrity and efficient operation of the market for nationally traded securities."[96] The IAD therefore seems to underlie a distinction between "securities" and "internal governance" issues in determining the scope of preemption when the federal statute is unclear.

The important question for present purposes is whether the Court *should* use the Commerce Clause (or perhaps the Full Faith and Credit or Due Process clauses) to forbid a state from imposing its corporate law on a firm incorporated in another state. A constitutionally mandated IAD cannot be based on the notion that multiple state laws would excessively burden interstate firms. Although it is necessary for *only one* state law to apply, that state need not be the incorporating state. Even if the incorporating state has the best claim to applying its law, this claim does not necessarily deserve constitutional protection.

Our analysis contributes to this issue by placing it in the broad perspective of the law market as a whole. Commerce Clause protection may not be necessary because of the roles of party mobility and of exit-affected interest groups. Since this mobility was enough to enable the IAD to develop without any direct constitutional support, it is not clear why the Constitution would be necessary to bolster it now.

Moreover, the IAD has no stronger policy basis than do other rules for enforcing choice-of-law clauses. It follows that, if the IAD has constitutional status, so perhaps should rules enforcing choice-of-law clauses in other types of contracts. For example, if the IAD has constitutional status, why not insist on the enforcement of clauses designating the applicable law in franchise, insurance, consumer, or employment agreements? After all, these are all agreements where courts are inclined to invoke the fundamental policy exceptions under general choice-of-law rules, as discussed in chapter 3. Any distinctions between these contracts and contracts dealing with corporate governance probably do not justify differing constitutional treatment. Given the close connections between the corporate and general law markets, there is no obvious way the Court could carve out a distinctly "corporate" area for constitutional protection. It would then have to immerse itself in state choice-of-law jurisprudence, an area it took up but quickly abandoned at the beginning of the twentieth century.

The Corporation as Contract

The law market has broad implications for how the government should approach regulating corporate governance. Since the inception of the modern publicly held corporation, there has been a lively debate between those who view the corporation as a political entity, consistent with its origins as a state-created franchise, and those who view it as the product of private contract.[97] An important basis for the state-creation position is that corporations are the beneficiaries of a choice-of-law rule that allows them to choose any state's law for their corporate governance. This state-created privilege seems to justify exacting the price of greater susceptibility to regulations than do other contractual relationships.

We have seen, however, that the IAD is actually a relatively narrow doctrine that leaves plenty of room for regulation by the states in which corporations carry on their activities. It follows that the IAD not only does not need to be justified by a political theory, but also does not itself confer a special privilege that should make the corporation, in effect, a ward of the incorporating state.

The relationship between the corporate law market and contractual choice of law generally is also significant in deciding how the IAD should be applied. Consider, for example, *Rosenmiller v. Bordes*,[98] where a Delaware court applied Delaware law to a Delaware corporation despite a New Jersey choice-of-law clause in the firm's shareholder agreement. Because the IAD is only a rule for enforcing contractual choice of law, it arguably should be interpreted like any other choice-of-law clause, consistent with the contracting parties' expectations. Incorporating in Delaware indicates the parties' intent to apply Delaware law to all corporate-governance-related matters notwithstanding a contrary choice-of-law clause in the shareholder agreement. Or, one might conversely argue that the later agreement trumps the earlier Delaware incorporation.

Even if the corporation is simply a contract, the state has the power to regulate it, just as it does other contracts. From this standpoint, the law market analysis provides a rationale for regulating corporate choice of law. Returning to *Rosenmiller*, the result in that case might be explained in terms of the law market processes discussed in this book. The Delaware court may have considered what could happen if it created a precedent that would enable other states to undermine Delaware's investment in corporate law. Delaware needs supply-side incentives in order to produce high-quality law. Delaware arguably can protect its significant investment in its corporate law infrastructure only if it can restrict the privilege of using Delaware law in Delaware courts to Delaware corporations, which have paid the full incorporation fee. This suggests that Delaware would hesitate to let parties circumvent the fee by incorporating elsewhere and agreeing to apply Delaware law.[99] To prevent firms from choosing Delaware law without incorporating there, Delaware's courts set a valuable precedent by disallowing a Delaware firm from doing the reverse by contracting for an alternative state's law.

The desirability of the precedent created by *Rosenmiller* ultimately turns on whether, on net, it facilitates the efficient operation of the corporate law market by protecting Delaware's investment in infrastructure, or hampers it by preventing a state from piggybacking on Delaware's investment to get to more efficient law. In either event, there is nothing special about the fact that this is corporate law. As we have seen, any law can be viewed as a product supplied by the state and therefore as potentially subject to the same law market analysis.

The Limits of the IAD

When should, and when will, states apply another state's corporate law to locally based firms? To see the outer edges of the IAD, let us look at some California cases that raise issues that fall at the intersection of the IAD and other areas of law. Consider first a California case that could have been treated as a run-of-the-mill contract case but was instead treated as a case falling within the IAD. *State Farm Mutual Automobile Insurance Co. v. Superior Court*[100] applied Illinois corporate law to determine the duty of the directors of an Illinois mutual insurance company to pay dividends. The insurance company had not incorporated, so the directors' duties could have been treated as one of simple contract, to which the usual contract analysis under the Second Restatement, section 187, applies. Instead, however, the California court seemed to recognize the general importance of the IAD for determining the duties owed by directors to shareholders.

Consider also some California cases that attempt to determine the line between the IAD and securities regulation. A California appellate court held in *Friese v. Superior Court*[101] that a shareholders' derivative action for insider trading brought on the corporation's behalf under the California securities law was not barred by the fact that the incorporating state (Delaware) did not allow such a claim. Meanwhile, a federal court held in *In re Sagent Technology, Inc. Derivative Litigation*[102] that the IAD *did* apply to this type of claim. And yet another California appellate court held in *Grosset v. Wenaas*[103] that the incorporating state's law trumped California's requirement that derivative plaintiffs hold their shares throughout the litigation, although it recognized that the California requirement that plaintiff own shares at the time of the transaction *would have* applied. The California Supreme Court affirmed, but managed to avoid the IAD issue and a confrontation with Delaware by holding that the California rule was, in fact, the same as the Delaware rule.[104]

The issues in these cases arguably do not concern the appropriate sphere of states' internal governance regulations, but only what issues the incorporating state has actually sought to regulate. Because the IAD is simply a contractual choice-of-law rule, a court need not decide whether the suit involves "securities trading" or "internal governance" in some fundamental sense. Thus, if Delaware decides that shareholders should be able to sue their firms derivatively to recover insider trading profits, this constitutes a contract among the shareholders to apply Delaware law to these suits wherever they are brought and wherever the shareholders and insiders reside. This would also be the case if Delaware clearly has determined to provide a breach of fiduciary action for insider trading.

California could, of course, decide to regulate Delaware corporations, including aspects that relate to internal governance, and thereby protect California residents. As we argued above, the Constitution would not preclude this regulation. States arguably should be able to invalidate choice-of-law clauses pursuant to a statute that clearly expresses their intent to do so.[105] Because the IAD is a contractual choice-of-law rule, the same principle should apply to the IAD.

The question, then, is when it would be *appropriate* for California to trump Delaware law, given that California has that power. California might reasonably decide that whether it trumps Delaware law depends on whether the case relates to a central aspect of Delaware policy and expertise—that is, to internal corporate governance rather than to securities regulation. California might wish to apply its policy, but might be constrained by several considerations, including the threat that Congress may intervene to preempt state corporate law. On the other hand, California could decide that it wishes to impose its law whenever the potential harm to California residents is enough to justify California regulation, irrespective of whether the matter involves corporate governance. These conflicting forces may have played a role in the California Supreme Court's Solomonic decision in *Grosset* to both apply its own law *and* avoid a confrontation with Delaware by reconciling its law with Delaware's. Rather than making an artificial distinction between internal governance and other issues, California should have the general power to apply its law, subject to several constitutional constraints on arbitrary choice-of-law rules.

If several states regulating Delaware corporate insiders impose undue burdens on multistate firms, Congress may have to step in. Indeed, the federal securities laws generally could be viewed as a reaction to burdensome state securities regulations. Although Congress did not preempt state law in 1933 or 1934, it did so in 1997 when California threatened to undercut Congress's attempt to limit securities class actions.[106] But whether Congress should act depends on whether the states can coordinate without federal help by reasonably construing the scope of the IAD. This book's analysis suggests that the law market can constrain aggressive state action in many cases without aggressive federal intervention.

7

Consumer Contracts

This chapter explores the use of choice-of-law, choice-of-court, and arbitration clauses in consumer contracts, including electronic commerce. Our discussion of the law market so far has been primarily confined to situations where both parties to the contract are sophisticated and knowledgeable. What happens when a contracting party cannot negotiate the terms of an agreement, may not understand the contract clauses or their import, and may not even have seen or read the contract terms? Should contracting choices effectively made unilaterally by firms be imposed on consumers?

The political context of consumer regulations also differs from that regarding business-to-business contracts. Recall that regulations are often the product of interest groups that (1) benefit from regulation; (2) are directly burdened by regulation; or (3) are benefited or burdened by the migration of businesses or people in response to state laws. Pro-regulatory groups may be more powerful in the consumer context than in the sophisticated contract context. To be sure, consumer groups have high organization costs because their members are inclined to free ride off the groups' legislative efforts. But consumers also have high benefits from organizing because political action may get these groups better contracts than they can get through individual bargaining with firms. Moreover, arguments for regulation may have more political traction in this context. Companies typically do business on the basis of standard-form contracts offered to consumers on a take-it-or-leave-it basis. Because consumers cannot bargain for the contract terms they might prefer, they appear to have a stronger argument for legislative relief. Thus, although regulated businesses and exit-affected interest groups are as powerful in this context as they are in others, the greater strength of pro-regulatory groups suggests that we might get more regulation of consumer than of business contracts.

As in other contexts described in this book, companies can respond to regulation by locating in less regulatory states and by inserting choice-of-law, choice-of-forum, and arbitration clauses in their contracts. States with strong consumer protection groups sometimes respond by refusing to enforce these contract clauses. Businesses can then decide to (1) continue existing operations under the super-mandatory regulation; (2) exit the regulating state's product markets (obviously difficult when dealing with a big state like California); or (3) lobby for federal laws that protect their interests.

We do not take a stand on the desirability of consumer protection laws. There are powerful arguments on both sides of the consumer regulation debate. Given the difficulty of determining both the utility and cost of consumer protection laws, the contractual choice-of-law approach seems preferable to a single federal regulation. Under our approach, which will be articulated in more detail in chapter 10, states must enforce choice-of-law clauses in consumer contracts unless a state *statute* explicitly provides otherwise. This lets a legislature protect consumers when the consumer groups in the state convince it that super-mandatory rules are appropriate. At the same time, requiring non-enforcement to take the form of statutes rather than ad hoc judicial determinations provides clear notice to companies that a particular state will not allow them to choose their governing law. Clarity enables firms to respond by either altering their business practices or exiting that state's product markets. Moreover, if states insist on imposing multiple regulations on interstate firms, businesses can seek relief through a federal statute. In short, we propose to preserve state regulatory authority while disciplining excessive regulation through the dual threats of firms' exit from the state and federal preemption.

This chapter discusses the supply and demand sides of the law market for consumer contracts generally. It also illustrates the law market in action by exploring some similarities and differences in the features of the law markets for credit cards, payday loans, insurance contracts, and electronic commerce. It is important to emphasize that our framework could apply to any consumer contract context. We have chosen these four contexts because their diverse market environments provide a range of law market lessons.

Regulating Consumer Contracts and Choice of Law

Choice-of-law clauses in consumer contracts can benefit companies in the same ways that we described in previous chapters. When the company transacts with many customers located in many states, a choice-of-law clause enables it to conduct business according to a single state's laws. Firms can more easily and cheaply set policies if they can refer to a single set of laws. Choice-of-law clauses also can help different types of companies to choose laws that best fit their business models. Finally, choice-of-law clauses can benefit companies by enabling them to avoid costly laws.

Competition may force firms to pass their benefits from contracting for law on to their consumers in the form of lower prices. However, consumers may not accurately evaluate the tradeoff between certain and present price reductions and possible future legal relief. Scholars have noted that consumers systematically underestimate the likelihood that they will have problems with a company's provision of goods or services.[1] Compounding this problem is the fact that consumers likely do not know what rights they are trading away with a choice-of-law clause.

To what extent should we worry about the effect of choice-of-law clauses on consumers? Markets sometimes protect even ignorant consumers. Knowledgeable consumers can reject products and services that come with burdensome contract clauses. Competitors that seek to sell to knowledgeable consumers have an incentive to provide fairer contract terms. If firms cannot discriminate in a mass market between knowledgeable and ignorant consumers, they have an incentive to provide terms no worse than those its major competitors offer to sophisticated buyers.[2]

Moreover, competition often protects consumers other than through contracts. Companies may fear that opportunistic consumers will attempt to use contract rights to get more than they paid or bargained for. A company therefore might provide few consumer rights in the contract but yet still behave generously when dealing with individual consumers. Put differently, the company's conduct may be determined more by its concern for its reputation than by contract clauses. Where the company's generous customer service fails to please unreasonable consumers, the company can fall back on its self-serving contract clauses for protection. As long as firms vigorously compete in their provision of service, we should not worry too much about contract terms.[3]

The invisible hand of the marketplace may not, however, always protect consumers adequately. There may be little competition to provide the product, or the competition may center on price and quality rather than on contract protection. A survey of first-year law students showed that, although many students read their electronic contracts for price and product features, virtually none read the choice-of-law, choice-of-court, and arbitration provisions.[4] Or, unscrupulous firms may take advantage of consumers with the intent of leaving the marketplace before they can incur reputational or other penalties. Whether or not these latter situations are prevalent or can be prevented by government regulation, they provide sympathetic stories that consumer groups can present to legislatures.

Now consider consumer regulation in the context of the market for law. Suppose that consumer groups in New Hampshire convince the state legislature to make it illegal for a company to limit its tort liability to consumers, or to charge more than a specified rate of interest on loans that it extends to consumers. In contrast, Delaware allows firms to limit their tort liabilities by contractually limiting both the damages and the warranties that are available to consumers, and has repealed its interest rate caps, permitting companies to charge any interest rate the market can bear. Because of different balances of interest-group influence, each state might see the tradeoff between price and protection differently. Some states, like Delaware in our hypothetical, ensure that their citizens have access to the cheapest goods, while others, like New Hampshire in our hypothetical, give their citizens broad protections against harm. Suppose that company X sells its products in New Hampshire with a standard form agreement providing that Delaware law governs any disputes between the company and a consumer. Will, or should, a New Hampshire court ignore the choice-of-law clause in an effort to protect its citizen-consumers?

The law governing the enforcement of choice-of-law clauses depends on where the contract is entered into and on whether the contract is for a good or a service. For sale-of-goods contracts entered into in the United States, virtually all courts will apply the Uniform Commercial Code (UCC), which, as currently enacted in almost all of the states, provides that contracting parties can choose the law of any state that bears a "reasonable relation" to the transaction.[5] In our hypothetical scenario, then, the company probably could successfully choose Delaware law under the UCC simply by locating its headquarters or its plant there.

As of this writing, state legislatures are considering 2001 amendments to the UCC that could change these rules. The UCC drafters removed the "reasonable relation" rule from the uniform law proposal because they concluded that it was simultaneously too restrictive for nonconsumer contracts[6] and too permissive for consumer contracts. Regarding consumer contracts, the revised UCC requires that the chosen law may not work to deprive the consumer of mandatory laws designed to protect consumers in the state in which the consumer resides or took delivery of the good. Thus, under the revised UCC, consumer protection laws trump the law chosen by the company regardless of the connection between the company and the state whose law it chose. To avoid undesired laws, it is not enough that the company remove its headquarters or assets to another state. It must refrain from doing business with consumers in that state altogether.

For consumer contracts for the provision of services, most U.S. courts apply the Second Restatement, section 187. Recall that, under section 187, the parties can choose the law of any place that bears a substantial relationship to the parties or transaction or for which there is another reasonable basis for choosing that law. Courts do not apply the chosen law, however, if this would violate a fundamental policy of the state whose law would otherwise apply and that state has a materially greater interest in the outcome of the case than the state whose law was chosen. Here too, mandatory consumer protection laws can trump the contractually chosen law even when the company relocates to a state with more favorable laws.

A problem with the consumer protection approach built into the revised UCC and (implicitly) the Second Restatement is that these standards do not provide clear notice or predictability as to which choice-of-law clauses are regulated. States often pass "mandatory rules" that cannot be varied by contract but can be varied by a choice-of-law provision. For example, though usury laws are mandatory rules in that parties cannot contract for an interest rate higher than the maximum amount permitted by law, courts often enforce choice-of-law provisions that get parties out from under the state's usury law.[7] In other cases, a regulation is mandatory as against both local law and contractually designated foreign law. As we discuss in chapter 10, states should be required to specify such super-mandatory laws through statutes rather than through case-by-case determination, thereby both increasing predictability and constraining excessive state regulation.

In contrast to the United States, Europe seems to be moving toward greater enforcement of choice-of-law clauses. As discussed in chapter 3, the European Parliament has adopted a regulation, which applies both in consumer and business cases, that restricts the enforcement of choice-of-law clauses only where they are prohibited by provisions of public law. This comes close to our proposal to give super-mandatory effect only to a limited category of laws. The main difference is that the EU Regulation's public law category may be somewhat ambiguous, whereas we propose to enhance clarity by forcing legislatures to specifically designate which laws have super-mandatory effect.[8]

Mobility and Regulation

When states do not enforce firms' choice-of-law clauses, firms shift to other means for evading unwanted regulations, as we have seen elsewhere in the law market. If a state's consumer protection laws become so burdensome that companies opt not to do business with its residents, the residents may lobby to lighten the regulation. Legislatures and consumer interest groups thus may have to consider the costs to local consumers of regulations intended to protect them.

Firms also can add clauses to their contracts that choose courts or arbitrators that are inclined to apply the chosen law. Consumers, for their part, might try to avoid these choice-of-court or arbitration clauses by suing in their home state courts. The following subsections show that, although courts are somewhat more hesitant to enforce choice-of-court and arbitration clauses in consumer than in business-to-business contracts, these clauses do help firms to increase the likelihood that their preferred law will be applied.

Choice-of-Court Clauses

Countries vary in their enforcement of choice-of-court clauses in consumer contracts. Some European countries are hostile to them. France and Germany, for example, enforce choice-of-court clauses in business contracts but not in consumer contracts (at least domestic ones).[9] Under their view, a consumer never should have to litigate claims away from home. In contrast, most U.S. courts enforce choice-of-court clauses, even in consumer contracts.

The best-known U.S. case, *Carnival Cruise Lines v. Shute*,[10] was decided by the U.S. Supreme Court as a matter of federal admiralty law, but has been applied broadly beyond this context. A resident of Washington state was injured aboard a cruise ship while in international waters. Eulala Shute had purchased a ticket for a seven-day cruise between California and Mexico. The contract, which was mailed to her after she purchased the ticket, included the following paragraph 8 buried in the fine print of the contract:

> It is agreed by and between the passenger and the Carrier that all disputes and matter[s] whatsoever arising under, in connection with, or incident to this Contract shall be litigated, if at all, in and before a Court located in the State of Florida, U.S.A., to the exclusion of the Courts of any other state or country.

Shute attempted to bring her claim in federal court in Washington state, but the Supreme Court ultimately forced her to sue in Florida, according to the contract's terms. The Court was unconcerned about the use of this choice-of-court clause in a standard-form consumer contract. The Court reasoned that a cruise line gets value from the provisions because it carries passengers from many places to many places, and the clause gives it some certainty regarding the place in which it might be subject to suit. In addition, the company saves litigation costs with these clauses, which can be passed along to consumers in the form of lower fares. Although Shute argued that litigation in Florida would be expensive, and the court of appeals had determined that Shute's suit would be effectively precluded if she were forced to litigate in Florida, the Court found no evidence that Carnival chose Florida in an effort to discourage legitimate claims, and therefore the clause was not fundamentally unfair.[11]

Other U.S. courts, however, have struck down choice-of-court clauses where the individual faced prohibitive costs if forced to litigate in the remote forum. In *Sudduth v. Occidental Peruana, Inc.*,[12] American employees contracted in the United States to perform work for defendant's subsidiary in Peru. The employment contract, which was written in Spanish, provided for adjudication of all disputes between the parties in Lima, Peru. After the work in Peru was completed and the employees returned to the United States, they discovered that they were entitled to paid vacation benefits under both the contract and Peruvian law. Rather than returning to Peru to sue, the plaintiffs sued in a federal district court in Texas. The district judge refused to enforce the choice-of-court clause because he found that the costs of traveling to Peru effectively deprived the plaintiffs of their right to relief.

A similar concern caused a California court to refuse to enforce a choice-of-court clause in a slightly different context. In *America Online, Inc.*

v. Superior Court of Alameda County,[13] plaintiffs attempted to bring a class action against AOL for charging monthly service fees after the plaintiffs had terminated their AOL subscriptions. AOL moved to dismiss on the ground that the service agreements provided that all claims must be brought in Virginia. While travel to Virginia was no worse and probably more convenient for some than was Eulala Shute's travel to Florida, the AOL plaintiffs faced a Virginia rule that bars class actions in Virginia courts. Because the lack of a class action effectively would deprive the plaintiffs of a remedy worth seeking, the choice-of-court clause was struck down.

On the other hand, *Forrest v. Verizon Communications, Inc.* upheld a provision substantially similar to that in the AOL contract.[14] The court noted that, while Virginia does not allow class actions, it does have small claims courts, as well as consumer protection laws that allow successful plaintiffs to recover reasonable court costs and attorneys' fees. The court also pointed out that the named plaintiff's preferred forum, the District of Columbia, was only a few minutes and a Metro ticket from the contractually chosen forum. The *Forrest* court accordingly concluded that the company's contract to litigate in Virginia trumped the consumer's desire to bring a class action in the District of Columbia.

The limitations on the enforcement of choice-of-court clauses are, therefore, more narrowly focused in the United States than in France and Germany. As we will discuss in the next section, this may be at least partly due to the enforcement of arbitration clauses under the Federal Arbitration Act (FAA).

Arbitration Provisions

Parties opt for arbitration for a variety of reasons (listed in chapter 5), most of which apply to the company's choice of arbitration in consumer contracts. However, recall that the vast majority of consumers pays no attention to arbitration clauses in their agreements. They also may not understand that these provisions could enable firms to circumvent their contracted duties. In particular, arbitration may deter smaller claims by eliminating class actions. Moreover, the limited discovery available in arbitration can impede consumers' access to information necessary to prove their claims. And because the company is typically a repeat player in arbitration, the arbitrator could be biased in favor of the company. These concerns serve as the basis for judicial scrutiny of arbitration in consumer cases.

On the other hand, markets can sometimes constrain the unilateral nature of the company's arbitration provision.[15] As a result, arbitration agreements may not be as unreasonable as their critics fear.[16] Markets also can induce firms to pass benefits from the clauses on to consumers in the form of lower prices.

In any event, courts have been willing to enforce arbitration clauses despite the apparent potential for consumer injury. This is at least partly because the FAA requires all U.S. courts, state and federal, to enforce arbitration provisions except on "grounds as exist at law or in equity for the revocation of any contract."[17] The FAA therefore prevents a state from developing a separate body of law to restrict the enforcement of arbitration clauses. Instead, any non-enforcement of arbitration clauses must stem from preexisting, generally applicable contract doctrine, such as fraud, duress, and unconscionability.

Under the unconscionability doctrine, a court may refuse to enforce a contract if both the procedure by which the parties entered into a contract and the substance of the contract terms fail to comply with norms of fairness.[18] An agreement is procedurally unconscionable if it is achieved through means that cast doubt on the meaningfulness of a party's assent. Some courts find procedural unconscionability in contracts of adhesion that a firm offers on a take-it-or-leave-it basis to an individual with little or no practical opportunity to understand or review the terms. These facts often seem to be present in consumer contracts.[19] Once a court finds procedural unconscionability, it can strike contract terms that it deems to be substantively unfair.

In practice, however, unconscionability is a rather narrow ground for refusing to enforce contracts, because courts tend to assume that the parties know what they are doing when they enter into a contract. In arbitration cases, courts are mainly concerned that arbitration not work to effectively preclude the consumer's right of redress by imposing prohibitively high costs. A particularly controversial type of arbitration agreement is one that prohibits class actions, thereby making it difficult for consumers to assert small-value claims.[20] Arbitration associations vary in their willingness to provide for class action arbitration. Prior to 2003, the American Arbitration Association (AAA), which is a popular forum for arbitration in the United States, took the position that class action arbitration was only available if the contract specifically provided for class action arbitration. In 2003, however, the AAA reversed the default rule, at which point firms began to contractually preclude class action arbitration. The shift in the AAA's default rule had the effect of at least forcing firms to clearly disclose any intent to preclude class actions in arbitration.

Even clear disclosure of the unavailability of class relief does not allay courts' concerns with preserving class actions as a device to deter firms' wrongdoing. A company might fraudulently overcharge each of its 1 million customers by $5 if individual customers have little incentive or ability to bring $5 claims. Potential class action lawsuits change the company's calculus, however. The deterrence provided by class action lawyers therefore can benefit even those individual consumers for whom the costs of complaining were more than their injuries. Thus, the Supreme Court of California has said:

> When the waiver is found in a consumer contract of adhesion in a
> setting in which disputes between the contracting parties predictably
> involve small amounts of damages, and when it is alleged that the
> party with superior bargaining power has carried out a scheme to
> deliberately cheat large numbers of consumers out of individually
> small sums of money, then, at least to the extent the obligation at
> issue is governed by California law, the waiver becomes in practice
> the exemption of the party from responsibility for [its] own fraud, or
> willful injury to the person or property of another.[21]

While California courts might strike down class action prohibitions merely because they might preclude consumers from pursuing small-value claims, other courts require a stronger showing. For example, the New Jersey Supreme Court looked past the class action prohibition to determine whether the *named plaintiff* would be prevented from pursuing her statutory consumer protection rights in the absence of a class action. The court nevertheless concluded that the enforcement of plaintiff's rights would be difficult if not impossible without the class action, and therefore struck the class action prohibition from the arbitration clause.[22]

Despite these concerns, most courts have upheld class action prohibitions in arbitration agreements. Courts often reason that plaintiffs can successfully arbitrate their claims without class actions. For example, courts have upheld class action prohibitions where the company offered to pay all of the consumer's costs associated with the arbitration;[23] the arbitration clause enabled the consumer to arbitrate at home, provided for the advancement of the consumer's fees and costs, and awarded attorney's fees to a successful plaintiff;[24] the successful plaintiff's attorney's fees were recoverable under the statutes that created the cause of action;[25] and the applicable law (the Truth in Lending Act) provided for viable individual and administrative claims.[26] These courts' narrowly tailored treatments of the issue no doubt result from their concern that the FAA limits their power to strike these clauses. In any event, the result is that arbitration, with its pressure on choice of law and forum, plays a significant role even in the context of consumer contracts.

Courts, however, sometimes refuse to enforce some arbitration provisions, including prohibitions on punitive damages and requirements that the parties equally share the arbitrator's fee, which can similarly work to make the plaintiff's claim prohibitively costly.[27] The AAA has responded to these court concerns by conditioning AAA consumer arbitration on a set of rights, known as the Consumer Due Process Protocol,[28] which facilitate consumer claims. For example, consumers retain the right to bring their claims in small claims court and are supposed to be notified of this right in the contract itself,[29] and companies are obliged to keep the cost of arbitration reasonable, including, if necessary, by subsidizing costs.[30] The AAA also provides lower fees for consumer arbitration and more opportunity for low-cost consumer arbitration.[31] These moves presumably represent a compromise between consumer groups and companies brokered by the AAA to preserve consumer arbitration against the risk that consumer groups will be able to persuade legislators to enact more stringent protections at the state or federal level. Thus, the same pressures and counterpressures that are present in the law market are also present in private arbitration.

As this book goes to press, the contest between law market forces and pro-regulatory interests is joined over Congress's consideration of the Arbitration Fairness Act. The proposed statute would amend the FAA to prohibit the enforcement of predispute arbitration clauses in all employment, consumer, and franchise contracts, as well as in other contracts where the dispute involves either a civil rights statute or a statute that regulates "contracts or transactions between parties of unequal bargaining power."[32] The United States thus may be poised to shift from narrowly tailored non-enforcement of the clauses to a broad ban on consumer arbitration.[33]

Effect of Mobility

States respond to the lack of one-on-one bargaining in consumer contracts by regulating the terms of such contracts more closely than those between sophisticated businesses. As with the other areas we have discussed, it is difficult to determine which of these regulations are reasonable and which are excessive. But a law market for consumer contracts helps to resolve these issues, albeit more weakly than in some other contexts. Firms can establish contacts with states that provide less consumer protection, making it more likely that these states' laws will apply to their disputes, and giving states an incentive to supply this permissive law. Firms also can attempt to obtain the benefit of permissive laws with choice-of-law, choice-of-court, and arbitration clauses. If courts or legislatures in pro-consumer states invalidate these provisions, firms can avoid contacts with, and therefore suit in, the non-enforcing jurisdictions.

States historically have been better able to regulate consumer contracts than commercial contracts partly because, since those regulations are imposed on all contracts formed with in-state consumers, firms could avoid the laws of a state only by completely withdrawing from a state's product markets. Larger states have a greater ability to impose regulations than do smaller states because larger states represent more lucrative product markets that firms cannot easily sacrifice. However, lower trade barriers have opened worldwide consumer markets, at least theoretically making it easier for a firm to exit jurisdictions and giving states less latitude to regulate. The key point is that statewide product markets enable states to regulate to protect their consumers, and firm mobility helps to constrain the excesses of such regulation. We cannot say how much regulation is optimal. But it does seem clear that the more populous a state is, the more protective its laws can be.

The Federal Role

As in other contexts, the federal government plays a role in the consumer law market. The federal government can regulate where the states have inadequate incentives to do so. Alternatively, Congress or the Supreme Court could protect firms under the Commerce Clause by striking or preempting unduly burdensome laws. And federal courts can enforce choice-of-law and choice-of forum clauses through their interpretation of state law. Federal jurisdiction is relatively rare in individual consumer cases because the $75,000 floor for diversity jurisdiction is above the damages sought in most consumer claims. Federal courts likely will have more influence in enforcing law market clauses in nationwide class actions because the Class Action Fairness Act (CAFA) allows federal courts to hear class actions where more than $5 million in total claims is involved even without complete diversity of citizenship.[34]

Any evaluation of the federal government's role in promoting the law market should take account of both the costs and benefits of enforcing law market clauses. Chapter 10 will discuss the potential for harnessing the federal government's power through enactment of a federal contractual choice-of-law statute.

The Consumer Contract Law Market in Action

This subpart briefly describes the current political and legal landscapes surrounding credit card agreements, payday loans, insurance contracts, electronic commerce (including contracts and Internet privacy), and product liability laws. In each context, we observe the potential for jurisdictional competition for businesses and hostility to that competition on the part of some states with strong consumer group interests. Firms sometimes may have to seek refuge in federal regulation in order to be free from a cacophony of state laws. And interest groups injured by underregulation in the face of firm mobility might also appeal to Congress for protection. For each of these contractual settings, our proposal—that choice-of-law clauses be enforced unless a state statute prohibits that enforcement—could sometimes provide an alternative solution that preserves both a state regulatory role and the potential for jurisdictional competition.

Credit Card Agreements

Look at the agreement that comes with your credit card. Odds are that the issuing bank is located in Delaware or South Dakota and that the agreement provides that your relationship with that bank is governed by the law of one of these two states. Without intending to disparage these states, we suggest that the banks have not chosen them for their weather, cultural amenities, or natural beauty, but rather because the states have enacted laws that attracted the banks. It also happens that, in this context, the other states have little power to thwart the application of these laws to their resident consumers.

The residents of Delaware and South Dakota now enjoy significant tax revenues and job opportunities from card-issuing banks, and they have Congress and the Supreme Court to thank for this. High inflation rates during the 1970s created a shortage of mortgage lending in states with fixed maximum interest rates. All states then had usury laws that limited the interest rate that banks could charge in contracts lending money to consumers. When the inflation rate rose into the double digits, banks in the states with low fixed rates of interest became unwilling to enter into mortgage loan agreements.

Rather than attempting to displace state usury laws, Congress opened up the lending market by providing in the National Banking Act (NBA) that all nationally chartered banks may charge any interest rate permissible in the state where the bank is located.[35] This is, in effect, a federally mandated choice-of-law rule. This rule, like most that focus on the location of the business, sparked jurisdictional competition to attract banks and their assets. Delaware and South Dakota responded by eliminating their usury laws altogether. Drawn by the prospect of being able to charge any interest rates that the market would bear, banks began flocking to these states.

Supreme Court decisions interpreting the NBA enhanced this federal choice-of-law rule. The Court held in 1978 that a national bank is located in the state where it is chartered even though some if its activities are located elsewhere.[36] As a result, banks can charter in Delaware and solicit credit card customers through branch offices located throughout the United States. The Court in 1996 construed the term "interest rate" in the relevant section of the NBA to include all charges that accrue pursuant to a credit card contract.[37] The banks therefore can charge any fees—including late, insufficient funds, overlimit, annual, cash advance, membership, and others—that are permitted in the states where they are located.[38] The same protections that apply to national banks may also apply to their wholly owned subsidiaries.[39]

The legislative contest among business, pro-regulatory, and exit-affected interest groups could better accommodate the competing interests of parties and states regarding credit card contracts. The NBA forces states to apply the law of a national bank's chartering state. Although consumer groups could lobby for federal laws that regulate credit card agreements, this strategy may not work because the NBA reflects Congress's intent to use choice-of-law rules to keep the federal government out of substantively regulating interest rates and fees. In any event, as we will discuss in chapter 10, the balance between the law market and state regulatory interests can be better preserved by a rule that generally enforces choice-of-law clauses except where state legislatures explicitly decide otherwise. Firms can respond to such super-mandatory laws by refusing to issue cards to these states' residents. The state can then decide whether the resulting costs to its residents outweigh the benefits of regulation. But the current rule leaves the states too little room to regulate consumer credit card agreements.

Although federal law ensures the application of the chartering state's law to interest rates and fees, battles rage on other credit card issues. As the consumer credit card market has matured, issuing companies have used questionable practices to stretch for profits. For example, First USA Bank apparently began charging an undisclosed fee whenever cardholders exceeded their limit, but without giving consumers adequate notice so they could minimize the fees. Discover Card apparently began charging accounts late fees whenever they posted credit card payments after 1 p.m. on the date that the payments were due without telling consumers that payments received and posted on the date due might nevertheless trigger the fees. And in some cases, banks changed the terms of credit card agreements despite agreements suggesting that those terms would not be changed except in specified circumstances.[40] In each of these cases, large numbers of consumers had each been deprived of small amounts of money—situations appropriate for class action relief. But the credit card agreements all provided either that claims must be brought in Virginia courts, a state that does not permit class action lawsuits, or that claims would be arbitrated without the benefit of class action arbitration.

Most courts have upheld the contract clauses. But some, following the unconscionability reasoning discussed earlier, have either refused to enforce the choice-of-court or arbitration clause, or have struck the class action waiver from the arbitration provision.[41] Discover Bank responded by providing in its agreements for the court resolution of disputes in the event that the court invalidates the class action waiver in the arbitration clause.[42]

Should class action waivers in credit card arbitration agreements be prohibited? As we have seen throughout the law market, there are powerful arguments on both sides. Samuel Issacharoff and Erin Delaney argue that class action attorneys help to ensure the fundamental fairness of credit card companies' behavior.[43] But unscrupulous lawyers can use class actions to line their pockets with fees while providing plaintiffs little value in settlement agreements. Indeed, settlement agreements often give plaintiffs coupons or other vouchers that ultimately go unclaimed or unused. Because the stakes can be quite high in large class action lawsuits, companies may pay a lot of money to settle even unmeritorious claims due to the inherent risks of litigation. Firms' savings from class action waivers can benefit consumers through lower prices. Meanwhile, reputational constraints and possible state unfair trade prosecutions remain to discipline the companies.

Our choice-of-law solution could help to resolve the debate over class action waivers by facilitating diverse regulatory approaches. Interest-group competition in California might create laws hostile to these waivers, while interest-group competition in Virginia created a statewide prohibition on class actions. But neither state's laws need govern the entire country. Firms should be permitted to choose the laws (and procedures) of the states they prefer, subject to state legislatures' ability to displace that choice through explicit statutory language.

Diversity becomes costly, however, when plaintiffs' attorneys can bring nationwide class actions in the state courts of, say, California knowing that the California courts will not automatically enforce a class action waiver and that firms cannot easily respond by avoiding the state. Two factors help to mitigate this problem. First, recall that the CAFA enables a defendant to remove nationwide class actions to federal courts. Federal courts might reach different conclusions than state courts regarding the unconscionability of specific class action waivers. Second, the Supreme Court's decision in *Shutts*, discussed in chapter 3, could constrain a California court from applying California law to credit card agreements having no connection to the state of California.

Payday Loans

Payday loans are short-term (a few days to 30 days) loans designed to help a consumer get access to quick cash in anticipation of paying off those loans on the borrower's next payday. Most payday loans provide for a "loan fee" ranging from $15 to $25 per $100 borrowed. The borrower provides collateral in the form of either a personal check postdated to the borrower's next payday or an authorization for an electronic bank account withdrawal, in either event empowering the lender to withdraw an amount of money equivalent to the amount borrowed plus the loan fee. If the borrower contacts the lender prior to when the loan comes due, the borrower can arrange to roll the loan over by paying only the loan fee on the original due date while the loan and a new fee roll over to the borrower's next payday. If the borrower does not contact the lender, but there is not enough money in the borrower's checking account to pay off the loan, then the lender may charge the borrower insufficient funds (NSF) fees, typically about $25, in addition to similar fees charged by her bank. If the lender attempts repeatedly to withdraw the amount due without success, then the borrower is charged a separate NSF fee for each unsuccessful attempt. The borrower also may be liable for late fees or other loan charges for not paying off the loan when it is due.

Payday loans are becoming an increasingly popular way for working-class families to get access to credit. In 2003, $40 billion of payday loans were issued, and the annual amount is rising rapidly.[44] Each year, an estimated 10 million working households, with a median annual individual income of about \$20,000 and a median checking account balance of \$66, borrow on payday loans.[45] Borrowers pay seemingly astounding effectively annualized interest rates of 400–1000 percent.[46] These facts suggest that payday lenders may be taking advantage of the working poor.

On the other hand, there are also arguments favoring the payday lenders. A study of payday lender returns indicated that they differ little from typical financial returns, indicating that the lenders might charge high amounts not because they are taking advantage of borrowers but because they face high per-loan fixed costs associated with credit checks, verifications, and bank transactions.[47] The fact that some employee credit unions have made payday loans available to employees at effective interest rates drastically smaller than those charged by commercial payday loan lenders[48] seems to indicate that commercial lenders earn supercompetitive profits from consumers. But the emergence of credit union loans itself suggests that the competition can bring short-term loan costs down, or perhaps that the loans are made to different types of consumers. Also, lenders that are state licensed and prepared to comply with local lending laws are beginning to advertise that fact on their Web sites in an effort to attract consumers.[49] These facts and competing arguments suggest that freezing regulation through federal law may be unwise.

The alternative to federal regulation, of course, is competition in the market for law. Consumer groups in some states are beginning to lobby their legislators for statutes to protect consumers against some of the terms in these lending agreements, including statutes that limit the size of the loans,[50] interest rates and other fees that lenders can charge,[51] and how many times borrowers can roll over loans.[52] Statutes also specify what lenders must disclose to the consumer[53] and other contract terms.[54] Some states have required lenders to obtain a license to provide payday loans in the state and to periodically report their activities.[55] Illinois has gone so far as to require the maintenance of a reporting system by which every lender knows the amounts that a borrower owes to other payday lenders.[56] Some states have imposed criminal sanctions on violators of payday loan statutes.

Payday lenders attempt to evade these regulations in two ways. First, some payday lenders move to and contractually choose the law of jurisdictions that do not regulate payday loans. Lenders in the United States have, for example, moved to Delaware or Nevada, where they trust the state legislatures not to regulate their agreements.[57] Several payday lenders have moved offshore and offer payday loans to consumers through the Internet. A quick perusal online indicates that Costa Rica is currently a popular site for payday lenders.[58]

Second, payday lenders can locate a store in a regulating state but act as a mere intermediary so that the borrower contracts with an out-of-state lender. The store then buys the contract from the out-of-state lender. The out-of-state lender can sometimes justify including a choice-of-law clause that chooses the law of its nonregulating home state. The store then buys the rights under the contract, which is generally enforceable to the same extent as between the original parties.

Consumer groups can fight payday lenders' efforts to evade local regulations. The Illinois payday loan statute, for example, defines a lender to include third-party intermediaries as well as persons or entities that buy interests in the payday loans. Moreover, the act purports to apply to all payday loans extended to Illinois residents, regardless of the lender's location. Although Illinois will find it hard to regulate entities based in other states, these lenders, in turn, may find it hard to reach the borrowers' assets for debt collection. Even federal regulations will not necessarily reach offshore lenders, though they can at least inhibit lender debt collection actions.

If state regulation of payday lending proves too troublesome for nation-wide firms, these firms may seek to eliminate the state law chaos through federal regulation. On the other hand, consumer groups may seek federal regulation to avoid the weakening of protective laws through jurisdictional competition. In any event, our basic point is that state regulation should be given an opportunity to seek the appropriate regulatory balance before embracing the one-size-fits-all solution of federal law.

Insurance Contracts

Insurance law lends itself to a strong regulatory approach that seems to leave little room for enforcing contractual choice of law. Consumers are at risk because they pay premiums long before the insurance company must pay a claim, at which point the insurer may refuse or be financially unable to pay. Insurance policies are even more difficult to understand and less negotiable than other take-it-or-leave-it consumer contracts. Consumers have little ability to judge insurers' financial strength.

Congress delegated insurance contract regulation to the states in the McCarran-Ferguson Act of 1945, which provides that "[n]o Act of Congress shall be construed to invalidate, impair or supersede any law enacted by any state for the purpose of regulating the business of insurance . . . unless such Act specifically relates to the business of insurance."[59] Insurers had reservations about being left to regulation by many states, but preferred this result to federal regulation under the antitrust laws.[60]

Unlike most other types of contracts, state courts are not required to enforce arbitration clauses in insurance contracts. Because the FAA directs state courts to enforce arbitration agreements in *all* contracts, it is not subject to the McCarran-Ferguson exception for laws specifically aimed at regulating the insurance industry. Twenty-three states and two territories have acted to either prohibit arbitration clauses in some or all insurance contracts or to permit but regulate the arbitration terms.[61] Firms' inability to use arbitration clauses to circumvent local laws and courts gives states less incentive to enforce choice-of-law and choice-of-court clauses than for other consumer contracts. Indeed, because courts are more inclined to strike choice-of-law clauses here than elsewhere, few insurance companies even bother to put them in their contracts.[62]

Firms unhappy with a state's regulations might withdraw from writing policies in that state. However, some state regulators have inhibited exit. For example, Florida limited firms' ability to raise their insurance rates after Hurricane Andrew and even restricted the companies' ability to refuse to renew existing insurance policies.[63] Barring exit restricts the one avenue of law market discipline that the McCarran-Ferguson Act permits.[64]

There is now considerable pressure to federalize the law of insurance. This is due partly to insurers' fears of excessive and duplicative state regulation and partly to consumer groups' concerns that state regulation and state guarantee funds do not provide adequate protection against insurer insolvency. Proposals include optional federal chartering, uniform best practices standards, and the consolidation of financial regulation under a broad federal umbrella.[65] The ferment in this area makes this a good time to consider a significant change in approach to insurance regulation.

Our suggested solution to the problem of state regulation of national firms is familiar by now: Congress should enact a federal choice-of-law statute that requires courts to enforce choice-of-law provisions in insurance contracts unless a state statute explicitly prohibits such enforcement. This proposal might be modified in the insurance area by explicitly giving only states where policies are sold the power to regulate, in order to give insurers predictability and the opportunity to avoid excessive regulation.[66] And, of course, states should not be able to bar insurers from exiting in response to excessive regulation.

Enforcing choice-of-law clauses would enable companies to choose the single law that best suits their business and to have that law govern their solvency and policies wherever they do business. Companies may gravitate toward a state law that becomes the "Delaware" of insurance. For example, Connecticut is known for developing high-quality insurance laws. Specialization also has occurred in the specific context of risk retention groups, or associations that provide insurance only for their owners, or members. These are a modern-day version of the fraternal benefit associations which, as we saw in chapter 3, are governed by the law of the place of the association's charter. Many risk retention groups have elected to charter in Vermont, apparently because Vermont has more flexible regulations and reduced capitalization requirements. In order to obtain these benefits, the associations accept Vermont's comparatively stringent regulations regarding financial integrity, which has kept the liquidation rate of Vermont associations relatively low.[67]

One might worry that a state like Delaware would try to attract insurance companies by reducing or eliminating regulation, just as it has done for credit cards. But consumer groups in other states can lobby their legislatures to refuse to honor choice-of-law clauses if Delaware competes in ways that substantially harm their interests. Our proposal permits this, while ensuring that super-mandatory laws have clear effect and significant political support. In any event, it is not clear that consumers would be made worse off by the "Delawarization" of insurance regulation. Dispersed regulators may have led to the inadequate regulation of problematic insurance contract terms.[68] Specialization by one or a few states therefore may actually increase the quality of regulation.

Insurers, in turn, may be concerned that preserving states' ability to regulate would not improve on the current system because it would leave them at the mercy of 51 state regulators. Our proposal to require state regulation to be embodied in statutes not only gives insurers predictability and a clear opportunity to exit overregulating states, but also ensures a forum for political opposition to super-mandatory laws. Moreover, states and consumer groups would remain subject to the ever-present risk that insurers frustrated with the state regime could turn to Congress for broad federalization of insurance law. Of course, a state choice-of-law regime is not perfect. But both insurers and consumers may be better off with the competition and experimentation possible in such a regime than under a single powerful federal regulator.

Electronic Commerce

Long before there was an Internet, businesses found ways to advertise their products to consumers in other states and to enter interstate consumer contracts. Television, newspaper and magazine ads, catalogs, and phone solic-itations provided information to consumers, who could then order goods by mail and telephone. To what extent, if at all, does the Internet change the appropriate analysis of choice-of-law issues? This section explores the extent to which the electronic environment might require a modification of the treatment of choice-of-law clauses.

Suppose that Larry goes online to purchase a book from Amazon.com that describes the recent research on the neuroscience of emotions. When he finishes his purchase, he searches online for and buys $5,000 worth of custom tiles to use in the renovation of his kitchen. Both sites present Larry with standard-form contract terms that he cannot negotiate: Larry must click on a button that states "I Agree" as a prerequisite to making his purchases. Is there anything about the use of the Internet for these purchases that suggests a dif-ferent legal treatment of choice-of-law and -forum provisions?

First, let us consider the offline situation. According to legal scholars Robert Hillman and Jeffrey Rachlinski, offline standard-form contracts pose at least three concerns that cause courts and commentators to question the meaningfulness of consumer assent to the terms in their agreements.[69] First, for a variety of reasons, consumers often rationally choose not to read the terms of their contracts: standard-form contract terms are often difficult to read and hard to understand, consumers may be in a hurry when they sign the presented forms, most of the terms on the form treat contingencies that are unlikely to arise, the consumer cannot easily negotiate changes, custom-ers expect that the company has chosen terms standard in the industry, and consumers may count on courts to strike down unreasonable terms.

Second, social forces may pressure consumers to sign standard forms without reading the terms. Consumers often get forms when an impatient agent indicates a desire to complete the transaction quickly. Compounding this perception, customers often feel that reading the form and questioning its terms would be considered unreasonably confrontational and untrusting, particularly if the agent presents the contract after giving the customer price and other concessions.

Third, consumers typically face cognitive limitations on their ability to assess the risks associated with assenting to the contract. Even when the con-sumer reads and can understand the form's terms, consumers cannot evaluate the situations in which the terms would apply. Also, at the point when the con-sumer is first buying the product, she might be inclined to underestimate the risk of defects. Consumers are also likely to focus their attentions on more salient aspects of the purchase, such as price and product features.

The online context mitigates some problems associated with standard-form contracts while exacerbating others. Consumers may be less hurried when they shop from their own homes, but may shop online precisely because they seek quick transactions. Consumers may feel fewer social pressures to sign forms online, but find it harder to read contract terms on a computer screen. Thus, consumers may evaluate only a few salient features of an online transaction, not including choice-of-law and -forum provisions. On the other hand, consumers may be better able to shop for desired terms over the Internet, and they have better potential access to consumer group warnings that some company terms are unfavorable to them.

Internet commerce has features that both help and hurt consumers compared to offline analogues. The dramatic rise in Internet commerce since the 1980s has somewhat increased the competitive pressures on contract terms.[70] On the other hand, firms freed from the need to maintain bricks-and-mortar stores may be more likely to be "fly by night." While consumers may be confident in relying on the reputation of Amazon.com to deliver a book, they may be more vulnerable when they buy tiles. Tile sellers are small and typically unknown, and their products are not homogeneous, raising questions about their quality. The cost of the tiles is substantial and likely not covered by credit card insurance terms. This argues for states' providing greater consumer protections for at least some online contracts than for equivalent offline contracts.[71] On the other hand, private verification and reputation systems are quickly arising online to take care of many consumer concerns, and these private mechanisms may turn out to be more effective than are attempts to add to an already comprehensive system of consumer protection laws. Moreover, data suggest that consumers are much more inclined to read contract terms when they purchase products online from unknown vendors or when the product is expensive.[72] As always, the regulatory debate has strong arguments on both sides.

Whatever forms that state consumer protection laws take for electronic contracts, firms will have some ability to avoid these laws as they do in other consumer contexts, including through choice-of-law, choice-of-forum, and arbitration clauses. For offline transactions, selling in or mailing the product to a particular state notifies the company that the state's regulations might apply to the sale, thereby letting the company decide whether and on what terms to sell to consumers in that state. But if a company sells music, movies, or software that buyers can download to their computers, neither party may know where the other is geographically located. Is it still appropriate to force the company to comply with the mandatory laws of the consumer's state?

The American Law Institute (ALI) and the National Conference of Commissioners on Uniform State Laws (NCCUSL) attempted to collaborate on a proposed uniform law for software sales. When controversy over the proposed law erupted, the ALI backed away from the project, but the NCCUSL began to shop the model law, called the Uniform Computer Information Transactions Act (UCITA), to state legislatures. The effort proved to be a dismal failure for a number of reasons. Most important, consumer groups in some states objected to the fact that the law of the licensor's state would apply to software sales conducted entirely online unless the agreement specifies a different governing law. This proposal would impede consumer group efforts to regulate these contracts by giving states incentives to design their laws to attract software firms.[73] On the other hand, for contracts that contemplate the physical delivery of software, the consumer protection laws of the consumer's state automatically became super-mandatory rules even without a clear legislative statement to that effect, thus working against sellers' ability to choose the applicable law.[74]

We argue throughout this book that states should be able to prohibit the use of choice-of-law clauses, and nothing suggests a different approach for purely electronic contracts. Although scholars once thought the Internet would undermine government authority, in fact geographic filtering technology, which enables sellers to correctly identify the geographic location of buyers with a high rate of accuracy, makes the Internet amenable to traditional territorial approaches to regulation.[75] These technologies are improving and getting cheaper, particularly as more states try to regulate Internet businesses.[76] A company that utilizes geographic filtering usually knows the law that applies to the transaction and therefore is able to decide whether and on what terms to transact. Although the company could be forced to comply with the laws of all of the jurisdictions in which it sells, it takes the same risk in offline transactions. Moreover, filtering technology enables firms to choose among physical jurisdictions even when doing business on the Internet.

To be sure, problems remain. For example, consumers might mask their location to take advantage of strong consumer protection laws while paying low-protection-state prices. Also, small firms like our tile seller may not be able to spread the cost of geographic filtering devices over many transactions. In these situations, firms could have a due diligence defense, perhaps requiring them only to ask consumers for their home addresses.

The feasibility of geographic filtering technology motivated the decision of a French court in *Licra and UEJF v. Yahoo! Inc.*[77] There, Yahoo! a U.S. company, operated an Internet auction site that offered Nazi memorabilia for sale. This sale is permitted in the United States and, indeed, is protected by the First Amendment to the U.S. Constitution. Under French law, however, it is a crime to exhibit or sell racist materials, including Nazi memorabilia. Plaintiffs sued Yahoo! for enabling French citizens to access these sale sites through their computers in France. The French court ultimately ordered Yahoo! to eliminate French citizens' access to the Nazi items by using the geographic filtering technology or face stiff fines. This decision accommodates both U.S. citizens' rights of access to these materials and the French government's policy against racism within France. Although the Yahoo! case was not about contractual choice of law, it shows how technology can be used to help enforce limits on the enforceability of choice-of-law clauses in consumer contracts.

Thus, geographic filtering makes feasible for electronic commerce transactions our general proposal for enforcing choice-of-law clauses except where state legislatures explicitly outlaw these clauses. The technology enables consumer groups in some states to push for super-mandatory rules that do not unfairly surprise vendors. At the same time, vendors can avoid states that adopt these rules. The rapidly changing nature of Internet commerce, and the fact that regulation of this commerce is still experimental and tentative, provides a strong argument for preserving the opportunity for jurisdictional competition and variation.

Internet Privacy

The technology of Internet shopping has generated new types of and markets for information, which present complications for our analysis. Consumers who move through a Web site leave behind two types of data trails they would not generate in a shopping mall: (1) the more conventional track from e-mail addresses or other information needed to enter a Web site, which can be linked with other information through databases and search tools; and (2) clickstream data, which are generated silently and therefore raise more significant issues about informed consent. Web sites place unique identifying numbers called "cookies" on the hard drives of most surfing consumers. Firms can use cookies to combine all of the information generated by visits to the site by a particular computer and thereby determine which pages the computer visited and how long it spent on each page. Most important, firms can link this information with identifying information the consumer has supplied, including e-mail addresses, passwords, and credit card numbers. This is how Amazon.com knows not only that you are "Larry" or "Erin" when you visit it, and what books you have bought in the past, but also your addresses and credit card information.

In general, consumer marketing information benefits both merchants and consumers by reducing information and transaction costs and, in turn, inefficient transactions and fraud.[78] This information helps merchants to target advertisements to consumers, which can have payoffs for both merchants and consumers.[79] Consumers may benefit from lower prices and more choices of products and services.[80] But consumers may want to keep such information private because they fear identity theft, or just because they fear threats to their autonomy.[81] Of course, there should be no problem if informed consumers agree to the use of their information because then we can safely assume that the value of the privacy is worth less than what the consumers get in exchange.[82]

Given the costs of making contracts with each consumer, it may matter which party has the burden of contracting, that is, whether the default rule favors privacy rights. This might depend partly on what the parties would have agreed to if there were no costs of agreeing,[83] which in turn depends on whether the value of the information exceeds the value of the privacy. The default rule for medical information (high consumer privacy concerns) therefore may differ from the rule for cookies (relatively low consumer privacy concerns). On the other hand, perhaps the default rule should reflect the fact that consumers may not be aware of the relevant choices. Thus, a state may restrict firms from gathering consumer data unless they explicitly notify consumers and get their consent.

Given this range of regulatory options, it would be particularly helpful in this area if parties could choose the law applying to their transactions from a number of alternatives. As in other areas, we propose to enforce choice-of-law clauses except where state legislatures explicitly adopt super-mandatory laws. States might adopt such laws at the behest of interest groups concerned that consumers have particular problems understanding what is at stake or that there is a social interest in privacy that extends beyond the contracting parties. States might protect consumers by permitting choice-of-law clauses, but require firms to specifically disclose the effects of the clause on their privacy rights. Alternatively, states might protect the social interest in privacy by forbidding use of cookies and making ineffective any choice-of-law clauses that would circumvent these restrictions.

Product Liability

As discussed in chapter 2, choice of law for product liability can influence the states' regulatory incentives. A place-of-manufacture rule attracts firms to states with low liability levels and sparks state competition for factories, which might result in too little regulation. In contrast, a place-of-consumer-residence rule could generate too much regulation because if firms cannot charge consumers more for greater legal rights, consumers in low-liability states may have to subsidize the consumers in high-liability states. To enable local consumers to reap these subsidies, states will compete to provide excessively high liability levels. A place-of-first-sale rule would enable firms to price their products in each state according to the product liability laws in that state, so that consumers would bear the costs of the regulation in each state. Unfortunately, no states apply a place-of-sale rule.

Our proposed treatment of contractual choice of law—generally enforcing these contract provisions unless the legislature explicitly provides otherwise—may serve a useful purpose here. A contract analysis might not seem to be relevant to product liability actions, which are normally characterized as tort cases. However, these torts occur in the context of a contract for the sale of a product, which theoretically could include a choice-of-law clause that provides for the governing state's product liability standard.[84] Indeed, the choice-of-law regulation enacted by the European Parliament explicitly provides for the enforcement of predispute choice-of-law clauses in nonconsumer tort cases.[85] Contracting for product liability law could enable a firm to conduct its business according to the law of a single state and therefore to price its goods to reflect that state's laws. That would not necessarily be the lowest standard: manufacturers of high-quality goods might opt for more stringent product liability laws to signal the quality of their products.

To be sure, contractual choice of law is not a panacea here. Sellers might take advantage of consumers' information and bargaining disadvantages to contract for lax laws. Conversely, multiple regulations could continue to be a problem as states take advantage of their power to adopt super-mandatory laws.

But before rejecting the choice-of-law approach, it is important to take a clear look at the alternative: federal laws and regulations that preempt excessively lax and overly burdensome state laws. Indeed, the preemption of state tort litigation by federal statutes and regulations is rising in response to rising tort litigation, prompting objections from trial lawyers, among others.[86]

A problem of federal regulation is that it blocks legal diversity and evolution, which is particularly important given the complexity of the issues in this area.

Our proposal has the important advantage of curbing overly burdensome laws while preserving states' power to regulate consumer transactions. Because states would have to specify any super-mandatory effect by statute, firms would receive clear notice of the applicable standards. Moving the issue from courts to statutes also would sharpen the competition among pro-regulatory, antiregulatory, and exit-affected interest groups. The result could be diverse state product liability regimes. Some states might decide that they prefer the employment benefits and tax payments that accrue from attracting plants into the state, while others could choose to protect consumers. That diversity could serve each state's local interests and enable states' experimentation with legal rules.

8

Marriage and Other Social Issues

We typically think of marriage as a status, or a way of presenting one's relationship to the world and to each other. But from a legal perspective, marriage also can be viewed as a kind of standard form contract, much like a corporation, where the parties also contemplate a very long-term open-ended relationship. In general, the law of the place where the ceremony is performed determines the marriage's validity. This is analogous to what happens when businesspeople incorporate in the sense that the parties can choose the place of ceremony, which need not have any other connection to the couple or the married life that they contemplate.[1] A couple therefore has considerable, though not unlimited, power to evade restrictions on marriage where they live just by traveling to a neighboring state. Although the couple is required to travel in order to select another law, the expense may be no greater than the fees and taxes that corporations must pay to the incorporating state.

The place-of-celebration rule serves the same need to settle important questions over the course of the relationship that business associations confront. If the validity of the marriage depended on the law of the state of a spouse's domicile, either spouse might shed obligations by moving to a state that did not recognize the marriage.[2]

In many ways, however, marriage is quite different from corporate law. States promote very different interests when they regulate marriages than when they regulate firm governance. Marriage is, among other things, a way of regulating sexual conduct, establishing the foundations of family life and child rearing, and generally setting policy that helps to shape the fabric of society. Accordingly, marriage has important implications for the couple; their children; their relatives, friends, and business associates; and society as a whole. Marriage is therefore of special interest in the choice-of-law analysis because here contract confronts fundamental social policy. Not surprisingly, the public policy of the state of the spouses' domicile can trump the law of the place of celebration. Examples of domicile state restrictions on marriage include (1) age requirements; (2) bigamy prohibitions (restricting marriage to a single spouse); (3) prohibitions on incestuous marriage (preventing marriage by closely related individuals); and (4) same-sex marriage prohibitions. Historically, some states also prohibited interracial marriages and marriages following divorce.[3] Moreover, even when the law of the place of celebration determines the validity of a marriage, the marital domicile determines the rights incident to the marriage. These domicile state rights can profoundly influence the parties' decision to marry.

Here, as elsewhere, we stress the political dynamics in contractual choice of law. Without party choice, state regulation is controlled by groups that are directly interested in the issues at stake. So, with marriage, some groups may seek the freedom to marry and to define their own relationships, while others resist certain types of marriage for others on religious and social grounds. However, as discussed below, if those seeking more freedom in marriage can move to permissive states, exit-affected interest groups can, at least in theory, influence the political balance.

As always, the federal government also can influence the potential jurisdictional competition for marriage law. Federal statutory or constitutional law can strengthen jurisdictional competition by forcing states to recognize marriages that are valid where celebrated. Conversely, federal statutory or constitutional law potentially can weaken competition by imposing regulations that supplant state law or by permitting or imposing a marital domicile rule.

This chapter provides a brief history of choice-of-marriage law and describes how the contentious issue of same-sex marriage has compromised the place-of-celebration rule. We then discuss the supply and demand of state marriage law. On the demand side, couples are seeking new types of marriage rules. On the supply side, legislatures have been urged to accommodate same-sex relationships not only by would-be spouses, gay rights groups, and social liberals, but also by businesses wanting to attract these clients or customers to their states. New forms of marriage have attracted strong opposition from social conservative and religious groups that wish to protect the traditional social fabric of their communities. In response to these latter groups, most U.S. states have modified the celebration rule to preclude the portability of same-sex marriages to other states of residence. But in Europe, more states have either legalized same-sex marriages or validated same-sex marriages performed elsewhere. This chapter also discusses the potential trend toward federal marriage rules. The policy question is whether federal government action is either necessary or desirable, particularly given the alternative of the state market for marriage law.

The chapter concludes by presenting a law market approach to divorce and to other important social policy issues, including surrogacy contracts and living wills.

An Overview of the Marriage Law Market

Choice-of-marriage law has developed in three distinct phases: (1) the adherence to traditional choice-of-law rules; (2) the influence of same-sex marriage in creating a nascent marriage law market; and (3) the constitutional and federal statutory response to same-sex marriage.

The traditional marriage rules were controlled by state, rather than federal, law, and the law of the state where the marriage was celebrated long has governed the validity of marriage.[4] However, this treatment is a mere rule of comity in the sense that a state with a connection to the couple can deny the validity of a marriage that violates its public policy.[5] In particular, the state where the couple resides sometimes rejects the validity of a marriage when the couple left the state temporarily to evade local marriage restrictions.[6] In general, apart from some restrictions on marriage to which there is widespread consensus, such as those barring incestuous or bigamous marriages, the local law invalidates foreign marriages that are valid in the celebration state only if the statute says so expressly, or strongly implies it, as by declaring the marriage "void."[7] Locally powerful interest groups therefore have difficulty overriding party choice unless they can persuade the legislature to make this intention clear.

The advent of the same-sex marriage debate has fostered the organization of interest groups that, at least theoretically, could fuel a market for marriage law. Although the potential of a market for marriage law is, at this point, more theoretical than real, it is well worth discussing, since the need to find some way to resolve the hotly contested same-sex marriage issue is as great as ever.

Choice of law regarding same-sex marriage loomed as a significant issue in 1993, when the Hawaii courts effectively concluded that limiting marriage to heterosexual couples unconstitutionally discriminated against same-sex couples.[8] Until a referendum reversed these decisions two years later, thereby confirming the state's power to refuse to recognize same-sex marriage,[9] it looked like state legislatures and courts across the country would have to decide on the local validity of Hawaii's same-sex marriages. The states' reactions to same-sex marriage, however, were largely hostile. Many states were concerned that permitting this very different form of marriage would threaten the coherence of their marriage laws, since the rights, or incidents, of marriage can depend on who may marry. But as of 2008, only U.S. states, California and Massachusetts, recognized same-sex marriage.

A choice-of-law approach to resolving the same-sex marriage debate would permit states that do not recognize local same-sex marriages to recognize the validity of a foreign same-sex marriage while providing those marriages with different local incidents than are granted to heterosexual marriages.[10] For example, a state could recognize the validity of a foreign same-sex marriage without permitting the couple to adopt a child.

States have expressed concern that recognizing foreign same-sex marriages would threaten the normative stature of traditional marriage. A state arguably could maintain this stature by refusing to let same-sex couples marry locally even if it enforces foreign same-sex marriages.[11] To be sure, state policies regarding same-sex marriage might be compromised by recognizing foreign marriages. But, at least in some cases, states' refusal to recognize these marriages would effectively thwart other states' efforts to provide their citizens with the ability to form valid same-sex marriages. In our mobile society, couples need certainty as to their rights and obligations as they travel from state to state. This problem is comparable to the spillover effect created when states ignore corporations' internal governance rules (see chapter 6) or apply local liability rules to nationally marketed goods (see chapter 7).

Thus, we face a conundrum. Enforcing the parties' choice-of-marriage law would prevent states hostile to same-sex marriage from imposing their policies on couples from other states. At the same time, forcing states to recognize foreign same-sex marriages could compromise the interests of voters in those states who are deeply offended by the idea. Put differently, marriage resists the choice-of-law solution because it is a subject in which society as a whole, and not merely the spouses, is deeply interested.[12] An effective solution to the policy debate must give certainty to same-sex couples regarding the validity of their marriages while protecting, to the extent possible, the strong policy concerns of states that have not recognized same-sex marriage.

A compromise solution might be preferable to these two extremes. Specifically, states could enforce foreign marriages for some purposes but not others. States might distinguish incidents of marriage that the parties can replicate by contract or other private arrangement from benefits that states provide to encourage people to marry.[13] The state-benefits category includes tax advantages, rights to public assistance, evidentiary privileges, creditors' rights exemptions, and the right to sue for wrongful death. On the other hand, parties can enter into antenuptial agreements or otherwise contract to obtain many marriage features, including the control and allocation of joint property, testamentary dispositions, payments after dissolution of the marriage, and various financial and control rights during the marriage. Indeed, the parties can now enter into these arrangements without marriage, for example, by entering into *Marvin* cohabitation agreements.[14] Under this compromise, states could limit the extent to which their laws encourage same-sex marriage while couples would have some certainty regarding their marital rights.

One function of marriage is to provide a bundle of state-provided default rules for a particular type of long-term relationship. Indeed, these rules are functionally similar to those applied in other contractual relationships, including business associations.[15] Moreover, the state, or even private parties, could provide for standard form relationships that include these rights without recognizing the validity of the marriage. The contract analogy has potential implications for contractual choice of law: if the parties can provide for rights by contract, a state arguably could enforce these rights even if it does not recognize the validity of the marriage. Conversely, a state could recognize the validity of foreign-celebrated same-sex marriages by providing only some but not all of the state-sanctioned benefits to these marriages.

To be sure, our proposal does not satisfactorily resolve all issues. Should residents who were married elsewhere but later moved to the state be given the same full-fledged marital benefits that their previous state conferred on them? Suppose a member of a same-sex couple married and living in Massachusetts is killed in a car accident in a state that does not provide wrongful death rights to same-sex couples. Could the surviving spouse sue in the state courts where the accident occurred? We do not claim that our proposed solution solves all problems that states confront in trying to accommodate competing policy concerns. We argue only that working toward this accommodation will provide better results than an all-or-nothing federal resolution. We turn now to an exploration of the extent to which a market for same-sex marriage law could arise.

The Demand for and Supply of Same-Sex Marriage Law

As we have discussed throughout this book, the law market involves four important elements. First, there must be some significant demand for alternative laws as evidenced by parties' ability and willingness to take the necessary steps to avoid undesired laws and to select the laws of other states. Second, some states must be willing and able to supply the desired laws. Third, political forces must respond to enhanced choice. States that do not themselves recognize same-sex marriage may respond to economic incentives with a willingness to enforce parties' attempts to select the law of a state that would provide same-sex couples with desired rights. Alternatively, pro-regulatory groups may prove to be stronger than the pro-law-market groups and may successfully press for restrictions on parties' ability to choose their governing law. Fourth, federal statutory or constitutional law may play a role in the competition by either facilitating or hindering party choice.

The demand for same-sex marriage has grown with the strength of the gay rights movement since the 1970s. The demand reflects the interests of not only the small percentage of the general population that wants to enter into same-sex marriages, but also a larger group of homosexuals who want this recognition of their lifestyle, and the still larger group in society that sees same-sex marriage as an important sign of tolerance and respect.

This demand has produced a supply of rights for same-sex couples, starting with the first judicial decisions in Hawaii that held the same-sex marriage ban to be unconstitutional. Other decisions striking state marriage bans followed in Massachusetts, Vermont, New Jersey, and California.[16] The Vermont and New Jersey decisions left the issue of precisely what to do up to the legislature. Vermont authorized "civil unions" for same-sex couples, which have the attributes of marriage.[17] The New Jersey legislature offered same-sex couples the same rights and benefits as those for opposite-sex couples. Incidentally, California, Maine, and the District of Columbia also authorize domestic partnerships, while Connecticut authorizes civil unions.[18] So far, same-sex marriage is permitted only in Massachusetts and California. The California decision permitted any same-sex couple to marry in the state. Massachusetts, in response, repealed a law that had long prevented non-Massachusetts residents from marrying unless their marriage would have been legal in their home state[19]—another example of the market for law in action. Given the ultimate role of political action in many states, the fact that the same-sex law reform process was started by the courts does not fundamentally differentiate this from other law markets, although court involvement may have affected the timing and extent of the development of this law market.

The third element of the market for same-sex marriage law focuses on regulating states' incentives to recognize the legal status of same-sex relationships formed in other states. In particular, state lawmakers may be motivated in part by exit-affected interest groups, including businesses involved in marriage celebrations[20] and those that want to adjust their benefits programs to attract talented gay employees.

The third element of the law market also involves a competition among interest groups (1) that favor the prohibition of same-sex marriage; (2) that support legal benefits for same-sex couples; and (3) that stand to gain economically if the state loosens its restrictions on same-sex marriage (i.e., exit-affected groups). To date, pro-regulatory groups have dominated the interest-group competition in most states. As of late 2006, 44 states had enacted laws and constitutional provisions denying recognition to same-sex relationships. Most of these statutes also deny recognition of relationships formed in the few states that permit them.[21] Several statutes bar recognition even of private arrangements short of marriage. For example, the Virginia act voids any "civil union, partnership contract or other arrangement between persons of the same sex purporting to bestow the privileges or obligations of marriage."[22] The states' general hostility to same-sex marriage deters same-sex couples from marrying even in states that allow these relationships, since each party knows that the other can avoid legal duties just by moving to another state.[23] Same-sex marriage has become a prominent example of how state regulation can sometimes survive the deregulatory pressures of the law market.

Despite significant setbacks, the potential for a marriage law market survives. In four states, same-sex couples can either actually or virtually marry. Massachusetts and California clearly authorize same-sex marriage. Vermont and New Jersey recognize same-sex relationships that are not "marriage," but that have the same rights and duties. Couples in several states can enter into civil unions, domestic partnerships, or some other kind of "marriage lite." Even without recognition of "marriage" or something like it, people in many states can enter into contracts that approximate some incidents of marriage. In addition, several countries, including Canada, the Netherlands, Belgium, and Spain, now recognize same-sex marriages, and several EU countries now offer registered partnerships.[24]

Indeed, the limits on same-sex marriage can have the side effect of promoting a market for residents rather than merely the less economically important market for marriage ceremonies. Marriage is important enough to some couples that they would be willing to move to permissive states to take advantage of their laws. Because of the risks of interstate non-enforcement, these migrants are likely to want to settle in the marriage state rather than just visit for the ceremony.[25]

Same-sex couples admittedly cannot yet obtain the whole package of reliably enforced and transportable standard form marriage rights. Some may find these limitations frustrating and socially undesirable. But the current law market at least has the virtue of encouraging the states to experiment with new types of rights to suit new types of relationships. The ultimate outcome may be preferable to the outcome that would result if each state unthinkingly poured these relationships into the marriage mold. And to be clear, we argue for reforms that enable legal evolution rather than for imposing a particular legal rule.

The current marriage market is undoubtedly nascent at best. Moreover, so far, states are competing only to attract residents willing to remain in the state rather than to provide a market for law unbundled from residents or investments. Marriage therefore resembles the market for corporate law that antedated the widespread recognition of the corporate internal affairs doctrine discussed in chapter 6. It is not yet clear whether a more wide-open market for marriage law will develop. This may depend to some extent on future federal government action, as discussed in the next section.

The Federal Law of Marriage

As always, the federal government is potentially an important component of the U.S. law market. Different forces have shaped federal law in the same-sex marriage context than in other choice-of-law contexts. The federal government often reacts when states unreasonably regulate interstate and international transactions. But in the marriage area, the federal government reacted to protect states' regulatory authority over relationships that had mostly local effect. Specifically, Congress adopted the Defense of Marriage Act of 1996 (DOMA),[26] which limits marriage to heterosexual couples for purposes of federal law benefits and, more important, provides that states need not give effect to same-sex marriages recognized in other states.

The DOMA resulted from a concern, probably misguided,[27] that once couples could enter into same-sex marriages in Hawaii, all other states would have to recognize their validity. This law was used as a model for state marriage laws,[28] sometimes referred to as "mini-DOMAs," which deny recognition of same-sex marriages celebrated elsewhere. Moreover, because the DOMA's definition of marriage has the effect of denying federal marriage benefits to same-sex couples, the demand for same-sex marriage is lowered throughout the country, even for couples who plan to live in a state that authorizes their marriage.

Future Supreme Court cases may have a significant opposing effect in promoting a market for marriage law. The validity and significance of the DOMA and the mini-DOMAs are potentially threatened by the Supreme Court's decision in *Lawrence v. Texas*,[29] which questions the constitutionality of regulating sexual relationships on purely moral grounds.[30] *Lawrence* invalidated a Texas sodomy statute, holding that gay people had a "liberty interest" in pursuing a homosexual lifestyle that was entitled to Due Process Clause protection. The Court concluded:

> The petitioners are entitled to respect for their private lives. The State cannot demean their existence or control their destiny by making their private sexual conduct a crime. Their right to liberty under the Due Process Clause gives them the full right to engage in their conduct without intervention of the government.[31]

It is not clear whether or how *Lawrence* creates a liberty interest in same-sex marriage. The Court qualified the liberty to pursue homosexual relationships by stipulating that this was "absent injury to a person or abuse of an institution the law protects."[32] It also noted that the case "does not involve whether the government must give formal recognition to any relationship that homosexual persons seek to enter."[33] Justice Sandra Day O'Connor, concurring, stated her view that gay couples had a right to equal protection, but added:

> Texas cannot assert any legitimate state interest here, such as national security or preserving the traditional institution of marriage. Unlike the moral disapproval of same-sex relations—the asserted state interest

in this case—other reasons exist to promote the institution of marriage beyond mere moral disapproval of an excluded group.[34]

Despite this cautionary language and the fact that *Lawrence* clearly does not hold that same-sex marriage bans are unconstitutional, the fundamental reasoning supporting the Court's result does point in that direction,[35] and in any event may limit the grounds on which states constitutionally can support these bans.[36] Specifically, states may not be able to justify outlawing same-sex marriage based on "mere moral disapproval." The *Lawrence* majority noted that condemnation of homosexual conduct "has been shaped by religious beliefs, conceptions of right and acceptable behavior, and respect for the traditional family"[37] and asked "whether the majority may use the power of the State to enforce these views on the whole society through operation of the criminal law."[38] This reasoning elicited a strong dissent from Justice Antonin Scalia, who said that the Court "dismantles the structure of constitutional law that has permitted a distinction to be made between heterosexual and homosexual unions, insofar as formal recognition in marriage is concerned" because such distinctions are based on "moral disapprobation of homosexual conduct," which is no longer a legitimate state interest.[39] Moreover, *Lawrence* might discourage more aggressive state efforts to restrict same-sex marriage. For example, even if states might constitutionally ban same-sex marriage, *Lawrence* might be interpreted as precluding non-enforcement of nonmarriage contracts because those contracts further the parties' liberty interest in maintaining their same-sex relationships.

Lawrence illustrates how judicial decisions might influence the law market and how this potential influence encourages strategic litigation by interest groups. Gay rights organizations have litigated several test cases on same-sex marriage and related issues, such as challenges to same-sex-only sodomy laws. When the groups are successful, the resulting judicial decisions create valuable precedents that support additional challenges in other courts.[40] Of course, opposing interest groups also can engage in strategic litigation, and they have political recourse through the constitutional amendment process. In the wake of *Lawrence*, Congress has considered constitutional provisions that would guarantee that the Constitution not be interpreted to compel the recognition of same-sex marriage.[41]

As a general policy matter, we believe that long-term consensus is better achieved through state judicial, constitutional, and legislative evolution than by federal constitutional determination. A state lawmaking process that evolves over time in response to changing social norms and practices can more effectively address the many questions concerning family relationships. The states could decide, for example, to offer various different standard forms of marriage, to permit a variety of private alternatives to marriage, and to outlaw others. Or states could decide to experiment with same-sex marriage in small ways, as New York has done, by recognizing the validity of same-sex marriages performed in California but continuing to refuse to recognize the validity of same-sex marriages performed locally. Courts and legislators can observe the results over time and get data as to how children and their parents fare under different arrangements.[42] To be sure, some state laws frustrate the development of the law market by sweeping away not only state-sanctioned marriages, but also various private alternatives, such as domestic partnerships. But as long as the states tinker with variations, there is room for the marriage law market to operate. A Supreme Court decision that strikes down a state prohibition or a restrictive federal definition of marriage could perversely affect this state law development. A congressional statute or constitutional amendment that mandates a nationwide prohibition on same-sex marriages could have the same effect.

While the benefits of a market for state marriage law are at least as clear as the benefits of a law market in other contexts, the costs of allowing state variation may be lower here. Marriage is not an area, like corporate or product liability law, in which a single state can effectively impose its law on a nationally or internationally marketed good. Although a state's restrictive marriage law can have effects beyond the state's borders by impeding the mobility of a same-sex couple married elsewhere, the couple does have some ability to obtain desired rights.

Divorce

A critical legal issue concerning the marriage relationship is the circumstances under which the parties can exit by divorce. Because the availability of divorce shapes the enforceability of marriage rights, it can also influence the parties' commitment to the relationship. In contrast to marriage, divorce is not traditionally governed by the spouses' mutual choice of a state of celebration or domicile. The U.S. Supreme Court has held that a state can enter a divorce decree if it is the bona fide domicile of one of the spouses even if the state of celebration, the couple's marital domicile, or both would not have allowed the marriage to be dissolved.[43]

The result of this rule was a market for divorce law. Local pro-regulatory interest groups that favored tough divorce were pitted against exit-affected groups, such as lawyers and commercial groups, which sought to attract the business opportunities from individuals seeking divorce.[44] At a time when big eastern states like New York permitted divorce only for adultery, Indiana permitted divorce for almost any reason to anybody willing to declare that they lived in Indiana, even for a single day. After social conservatives got Indiana to tighten the grounds for divorce, Sioux Falls, South Dakota, picked up the slack. When social conservatives successfully promoted a tightening of South Dakota's divorce laws, Nevada took over. Nevada competed for divorce business by cutting its residency requirement to six weeks and offering absolute divorce on many grounds, all of which could be proven by unsupported testimony.[45] This brought a significant influx of wealthy people seeking quickie divorces, each of whom spent money in the state. Nevada's divorce business dried up (at which time, Nevada switched to creating marriages) in 1966 when New York, which had supplied much of Nevada's divorce business, liberalized its divorce law. The ready availability of liberal divorce has made no-fault divorce the governing rule across the United States.[46] Moreover, the legal move to no-fault divorce has apparently increased the rate of divorce.[47]

Allowing parties to escape readily from marriage is not self-evidently the best rule for all families or for society as a whole. In the marriage relationship, just as in any long-term contract, the parties' inability to enforce the continuity of the relationship can allow one party, by exiting, to take advantage of the other party who has made substantial investments in the relationship. In marriage, often the wife forgoes career opportunities in order to produce and raise children. Her investment in the home enables her husband to accumulate assets that they both expect to enjoy in later life. However, the husband may opportunistically withdraw from the marriage after his wife has made the investment in the children but before sharing the payoff from the husband's career.[48]

This risk of opportunism has potential social consequences. If both parties understand at the outset that marriage is easily ended, they may be less willing to fully commit to the relationship and to make long-term investments in having children. To be sure, easy exit also theoretically could make people more willing to enter into marriage. However, available evidence indicates the opposite: easier divorce has been associated with fewer marriages.[49]

More important, no-fault divorce changes the contours of those marriages that are entered.

To be sure, strong arguments also favor allowing parties easily to exit marriage. People usually marry when they are young and may lack the wisdom and maturity to evaluate the risks that their marriage will be unhappy. For example, there is evidence that newlyweds are unrealistically optimistic about whether their marriages will be successful.[50] Moreover, some children are harmed more by their parents remaining in an unhappy marriage than by the breakup of the family.[51]

In short, the divorce laws at least historically involved a clash of competing policies. Some states wished to free spouses from the fetters of their unhappy marriages, while others sought to promote investments in long-term family relationships. Mobility gives parties more ability to free themselves, but at the expense of states pursuing different policies. This raises the question of whether the law market might offer a compromise solution to the problem of divorce just as it does to the problem of same-sex marriage. A state could enable parties to commit themselves by entering into a form of marriage that does not permit no-fault divorce. Other states could then enforce this relationship by refusing to divorce the parties to such a marriage even if one or both of them resides locally and even if the domicile state's law provides for no-fault divorce. In effect, then, this alternative divorce form could create a super-mandatory rule whereby contrary policies are trumped by the law (and courts) of the state of celebration.

This potential for a state competition in divorce laws is not merely hypothetical. Louisiana has enacted a "covenant" marriage law that lets the parties waive their rights to a subsequent no-fault divorce.[52] The law permits the spouses in such a marriage to divorce only upon a showing of adultery, abandonment, crime, one-year separation, or a judgment of separation on a showing of abuse.[53] Other states have followed with similar laws.[54]

Will covenant marriages be enforced in other states to which a spouse moves? If not, these laws could meet the same fate as the earlier version of fault-based divorce. On the one hand, states might decide to permit no-fault divorce for marriages celebrated locally, but enforce other states' covenant marriages. This would reflect the parties' strong need for certainty regarding the durability of their marriage and the fact that they have clearly expressed their expectation of durability by entering into a covenant marriage.[55] It would also give effect to other states' policies intended to encourage investments in marriage relationships. On the other hand, states may decide to enforce their local policies that enable exit from marriage even as to couples that have been married under another state's covenant marriage law. The state may want to protect local spouses and children, as well as its own courts and welfare agencies, from the costs of binding spouses to unhappy marriages.

Apart from states' policy decisions, law market dynamics may work against a market for durable marriage. Although the history of no-fault divorce shows that there are obvious beneficiaries of local divorce business, it is not obvious who would pressure lawmakers to honor foreign covenant marriages. Perhaps the marriage counseling industry could benefit from advising would-be spouses regarding such marriages, but any such benefit would be felt in the states in which these marriages are celebrated. The states where parties to a durable marriage live incur the costs of unhappy marriages but not necessarily the benefits of offering a durable marriage option.

A further compromise could salvage a law market approach to divorce. By analogy to the solution suggested above for same-sex marriage, states might enforce only those aspects of durable marriages for which the parties could provide by contract even in the absence of covenant marriage. Parties might, for example, contract for greater support amounts unless certain contractual conditions for divorce are satisfied.[56] The parties also might contract to some extent for child custody rights.[57] Since many states already take marital misbehavior into account in assessing financial obligations,[58] it is arguably not much of a stretch to enforce an antenuptial agreement that provides for fault standards and damages. Or parties might be able to contract that any support or custody determinations be made by courts in the state of celebration.[59] If states are willing to enforce at least some types of durable marriage contracts, they may also be willing to enforce choice-of-law clauses that apply the even more permissive laws of other states. Given the important and contentious social policy issues at play in divorce and family law, social liberals and conservatives might agree to one of these compromises. To be sure, this contractual approach to durable marriages would not offer the same level of assurance, and therefore opportunity for commitment, as a covenant marriage. Damages for divorce are not the same thing as the specific enforcement of the marriage relationship offered by covenant marriage. On the other hand, the lack of strong enforcement may be an advantage. The parties would be able to make a contractual commitment that encourages some investments in the relationship, but not one that is so strong as to engender the social costs of forcing people to remain in unhappy marriages.

The law market may encourage the enforcement of durable marriage contracts notwithstanding the apparent lack of interest-group impetus to provide competing laws. Under the choice-of-law statute we propose in chapter 10, states would have to enforce choice-of-law clauses unless they state explicitly otherwise in their statutes. The debate over the enactment of such a super-mandatory clause might engage participation by the same pro-marriage groups that favor the enactment of the durable marriage law. This may be significant in states where the other relevant interest groups are closely balanced.

In sum, there is a potential market for divorce law in the United States just as there is one for marriage. The market so far has been shaped by a Supreme Court decision that protects states' decisions to permit exit from marriages celebrated elsewhere. But this means only that the Constitution protects states' refusal to enforce durable marriage just as it does the refusal to enforce other choice-of-law contracts. The states remain free to enforce durable marriage, and the market for law eventually may give them reason to do so.

The Law Market and Other Family and Social Regulation

In addition to marriage and divorce, other social policy issues regarding important personal decisions may be subject to resolution through choice of law. Here, we illustrate two of the many potential applications by briefly discussing issues that arise at the bookends of birth and death—that is, gestation contracts and durable powers of attorney.

Gestation Contracts

Suppose a couple wants biologically related offspring but faces difficulties because the woman is physically unable to carry the fetus, one or both is sterile, or it is a same-sex couple. The couple could arrange to have a surrogate mother carry the fetus produced by sperm and egg, at least one of which belongs to one member of the couple. The surrogate mother contracts to turn the child over to the couple after its birth. Suppose further that the couple lives in Connecticut, where the legal treatment of surrogacy is unsettled, and the surrogate lives in New York, which has a public policy against surrogacy contracts based on concerns about exploiting the surrogate. The parties enter into a "gestational carrier agreement," which provides that the child will be delivered in a specified Massachusetts hospital, that the parties will take the necessary steps to give the couple physical custody and have them named as the legal parents on the birth certificate, and, most important for present purposes, that the agreement would be governed by Massachusetts law. To prevent the need to institute postbirth adoption proceedings, the genetic parents want a court order clarifying that they are the legal parents of the unborn child and ordering the birth hospital to issue a birth certificate naming them as the parents. This is obviously a situation in which the parties' need for certainty may clash directly with strong public policies.

Responding to these facts, a Massachusetts court in *Hodas v. Morin*[60] held under Massachusetts law that the genetic parents were entitled to the requested court order. This was only six years after *R.R. v. M.H.*,[61] in which the same court ignored a choice-of-law clause that selected Rhode Island law and refused to enforce the surrogacy agreement. In *R.R.*, the gestational carrier and genetic mother was a Massachusetts resident and the child was born in Massachusetts, but the genetic father and his wife resided in Rhode Island. In the earlier case, the court relied on a Massachusetts public policy against surrogacy for pay (the carrier was to be paid $10,000).

The cases can be distinguished on several grounds, including the facts that, in *R.R.*, the surrogate was to be paid, she was the biological mother, and she changed her mind during the pregnancy and decided she wanted to keep the baby. In *Hodas*, the surrogate fully complied with her agreement, did not contest the requested court order, and was not performing her services for pay. But the cases also can be distinguished by the way the Second Restatement, section 187, applies to the facts. The *Hodas* court found a "substantial relationship" in Massachusetts because of the birth and prenatal care (i.e., "performance") there. Moreover, Massachusetts was interested in "establishing the rights and responsibilities of parents [of children born in Massachusetts] as soon as is practically possible" and in "furnishing a measure of stability and protection to children born through such gestational surrogacy arrangements." Unlike Massachusetts's interest in *R.R.*, New York's interest in *Hodas* was not controlling, even if "materially greater" than the interests of the other states, because it was not clearly the applicable law in the absence of a choice-of-law clause. Applying the Second Restatement, section 6, factors (see chapter 3), the "place of contracting" and the "place of negotiation" were not determinable, but probably both New York and Connecticut could lay claim; the "place of performance," as just noted, was Massachusetts, or possibly New York, "where the pregnancy evolved," or Connecticut, where the carrier was inseminated. Only God knows where the "subject matter of the contract" is, and the domiciles of the parties are in both New York and Connecticut.

So, the court concluded that it was "doubtful" that New York law would apply if there were no clause. The court cited the Second Restatement, section 187, comment g, which provides for enforcement of the parties' choice "where the significant contacts are so widely dispersed that determination of the state of the applicable law without regard to the parties' choice would present real difficulties."

This analysis highlights the difficulty of determining the governing law for interstate contracts. This indeterminacy contributed to the court's final resolution, which seems almost disingenuous. Was not the dominant interest here the protective policy of New York, which, just like Massachusetts, seeks to protect poor mothers from giving over the babies from their wombs? The most substantial basis for overruling that choice is the "justified expectations of the parties" factor under the Second Restatement, section 6, given the expectations expressed in the agreement. If the court just wanted a simple test, or one that would foster uniformity, to cite two of the other factors the court stressed, why not just apply the protective law of the protected party's residence? But if enforcing the parties' "justified expectations" is what the court wants, the only way to accomplish that is a clear rule favoring the contract, rather than the muddy multifactor test the court applied. On the other hand, perhaps these expectations should not control in situations where the gestation mother's preferences can change from contract to childbirth.

The law market factors we emphasize throughout this book—here, the demand for and supply of surrogacy law—could potentially be significant in these cases. The demand side is driven by party mobility and legal variation. The contract parents, like those in *Hodas*, can choose hospitals in states that enforce gestation contracts. The gestation mother who has a timely change of heart can give birth in or take the baby to a non-enforcing state, as the *Hodas* court implicitly acknowledged,[62] though the contract parents have some leverage through their agreement to pay the gestation mother's expenses. The contract parents also can choose gestation mothers who reside in states that are hospitable to these contracts, which may be significant to the extent that the courts emphasize the protective policies of the gestation mother's residence state.

On the supply side, state laws regarding the enforceability of surrogacy agreements vary significantly. Some states will not enforce any surrogacy agreements, some will not enforce surrogacy-for-pay agreements, some impose other regulatory restrictions on the agreements, and still others enforce them fairly freely.[63] Support both for surrogacy contracts and for enforcing choice-of-surrogacy law comes from all those who benefit from these contracts: doctors, hospitals, gestational service intermediaries, gestation mothers, and contract parents. These parties might encourage even states that do not enforce surrogacy contracts to enforce their contractual choice of law. The result of these supply- and demand-side forces would be greater certainty, which is ultimately valuable for all parties involved.

Because the states may have strong regulatory interests in these arrangements, they are unlikely to permit the open-ended choice of an unconnected state's law. The *Hodas* court expressed a concern for this problem, since the parties admitted that they chose Massachusetts law partly because it enabled them to obtain a prebirth order. But the court was satisfied by the fact that the parties also had chosen Massachusetts as a convenient midway point between the parties' residences, which enabled the genetic parents to attend prenatal doctor visits. The choice-of-law rule could address the parties' interests in certainty by specifying the requisite connection with the designated state. For example, the parties might contract for the law of the residence of the gestation mother at the time of the contract. This rule would enable contract parties to shop for law at the same time as they are choosing a gestation mother.

If the demand for surrogacy contracts grows but states continue to differ on whether to enforce the contracts and their accompanying choice-of-law clauses, there is always the potential recourse to federal law, just as we have seen elsewhere in the law market. As always, Congress has the basic choice between legislating on the merits by declaring the validity or invalidity of these contracts, and simply clarifying the governing state law. The latter course seems more attractive in this setting given the deep roots of parentage issues in state family law. In addition, by not regulating surrogacy contracts, Congress enables the states to experiment with various types and levels of regulation. States might differ on such issues as the need to prohibit paid surrogacy, whether enforcement should depend on counseling the parents and the gestation mother, and restrictions, including age, on who can enter into these contracts. But both experimentation and clarity could be achieved with clear rules governing choice of law, including the enforcement of choice-of-law clauses.

Surrogacy contracts only scratch the surface of the life-creation issues that loom on the horizon, from test tube babies to cloning. States are very likely to take years working out the answers, and these answers will surely differ.[64] Meanwhile, the parties have a desperate need for certainty, since the creation of life triggers a lifetime's worth of legal and other rights and obligations. Relying on federal law to produce this certainty sacrifices the experimentation that will be necessary for the law to ultimately generate sound policy. Contractual choice of law offers a potential alternative solution.

The Right to Die

In early 2005, the nation watched the spectacle of a brain-damaged woman, Terri Schiavo, lying in a hospital bed while her relatives and others fought for her life and death. Eventually, Schiavo's life was ended as a result of a court order. The Schiavo case stirred up a controversy containing echoes of the abortion debate, with the comatose Schiavo as the fetus. An important difference is that people who come to Terri Schiavo's position are potentially able to make an advance choice through a legal instrument, such as a living will or durable power of attorney, that instructs family members and medical personnel what its maker would want to happen if she comes to be in Schiavo's state. State law can encourage this advance resolution by enforcing these instruments.

These instruments present difficulties. Like a gestation mother in the surrogacy situation who may have a change of heart when the baby is born, people may not be able to accurately foresee either what they want done in an end-of-life situation[65] or who should be trusted to make the decisions. The law must decide how to interpret living wills or durable powers of attorney, particularly when the documents fail to specifically anticipate the end-of-life situation that actually occurs.

The important point for present purposes is not to settle the normative debate over whether and to what extent to enforce these instruments, but to show how a state law market might work in this context. A power of attorney or another instrument might specify the governing law to be the state of residence of the person who is executing the relevant instrument. What happens if the person moves between the time she signs the instrument and the end-of-life events that trigger the clause? What if the person falls ill while on vacation and ends up in a hospital in a nonresident state? In either of these situations, a court might decide that the location of the hospital and not the contractually selected state should provide the governing law.

As we have shown throughout this book, the law market will not necessarily accept the verdict of a non-enforcing court. On the buyer's or demand side, the dying person or his family may choose a hospital or hospice in a state that will enforce the underlying contract, or at least the choice-of-law clause. If a person enters a hospital outside an enforcing state, the family might arrange to have the patient transferred to a hospital in a state that will enforce the instrument. These scenarios, of course, assume that people care enough about the enforceability of these instruments that they are willing to relocate to ensure their enforcement. But if the stakes in the choice-of-law issue are high enough, it is reasonable to assume that people will incur costs to ensure that the law they prefer applies.

On the supply side of the law market are lawyers who may benefit from promoting durable power-of-attorney laws. To the extent that people use lawyers in drafting these instruments, durable powers of attorney could be a source of legal business, perhaps as a "loss leader" in generating estate-planning business. Standard forms might minimize the need for lawyers and thereby mute lawyers' interests. But people's wishes might not lend themselves to standardization. Interpretation issues therefore are very likely to arise, in which case lawyers would be glad to help litigate the documents, as well as to help people forestall litigation by drafting customized provisions. Also, hospitals and other caregivers have an interest in documents that will clarify their responsibilities.

This analysis leaves the question of whether states that restrict the enforcement of these devices might have an incentive to enforce choice-of-law clauses that select other states' permissive laws. As in other contexts, it is necessary to consider the role not only of pro- and antiregulatory interest groups, but also of exit-affected groups that want to attract or not repel people who care about enforcement of these clauses. Of course, people usually do not think about being rendered incompetent when they are choosing where to live. But retirees might be thinking along these lines. States that seek to attract retirees would have an interest in enforcing their wishes about end-of-life decisions. Even if strong pro-regulatory groups in the state oppose the enforcement of these documents, these groups may be weaker than the combination of anti-regulatory and exit-affected groups.

A state's most straightforward course might seem to be to enforce the power of attorney itself rather than continue to prohibit at least some parts of these documents while nevertheless enforcing those that contain a choice-of-law clause. However, if the balance of interest groups is close enough, prohibiting or regulating the enforcement of purely local documents while enforcing the choices made by mobile people who designate another state's law might be a reasonable compromise. In all of these contexts—same-sex marriage, surrogacy contracts, and end-of-life arrangements—the state could draw the line at "tramp" contracts or documents that designate the law of an unconnected state. States might, for example, enforce only instruments that designate the law of the state where the dying person resided at the time of executing the instrument. Indeed, a court might look to that state's law even in the absence of a contract, on the theory that the executing party wanted a valid document and could reasonably assume that validity depended on the law where he lived at the time of executing it. Moreover, the residence state sometimes has enough interest in the contract to outweigh the regulatory interest of the state where the party happens to be when he is dying. This approach would give some weight to the regulatory policy of the state where the party resided while he was dying by restricting the choice of an alternative state's law to one that has a connection to the instrument. At the same time, this approach also helps to effectuate the law market by more generally facilitating state competition for residents with policies promoting choice regarding end-of-life scenarios.

As with surrogacy and related contracts, contracting for death arrangements is likely to become increasingly important with technological advancements. Science's ability to prolong life may far outstrip its ability to maintain life's quality. People may not wish to trust their caregivers because these third parties may be more concerned about their own potential liability or, more cynically, about getting paid to prolong life than about the dying person's quality of life. Conversely, medicine is developing so fast, and becoming so complex and inexact, that people may decide that it is better to exhaust medical science than to give a doctor the right to pull the plug. This is therefore a troubling issue for which there is no easy answer. As in other law market contexts, a variety of state laws can provide the necessary mechanism for experimenting with possible solutions. Moreover, enforcing contracts can reduce some of the uncertainty inherent in the brave new world of medical science and give to at least highly motivated individuals the power to make these very difficult choices for themselves.

9

Property

A law market, both potential and real, exists for legal rules regarding property. We focus on three aspects of that law market. The first is the market for trusts, which are created when the original owner, or *settlor*, places assets in the control of a *trustee*, who supervises the assets for a *beneficiary*. Giving power to a trustee to act on behalf of the beneficiaries can be an important tool for transferring wealth while constraining the unreasonable use of the assets. We discuss the rise of state competition for trust funds and how this market led to the demise of a universally followed rule that restricted their duration.

The second aspect of the property law market is state competition for asset protection trusts and business associations. These vehicles are used by asset owners to avoid responsibility to creditors, so the owners' ability to choose the governing law here is somewhat more troubling, given possible socially undesirable spillover effects on third parties.

Finally, we turn to a proposal to create a market for real property law similar to that for corporate law. While, at this point, the idea is only a theory, it provides a good basis for developing the law market concept.

The law markets for property follow the pattern discussed throughout this book in that they are driven by (1) individuals' and firms' demand for laws, or their ability to, in effect, shop for legal rules; and (2) states' and countries' willingness to supply the laws demanded, or at least to enforce contract clauses or equivalent devices that enable people easily to choose laws. Choice of legal rules is, in turn, limited by interest groups acting at the state level to preserve the effects of local regulations against erosion through the law market. Moreover, federal or international lawmaking efforts can hinder or eliminate the law market by imposing partial or complete uniformity on the states.

One might argue that many of the devices discussed in this chapter are not examples of the law market at all because they are attempts by a single individual or entity to evade restrictions on the use of property rather than the product of an agreement between affected parties. But in each case, the way in which a party holds property provides a basis for determining the rights inherent in later voluntary transactions involving the property. This is similar to the rights specified in articles of incorporation, which apply to all officers, directors, and shareholders of the corporation and may bind others who deal with the corporation. The property law market also neatly illustrates how a law market can provide an exit option from arguably costly products of the political process: the federal estate tax, sharp rises in liability costs, and limits and restrictions in state property law. To be sure, these mechanisms also can produce a harmful evasion of taxes and regulations. We ultimately leave it to the states to determine which is the proper characterization of exit efforts here, as elsewhere.

Competition for Trust Law

Property owned by individuals for nonbusiness use is now increasingly held and managed on behalf of its beneficiaries by trusts. When a trust is created, the original owner (the settlor) of the property, real or personal, directs the property to be held by a trustee and administered for the benefit of another (the beneficiary). The beneficiary can be either a third party or the settlor herself. The standard contractual choice-of-law rule for trusts is analogous to that for contracts generally. The settlor can choose the governing law provided that (1) the choice is designated in the trust instrument; (2) there is a substantial relation between the trust and the designated state; and (3) the law chosen does not violate a strong public policy of the state with the most significant relationship to the trust.[1] However, the courts and legislatures have significantly enhanced party choice by permitting the settlor to choose the governing law as long as the *trustee*, which can be a bank, is located in the designated state.[2] That choice is limited by the standard public policy exception that limits most other choices of law. As with other law markets, the market for trust law has both supply and demand sides and is limited by state and federal super-mandatory rules.

Demand Side

All markets for law require that parties or their assets be sufficiently mobile to generate a meaningful demand for desirable laws. New demands arise from the declining costs of mobility, the increased benefits from choice, or both. The demand side of the trust law market was ignited by a development that drastically increased parties' gains from contracting for law. In this case, the trigger was a 1986 law that imposed federal taxes on wealth transfers to succeeding generations, but exempted certain transfers in amounts rising to $3.5 million by 2009.[3] Under this law, by putting money into a trust to be held at least until her death, a settlor might be able to pass to her heirs millions of dollars in wealth, *plus* appreciation on the trust's assets, forever free of federal taxes if the trust could last into perpetuity.

The catch to using this tool was an arcane state property law known as the *rule against perpetuities* (RAP), which had stumped law students and stymied estate planners for hundreds of years. The RAP provides that a restriction on property, particularly including placing property in trust instruments,[4] is invalid from its inception if the restriction lasts for longer than the life of anyone alive at the time of the transfer (a "life in being") plus 21 years. This rule ensured that property would not be encumbered for long periods. It thereby enabled property to be transferred to a person who might use it more productively than someone in the original line of succession. It was always questionable whether the rule's supposed benefits warranted either its restrictions or the resulting confusion. Yet no powerful group organized to change or abolish it.

The new, potentially perpetual tax benefit for trusts created a strong demand for trusts freed of the restrictions imposed by the RAP. State legislatures met this demand by adopting legislation friendly to perpetual trusts, particularly by abolishing the RAP. Delaware abolished the RAP in 1995, explicitly acknowledging its intent to participate in a competition for trust law, and several states followed suit over the next three years.[5] Because settlors were already significantly able to choose their governing laws, many naturally began to move their trust assets to states that had abolished the RAP. According to Sitkoff and Schanzenbach, states that abolished the RAP reported an average of about $6 billion, or 20 percent, more in trust assets than states that retained the RAP.[6]

Supply Side

One really interesting aspect of this state competition is the *reason* that states chose to supply perpetual trust laws. One might think that they wanted to levy taxes on the trust assets, analogous to the standard franchise tax explanation for the corporate charter competition discussed in chapter 6. But Sitkoff and Schanzenbach convincingly refute this explanation by showing that *only* the states that did *not* tax trusts saw an increase in trust assets after abolishing the RAP. This is not surprising from a demand-side perspective: as long as some states eliminated the RAP but did not charge a tax, settlors would have little incentive to move their assets to a state that charged a tax. The puzzle is on the supply side: why would states participate in the competition if they were not reaping tax revenues?

The answer should be obvious from our analysis in earlier chapters. Even if a state stands to gain from attracting out-of-state tax revenues, taxpayers as a whole are too diffuse and disorganized a group to lobby effectively for laws that increase state revenues. The more politically important beneficiaries of the competition for trust law are well-organized lawyers and bankers, who reap significant fees from creating and managing trusts. Sitkoff and Schanzenbach show that states that abolished the RAP garnered a total of $100 billion in additional trust assets, which, based on standard fee schedules, translates into about $1 billion a year in trustees' commissions.[7] Lawyers undoubtedly earned significant fees from setting up and managing trusts and correctly guessed that those fees would decline if states taxed the trusts.

The competition for trust funds clearly illustrates both how a law market can develop in response to increased benefits from choosing law and how the market can change the law. In particular, this competition suggests that the development of the market for corporate law discussed in chapter 6 was not a fluke attributable to the idiosyncratic features of corporations, nor was it dependent on the ability of a leading state like Delaware to charge a significant fee for using its law.

The relative unimportance of state tax revenues in motivating trust competition may turn partly on the fact that the corporate franchise tax arguably serves a different function for corporations than the fiduciary income tax serves for trusts. As discussed in chapter 6, the reliance of the small state of Delaware on the corporate franchise tax bonds its future performance as a provider of high-quality corporate law. This, in turn, gives Delaware a unique edge over other potentially competing states. There is much less concern about a state's future performance as a trust regulator because state trust law is far less detailed and variable than state corporate law. Moreover, trusts produce far fewer lawsuits by beneficiaries than do publicly held corporations by shareholders. As a result, trusts do not need the significant legal infrastructure that is necessary to maintain Delaware corporate law.

Super-Mandatory State and Federal Laws

As with other law markets, the market for trust law helps parties to evade mandatory rules. The competition for trust law might be viewed as a race to the bottom to the extent that settlors, lawyers, and bankers have induced states to abolish a rule—the RAP—that arguably protects society as a whole against the inefficiencies of assets being bound up in a perpetual trust.

Even if the costs of the trust law market might be imposed on nonconsenting parties, it seems unlikely that this will lead to super-mandatory state rules. As the arguable locus of the trust property, the designated state has as much interest as any other state in freeing property for its potential transfer to more highly valued uses. While it is theoretically possible that states would still disagree about the RAP, in fact the vast majority of states have abolished it. Perhaps the states could not resist the tide sweeping over the RAP, in which case super-mandatory rules here are a job for Congress rather than the states. Accordingly, to the extent that the abolition of the RAP creates significant social costs, it would now take a congressional act to reimpose the RAP as a super-mandatory rule.

The abolition of the RAP also combines with current federal tax rules to enable wealthy families to establish dynasty trusts that some fear will further cement wealth disparities in the United States.[8] This is not a problem with the RAP alone, of course: wealthy families are perfectly capable of keeping their wealth within the family even under the RAP.[9] Rather, it is a problem that was created when Congress decided to permit the creation of tax-free trusts subject only to state limitations on their duration. Unlike the usual law market scenario, where the federal government is called on to protect interests jeopardized by states' enforcement of contractual choice of law, in this case the United States put its own interest in tax revenues on the line when it assisted this state competition. Congress has an opportunity to act again when the tax rule comes up for renewal in 2011.[10]

Asset Protection Vehicles

A law market for trust funds also has been spurred by settlors' demands for the protection of personal assets from liability, which some states have been willing to supply. The market has been constrained both by state supermandatory and federal bankruptcy laws.

Demand for and Supply of Asset Protection Vehicles

The rise of large firms and mass production since the industrial revolution has contributed to a significant increase in tort liability. This liability creates a demand by corporate owners for protection. In response, the corporate rule of limited shareholder liability evolved, under which the shareholders' personal liability for the firm's obligations is limited to the amount they have invested in the firm. The benefits of limited liability have traditionally been offset by the double corporate tax.[11] However, as discussed in chapter 6, the law market for unincorporated firms eroded the tax constraint on limited liability in the late 1980s and 1990s.

Limited liability protects people only from *vicarious* liability for the debts of their firms. They are still personally liable for injuries caused by their own acts. While insurance adequately protects most people from these liabilities, some—particularly doctors and other professionals—face a risk of significant liability that might not be fully insured. Moreover, small business owners may find it hard to secure significant credit on behalf of corporations or limited liability companies (LLCs) without personally guaranteeing the firm's debt. These people might find it worthwhile to protect at least a portion of their personal wealth from creditors' claims, particularly if they can do so without having to secure their loans or pay higher credit charges.

A large industry of "asset protection" vehicles has grown to meet this demand. Individuals can transfer their property to entities that they control but that their creditors cannot reach. It has long been possible to do this through a "spendthrift trust," which was created initially to enable settlors to pass wealth to improvident beneficiaries while protecting those assets from the beneficiaries' potential creditors. The law in the United States at first did not let debtors evade creditors by placing their assets into trusts and naming themselves as beneficiaries.[12] Put differently, under traditional trust law principles, the settlor and the beneficiary could not be the same person.

The law market for asset protection trusts initially appeared outside of the United States. This competition took the form of *offshore* asset protection trusts, which were invented in the Cook Islands in 1984[13] and spread to Belize, the Cayman Islands, Gibraltar, Bermuda, and Jersey (Channel Islands).[14] Total assets in these trusts have been estimated to exceed $6 trillion.[15]

Despite the rise of offshore trusts, many American property owners were reluctant to use them. Some early U.S. cases refused to apply the law of offshore formation jurisdictions,[16] and debtors themselves were uncomfortable with foreign laws and possibly untrustworthy foreign trustees and unstable governments.[17]

The U.S. states began competing for domestic asset protection vehicles starting in the late 1990s.[18] Alaska, Delaware, Nevada, Rhode Island, Utah, Missouri, Oklahoma, and South Dakota each passed laws enabling the creation of domestic asset protection trusts.[19] But these U.S. trusts did a poor job of protecting assets. For example, they did not protect assets from some claims, such as for child support, alimony, and personal injury or wrongful death claims arising prior to the transfer into the trust. More important, debtors could not guarantee that the enforcing state or a bankruptcy court would apply the law designated in the trust instrument. Finally, some U.S. legal principles make it difficult for asset protection laws to fully protect settlors. For example, the Full Faith and Credit Clause of the U.S. Constitution requires states to enforce other states' judgments regarding the disposition of assets in the trust. This means that states without asset protection laws can order that creditors be given access to trust funds, and the protecting state cannot issue contrary judgments. Because the offshore states are not similarly constrained, they can more effectively refuse to turn over trust assets. In addition, bank secrecy laws are tolerated in offshore jurisdictions but not within the United States.

However, the law of unincorporated firms was used to create another twist on jurisdictional competition.[20] As discussed in chapter 6, the state-of-organization rule is clearly recognized for unincorporated firms in the United States. Accordingly, if the debtor could place assets in a business association whose governing law shields the assets from creditors, courts everywhere in the United States probably would enforce this protection.

The traditional unincorporated firm, the partnership, offers asset protection by restricting the transfer of partnership interests. Partnership statutes provide that, in the absence of contrary agreement, partners can transfer only economic and not management rights.[21] The limited transferability of partnership interests reflects partnerships' traditional nature as close-knit associations of individuals who could be expected to want to control with whom they had to share management rights.[22] This contrasts with corporations, which are designed for widespread ownership and permit transfer of both voting and economic rights. An owner of a partnership interest, including a partner's creditor who has obtained ownership of the interest by foreclosure, therefore can receive only the distributions that the owners choose to make.[23] At best, a creditor or other transferee may be able to petition a court for dissolution of the partnership.[24] Similarly, a partner's creditor can get a "charging order" on any distributions the partnership makes,[25] and by foreclosing on the interest get the right to petition for dissolution.[26] By contrast, creditors of corporate shareholders get an attachment remedy,[27] by which they can obtain or sell the shareholder's management as well as financial rights.

Despite these restrictions on creditors' rights, the partnership has limited utility as an asset protection vehicle. A debtor-partner may not be able to stop her co-partners from having the firm make distributions that the debtor's creditors can obtain. If the firm cuts off distributions just to the debtor, this could be considered an evasive tactic that is disciplined by one of the creditor protection remedies discussed below. A debtor cannot avoid these limitations by forming a single-member partnership because a partnership is *defined* as "an association of two or more persons to carry on as co-owners a business for profit."[28] More important, because a partnership is defined in part as a "business for profit," a debtor cannot use a partnership to protect houses or other nonbusiness assets that a debtor might want to shield from creditors.

Instead, the partnership's asset protection qualities have flowered in its offshoot, the limited liability company. The LLC statutes started out with the partnership features of limited transferability discussed above and then added important features that the partnership form lacked, including the ability to form LLCs with only a single member and to hold nonbusiness assets.[29] These provisions made LLCs available for uses that were new to partnership-type firms, including asset protection. Most important, debtors could lock up personal assets in solely owned LLCs, and their creditors would have only a very limited right to judicial dissolution of the firm, and often not even that.[30]

The asset protection features probably are a by-product of the general market for LLC law rather than the result of debtors lobbying for asset protection. The LLC statutes dropped the limitations of the partnership form mainly to eliminate troubling uncertainties that could impair the LLC's flexibility, such as whether the LLC in fact had multiple members or was organized for a purpose that fit the statutory definition. Debtors then capitalized on this flexibility to get the protection they could not get through asset protection trusts.[31]

In short, the demand for asset protection has led both to the development of asset protection trusts and to the use of existing business associations for asset protection purposes. As elsewhere in the law market, mobility fed demand: debtors could put their mobile assets into a variety of property-holding vehicles made available by states throughout the world. This, in turn, pressured other states to offer these forms in order to stem the outflow of clients and assets.

As has been the case throughout the law market, the development of asset protection forms was led by lawyers, both as statutory drafters and as debtors' advisers. In particular, as discussed in chapter 6, lawyers drove the state competition to develop the LLC in the 1990s. Lawyers gained from the fees they received in setting up LLCs and in advising their clients on this new business form. The LLC features that lawyers sold to their clients included not only the ability to combine limited liability with partnership-type taxation, as discussed in chapter 6, but also asset protection. Although the use of LLCs for asset protection purposes was primarily a matter of exploiting existing forms for new purposes, this flexibility was a by-product of lawyers seeking user-friendly forms to attract and better serve clients. Banks and other trustees assisted lawyers in promoting the self-settled spendthrift trust laws.

Super-Mandatory Rules

In response to the developments discussed above, creditors and their lawyers, including the plaintiffs' bar, have fought hard to mitigate the harms created by the new forms of asset protection. The largest creditors can protect themselves in various ways, such as by obtaining security interests in particular assets that asset protection vehicles cannot circumvent. In contrast, smaller creditors and tort plaintiffs often need state assistance to protect their interests.

Creditors have sought relief through general equitable remedies applied in both state courts and federal bankruptcy proceedings, including rules related to fraudulent conveyance and "reverse veil piercing."[32] But these remedies require creditors to show fraud or similar misconduct, particularly including a transfer that is intended to foil creditors or that is likely to have that effect because it is made when the firm or the settlor is insolvent. It might not be enough for a creditor to show that a doctor, for example, put her vacation house in an LLC when she was quite solvent and left it there after committing malpractice. These creditor protection remedies might mitigate the most serious asset protection abuses, thereby dampening pressure from creditors and trial lawyers to seek more drastic limits on trusts or LLCs. Importantly, for current purposes, state and federal bankruptcy courts seem willing to apply local fraudulent conveyance rules notwithstanding the settlor's efforts to choose the law of a state that provides relatively little by way of fraudulent conveyance protections.[33] Even with these limits, offshore asset protection trusts continue to provide a vehicle for some who are determined to shield their wealth.

A Market for Real Property Law?

The jurisdictional competition for legal rules affecting the ownership and rights to property has so far been indirect, through the rules governing the legal entities, such as trusts and business associations, that hold the property. However, a viable law market conceivably could develop in the rules that govern the ownership and disposition of real, or immovable, property itself. This section considers what that market might look like.

Legal and Theoretical Considerations

The default choice-of-law rules regarding real property are well established. Disputes relating to use, title, ownership interests, and the transfer of real property are subject to the law of the state where the property is located: the *situs rule*.[34] This rule reflects the situs state's interest in promoting the efficient use of land and in ensuring clarity of title. The rule also provides clear notice as to which state's law applies, since the affected parties at least know where land is located, and the location does not change over time.

Should property owners be permitted to choose a law other than that of the situs in a land-sale contract or other instrument relevant to land, such as a will or deed transferring an interest in property?[35] The choice of law could be recorded with the title to the property to provide the same notice of the governing law to interested parties that the situs rule provides. A similar device might work for titled personal property, such as automobiles.

Although contractual choice of law in this context might seem odd at first glance, a law market here is not much different from the state-of-formation rule for business associations. Like the internal governance of a corporation, the rule would apply only to matters that affect property ownership and the allocation of rights among owners. As with corporations, it is necessary to distinguish between rules that affect the parties to the choice-of-law clause and rules that impose consequences on parties that do not participate in the contract. The choice-of-law clause arguably presents little problem as to potential owners who can take account of the rules in their dealings. Thus, parties arguably should be able to choose the governing law for rules regarding transfer and title so long as a public record reflects both the ownership and the choice of governing law.

More problematic are parties' choice of laws providing for redress by nonowners injured by the use or maintenance of the property, such as neighbors who assert that the land use creates a nuisance. Similarly problematic are parties' choice of rules regarding the creation of interests without owner consent, as through adverse possession or finder's rights.[36]

The advantages of enforcing choice-of-law clauses for property ownership and disposition (but not use) are by now familiar from our analysis of other aspects of the law market; they foster variety, experimentation, and competition. According to the *numerus clausus* principle, property owners can choose only from the limited menu of property ownership forms provided by the state where their land is located. They are not permitted to create new or different rights by contract.[37] Even if it is clear that the number of property forms should be limited, no one knows how many or which of these forms are optimal. The limited menu of property rights also constrains property law's ability to create rights to deal with new social demands. One example is a state conservation easement that lets owners perpetually protect their land from developers.[38] While property owners or others might try to persuade local legislators to pass statutes to provide for these easements, legislators may be leery of innovations that have uncertain effects for which they would take political heat. Getting the right mix of rules for the many different types of potential situations is arguably an appropriate task for the law market, because it fosters state experimentation.

Enforcing choice-of-law clauses also would eliminate uncertainties that can arise in choice of law for property. In general, since land is immovable, under the situs rule it is usually clear which state's law governs. However, when interests in property are created, transferred, or terminated through contract, will, marriage, or divorce, a dispute over the interests could be characterized as a dispute about contract, estate, or family law, in which case nonsitus law could potentially apply to resolve those disputes.[39] Moreover, if a person owns property in several states, multiple states' laws could apply to interpret a will or prenuptial agreement that attempts to dispose of that property on death or divorce, respectively.[40] For obvious reasons, the owner might strongly prefer to have all of the property distributed under the rules of a single state's law. Contractual choice of law enables parties both to determine the law in advance and to select a single set of rules for multistate transactions.[41] The contract option also can constrain situs states that have a kind of "monopoly" on scenery or other unique geographic advantages from adopting ownership laws that unduly favor some interest groups over others.

One problem with contracting for property law is its potential to affect third parties who did not actually or constructively consent to the choice, even where the rules seem to relate directly only to the owners or other contracting parties. Property law settles interests in the property as to the whole world, that is, *in rem*.[42] An heir, donee, or transferee otherwise might be subjected to claims by those who were not parties to the instrument but who claim to have interests in the property. In other words, it may be futile to try to distinguish particular property rules that have third-party effects because *all* property law has broad effects that make it inherently inappropriate for contractual choice of law. Even a landlord's implied warranty of habitability, which might seem to be a contract solely between landlord and tenant, may sufficiently affect the general social and physical environment that courts or legislatures would not want to apply rules adapted to a quite different environment. In other words, we may not want parties to create a "private Idaho in Greenwich Village."[43] Similarly, permitting a landowner to place a conservation easement on her property that forever bars development might seem unproblematic because it binds only the property owner and future owners who know of the restriction. But these easements arguably are socially objectionable because they constrain future valuable uses of the property, much like the rule against perpetuities limited how long a trust could endure. If, for example, land becomes scarce, a community might want to preserve the power to revisit the tradeoffs between environmentally desirable density and affordable housing.

At the same time, enforcing contractual choice of law is arguably less necessary for property than for other types of law. Precisely because property law is so rooted in the property's locale, this state arguably bears both the benefits and costs of its property law. Spillovers of regulatory costs therefore are less a problem in this context than they are, for example, with respect to the governance of a global corporation or franchise network. Even domestic relationships have more of an interstate dimension than does real property because of the spouses' ability to move between states.

Property rules also arguably raise distinct information cost issues that bear on enforcing contractual choice of law. Property rights are subject to infinite variations. This complexity may explain why lawmakers traditionally have been limited by the *numerus clausus* principle from creating new property interests. Yet choice of property law threatens to multiply this complexity by the legal menus available in all other potential jurisdictions. As a result, parties might be forced to incur costs of investigating their rights that outweigh the potential benefits of allowing variations.

Demand for and Supply of Real Property Rules

Apart from whether there is a suitable domain for a market in property law, how might such a market arise? As always, this market requires (1) parties that demand property rules other than those provided by the situs state; and (2) states that are willing to meet this demand by participating in a competition for property rules.

The demand side seems absent as to real property. Even if property owners might want to use property rules from other states, the situs rule locks them into the state where the property is located. If they cannot move the property, how can they exert the necessary leverage to press for an alternative choice-of-law rule under the law market dynamic we have discussed throughout the book? People might leave and buy property in a new state, but they cannot take real property with them nor expect to find precisely comparable property in the new state. Indeed, as discussed above, it is the fact that real property is not fungible that makes a market for property law detached from physical location attractive. Although a market for law provides a way to skirt states' monopoly on their geography, the fact of the monopoly also inhibits the mobility necessary to create a market for law. A quarter-acre residential lot in Boulder in the shadow of the Rockies is not the same thing as a residential lot in central Illinois. Even otherwise identical residential properties differ because of the proximity of particular jobs and amenities and the preferences and needs of particular owners. Moving to take advantage of property law is therefore less feasible than the sort of mobility that has driven the corporate law market and the mobility that may ultimately liberalize same-sex marriage laws.

But all is not hopeless for the property law market. First, property is more vulnerable to mobility than might first appear. The rights of property owners can be controlled by giving them to mobile entities and relationships like trusts, corporations, and marriages. Also, property owners' mobility can affect a property's value even if the property itself is immobile and nonfungible. As discussed in chapters 4 and 6, markets in contract and corporate law have been driven partly by firms' willingness to relocate their headquarters in response to regulation. Similarly, real estate developers surely choose where to conduct their activities in part based on local property rules.

Second, law markets can be galvanized by events that create a new incentive to contract over the law. Developments in corporate finance and industry created a demand for new corporate law (see chapter 6), a federal estate tax rule that favored durable trusts triggered a market for trust law (see above in this chapter), and the gay rights movement and a Hawaii court decision triggered a potential market in marriage law (see chapter 8). An equivalent event could have similar consequences for property law by increasing either the costs or the benefits of the menu of rules that states currently offer. For example, the joint tenancy with right of survivorship was revived in property law when it was perceived as a way to avoid the expense of probate.[44] If some states lag in property law reform, parties have incentives to seek out more permissive laws.

Assuming that there is sufficient mobility to generate some demand for new property rules, would any state seek to supply the demand? Bell and Parchomovsky draw an analogy to corporate law and suggest that states would have the right incentive only if they could charge a fee for use of their law, analogous to the franchise tax that has been so important to Delaware.[45] This would require registration of the property not only in the situs state, but also in the state that is supplying the law. However, as we have noted, such fees are not essential, and perhaps not even important, to the development of law markets. Lawyers in particular have incentives to push for laws that would bring them new transactional work or litigation. A state that competes in a national market for property law may be able to attract property cases to its courts, where locally licensed lawyers would have an edge in competing for business. Indeed, a state might condition use of its property law on litigating the case in the local courts. Unfortunately for those lawyers, however, a nonsitus state probably lacks the constitutional authority to exercise *in rem* jurisdiction over property located elsewhere.[46] This limitation could seriously hamper the development of this law market. Nevertheless, the nonsitus court probably could exercise jurisdiction over some property disputes if it possesses personal jurisdiction over the people who are disputing the property rights.[47] Because consent is a basis for personal jurisdiction, two parties to a contract involving land could consent to jurisdiction in the chosen state's courts.

Super-Mandatory Laws

The remaining question for the property law market is whether, if property owners inserted a choice-of-law clause in a deed or other instrument that chose the law of a nonsitus state, states other than the designated state would enforce the clause. In other words, to what extent are states likely to deem their property rules to be super-mandatory and therefore to trump choice-of-law contracts? Note that, traditionally, only the state where real property is located could render judgments affecting the property, particularly regarding title to the property.[48] However, a nonsitus state could adjudicate the claim and apply its law pursuant to contractual choice-of-law and choice-of-forum clauses, including those entered into by constructive consent through appropriate notice of the applicable law filed with the property records in the situs and designated states. The designated state would have personal jurisdiction over both owners who reside locally and those who have consented to jurisdiction in the designated state. A judgment by the designated state pursuant to these agreements might provide substantial contract enforcement among the parties even if the court lacks jurisdiction over the property itself.

As is typical in the law market, states might be willing to enforce choice-of-law clauses if the alternative is that people and firms will avoid the state or its courts. A state might retain restrictive rules to its own property but allow the owners to choose a less restrictive state law. States might enforce at least those choice-of-law clauses that designate nonsitus state law if it is the law of the owner's state of residence. This limitation would reflect the need to obtain personal jurisdiction over the property owners in order to be able to compel transfer of the deed, as suggested above. Enforcing the choice of the law of the owner's residence also would allow a form of "price discrimination" by giving flexibility to out-of-state owners, who may have more choice as to where to invest in property, while insisting that locally based owners abide by local law. For example, an interstate developer might be encouraged to operate locally if it could contract for the law of its headquarters' state. At the same time, this discrimination in favor of out-of-state parties would minimize states' ability to impose costs on these parties for the benefit of more politically influential locals.[49] And recall that choice-of-law clauses would only be used to determine the rights of the contracting parties. Third parties would continue to be able to sue under situs law to enforce their rights. Thus, as with the corporate internal affairs doctrine, party choice can be confined to avoid interfering with states' policy concerns.

Even if states are willing to enforce some clauses that designate the laws of other states, they are likely to impose their own laws in some situations. For example, a New York court might refuse to compromise New York's implied warranty of habitability (which imposes a duty on the landlord to provide habitable housing to tenants) in favor of an Idaho choice-of-law clause.[50] To the extent that states resist enforcing efficient choice-of-law clauses, a federal choice-of-law rule may be necessary. A federal law also might be desirable as a way of promoting the recognition of specific types of conservation and environmental laws at the state level without imposing substantive federal regulation. For example, Congress might adopt a law to enforce choice-of-law clauses for conservation easements[51] if states resist enforcing these property rights.

10

A Federal Choice-of-Law Statute

So far, we have primarily treated the law market as a self-ordering phenomenon. Those who are adversely affected by state regulations can impose costs on regulating states and confer benefits on states that enforce contracts by moving from the former to the latter states. Exit-affected interest groups in the states exited can exert pressure on state lawmakers to moderate their regulation and to permit enforcement of other states' laws. Where regulation otherwise would be inefficient, the resulting competition can improve the substantive content of state legislation by forcing state lawmakers to take account of the costs they impose.

The competitive pressure that the law market can exert on states is necessarily limited. Exit-affected groups, such as the potential employees hurt by franchise regulation, are often not coordinated enough to effectively influence legislation. There is therefore no guarantee that the addition of exit-affected groups will serve as an effective check on inefficient regulation. Nevertheless, we claim that exit-affected interest groups can affect the outcome of otherwise closely contested political issues.

We have also seen that a potential federal law can be viewed as a silent constraint on states' lawmaking efforts. State lawmakers and interest groups know that if they insist on imposing costs on interstate transactions, including by allowing little contractual freedom, Congress might oust state law with federal regulation. Yet, when actually imposed, federal government discipline comes at the cost of eliminating the benefits of state competition and experimentation.

In theory, uniform state laws can be a compromise between the chaos of multiple state regulations and the sometimes mistaken judgments of federal law. If the states can somehow coordinate around a single rule, this rule might accommodate interests at the state level while mitigating individual states' incentives to ignore regulatory benefits and burdens that occur elsewhere. The primary mechanism for coordinating the U.S. states is an organization called the National Conference of Commissioners on Uniform State Laws (NCCUSL), which was discussed in chapter 7. The NCCUSL commissioners are appointed by state governors and serve part time without pay, although each state contributes toward funding NCCUSL drafting projects.

The uniform lawmaking process poses several problems. Even where uniform laws are desirable, the NCCUSL might not produce the best set of uniform laws. The NCCUSL, like any lawmaking body, has its own agenda. One study argues that NCCUSL commissioners benefit by maximizing the number of uniform law proposals, so they typically draft the proposals to minimize interest-group opposition rather than to craft efficient public policy.[1] Alternatively, the NCCUSL can be a way to enhance the power of specific interest groups by effectively assisting their lobbying.[2] Moreover, this lawmaking process could promote uniformity in substantive law even when a diversity of substantive laws coupled with the enforcement of choice-of-law clauses would be a superior solution.

Nor is a formal uniform lawmaking process necessary. Uniformity can sometimes spontaneously evolve through the law market.[3] Indeed, if uniformity is efficient, a robust market for law often will generate it. There is evidence that spontaneous evolution is more likely to produce uniformity in the circumstances when it is needed, but not in circumstances when it is inappropriate, than will a NCCUSL-aided process.[4] But it is far from clear that either NCCUSL or state competition will produce uniformity whenever it is appropriate.

We propose a way to preserve the benefits of the law market while eliminating some of the impediments to its efficient operation: a federal statute that compels states to enforce choice-of-law clauses. Congress has the power to enact such a statute under the Commerce Clause (at least to the extent that the statute affects interstate transactions). Alternatively, Congress has the power under the Full Faith and Credit Clause[5] to specify the obligations of each state to apply the laws of other states, including by enacting a general choice-of-law statute.

For such a statute to work effectively, however, Congress also must enable the states to retain their power to enact super-mandatory rules that trump choice-of-law clauses. Because choice-of-law clauses can circumvent efficient regulations, their overenforcement can be as costly as their underenforcement. Indeed, one virtue of the spontaneous law market (one without federal substantive standards) is that it preserves a regulatory role for the states at the same time that it erodes states' power to overregulate. Unless carefully crafted, a federal choice-of-law statute could fail to produce this delicate balance.

Indeed, if the federal statute is carefully crafted, it could more effectively preserve state regulatory authority than does the current regime. As discussed in chapter 4, the federal courts currently are an important venue for enforcing contractual choice of law. Some might argue that federal courts' enforcement of choice-of-law clauses undermines appropriate exercises of state regulatory authority. A federal choice-of-law statute like the one we propose could better protect the balance between competition in the law market and states' power to regulate because federal courts would be required to strike choice-of-law clauses when a state enacts a super-mandatory law.

The following proposal and analysis attempt to balance state regulatory concerns with the benefits of jurisdictional competition. We preliminarily show why our proposed solution needs to be initiated by Congress rather than the state governments and why a statute is necessary to provide needed clarity and predictability for contracting parties. After laying that groundwork, we present and analyze a proposed federal choice-of-law statute.

State or Federal Law?

We argue later in this chapter that enforcing choice-of-law clauses with clear exceptions is an appropriate way to promote a more efficient balance of state regulations. As discussed in chapter 4, a handful of states already have passed statutes that clarify the enforceability of certain choice-of-law clauses. Each of these statutes ensures that choice-of-law clauses will be enforceable in that state's courts. But current statutes cover only certain large commercial contracts, and currently other states are free to ignore these statutes. In general, choice-of-law clauses are broadly enforced in the United States, across virtually all states and contract types. However, the standards-based approach to the typical common-law treatment of these clauses has prevented most states from achieving the clarity regarding exceptions to enforcement that is essential to healthy law markets. This clarity is better promoted through federal action than by leaving the process entirely to the states.

State law reform could occur through a uniform law. The likely coordinating mechanism is a choice-of-law statute proposed by the NCCUSL. A widely adopted proposal could clarify the enforceability of choice-of-law clauses. However, to ensure widespread adoption, the NCCUSL might well tailor the proposal with exceptions or vague language that attempts to accommodate opposing interest groups. The result could be no better than the existing Second Restatement rule.[6]

To be sure, a federal choice-of-law statute likely also would be shaped by similar political compromises. If the balance of politics in Congress differs from that of the state legislatures, Congress could end up insisting on the overenforcement of choice-of-law clauses. Alternatively, political concerns could keep Congress from acting at all. Enacting neutral rules for choice-of-law clauses designed to enhance the quality of state lawmaking might not generate sufficient political benefits for federal legislators to justify the political risks of interfering with the traditional state prerogatives.[7]

On the other hand, a federal statute could attract international commercial opportunities and arbitration proceedings to the United States. As discussed in chapter 5, Congress responded to substantially weaker international competitive pressures in 1925, when it enacted the Federal Arbitration Act. To encourage foreign firms to avail themselves of U.S. markets, Congress further amended the FAA to reduce the likelihood that international firms would be forced to litigate contract claims in U.S. courts. A choice-of-law statute would help to maintain U.S. competitiveness by providing international firms with an additional tool to avoid the costs of complying with undesirable and multiple state laws. At the same time, a choice-of-law statute would relieve Congress from having to make an all-or-nothing decision to either dictate substantive legal standards or let costly state litigation continue unabated. Moreover, with a strong federal policy in favor of choice-of-law clauses, parties should feel more comfortable resolving their disputes within the United States.

Even if Congress is unwilling to adopt a general choice-of-law statute, it might be willing to facilitate the operation of the law market with respect to particular types of legal disputes through use of its power to preempt.[8] In particular, Congress might preempt state laws *unless* states permit parties to contract for the applicable law. This approach prevents the operation of state laws that unduly interfere with national and international commerce while at the same time preserving some scope for state regulation that is constrained by the law market.

Congress adopted a somewhat similar approach in the Securities Litigation Uniform Standards Act (SLUSA).[9] That act attempted to prevent plaintiffs from filing state securities claims in state courts as a device to evade restrictions on federal private securities law actions. However, in response to pressure from the Delaware bar, and acknowledging the important role of state corporate law under the internal affairs doctrine, SLUSA included the so-called Delaware carve-out, which continued to permit certain actions brought under state corporate law. As discussed in chapter 6, state corporate law is subject to the internal affairs choice-of-law rule that applies the law of the incorporating state to matters concerning the governance of the corporation. Consistent with our suggested approach, SLUSA essentially says that state law controls as long as the parties can select this law by contract.[10] Otherwise, cases must be brought in federal court, where federal law applies.

As an alternative to qualified federal preemption, Congress could simply adopt a federal choice-of-law rule that facilitates the state law market. For example, the National Banking Act enables banks to charge interest rates and other fees permitted by the state where the bank is chartered.[11] This in effect enables contractual choice-of-law by letting banks choose the chartering state and then enter into contracts with borrowers that are subject to the chartering state's law. Unfortunately, as discussed in chapter 7, this federal choice-of-law rule gives the states too little power to regulate loan contracts, because it fails to allow regulating states to prevent the enforcement of choice-of-law clauses in contracts with their residents.

Congress instead could enact a statute to compel the enforcement of choice-of-court clauses. These clauses would enable parties to confine litigation to courts willing to enforce their choice-of-law clauses. In addition to promoting law markets, there are strong advantages to having the state whose law is chosen also control judicial decisions interpreting that law (which we presume will generally be the case), because these decisions are part of the legal package that states compete to provide.[12] The difference between forum and law may matter to Congress because mandating the enforcement of choice-of-court clauses avoids the need for Congress to make a policy judgment of which state's law should be enforced. A federal choice-of-court statute easily could be squared with congressional policy as expressed in the Federal Arbitration Act and with Supreme Court cases favoring the enforcement of choice-of-court clauses. However, mandating the enforcement of choice-of-court clauses could interfere with judges' litigation management decisions, and the clauses could force one of the parties to litigate in an inconvenient location.

In general, therefore, a federal choice-of-law solution that preserves state regulatory authority appears to be the best mechanism for promoting experimentation with legal regimes without unduly hampering contracting parties. Congress might have an incentive to enact such a statute. Indeed, it has adopted the equivalent of a limited choice-of-law statute with its Delaware carve-out to SLUSA. Perhaps Congress will enact only subject-specific choice-of-law statutes instead of the generally applicable choice-of-law statute that we propose below. If so, our choice-of-law analysis also can usefully guide an incremental congressional approach to regulatory problems.

Federal Common Law or Statute?

The federal courts might promote contractual choice of law through common-law rules. We saw in chapter 4 that federal courts are significantly more likely than state courts to enforce choice-of-law and -court clauses. This is not surprising, since federal courts have less incentive than do state courts to insist on the application of local state regulation. However, federal courts face the significant constraint that, in diversity jurisdiction cases, they must apply the forum state's choice-of-law rules under *Klaxon Co. v. Stentor Electric Manufacturing Co.*[13] Although these state rules are flexible enough to give the federal courts significant leeway, the courts still are able to work only on the margins. Moreover, whether state or federally crafted, common-law choice-of-law rules are inherently unpredictable.

The federal courts might have some room to apply their own choice-of-law rules despite *Klaxon*. One possibility is triggered by the Class Action Fairness Act, which, as discussed in chapter 3, permits removal of large class actions to federal court even with only partial diversity between the defendant and a single plaintiff. Congress did not settle the question of what state law applies in these cases. However, the fact that Congress provided a federal venue arguably indicates its intent to provide a federal solution to the problems posed by mass market class actions. Samuel Issacharoff suggests the specific approach of applying the law of the defendant's home state.[14]

Issacharoff's proposal is unsatisfactory for several reasons. First, the federal courts likely are not empowered to apply a special choice-of-law rule in CAFA class actions. More likely, Congress did not promulgate a special rule because it assumed that state choice-of-law rules would continue to apply. Second, even if Issacharoff is correct that *Klaxon* no longer constrains the federal courts' hearing class actions, his proposed treatment of choice of law is troubling. Freeing the parties to contract for the law of any state is arguably preferable to binding them in all cases to the law of defendant's home state or another across-the-board rule. Across-the-board rules can unwittingly bias state substantive laws toward one party or the other—as with the place-of-manufacture rule for product liability or the place-of-bank-charter rule for credit card contracts.[15] Enforcing choice-of-law clauses at least mitigates this problem by making it more likely that both parties' preferences are reflected in the choice of governing law.

The important point for present purposes is that both federal and state courts are worse situated than legislatures to provide the appropriate rule. As we have argued throughout the book, an important benefit of enforcing choice-of-law clauses is that they provide predictability as to the governing law. Common-law rules necessarily compromise predictability, however, because they tend to take the form of open-ended standards applied on a case-by-case basis to particularized facts, as illustrated in the Second Restatement's treatment of choice-of-law clauses. Moreover, even if the Supreme Court were to fashion a detailed rule for application in all state and federal courts, the Court likely lacks the institutional capability to promulgate a rule that can efficiently reflect the large variety of circumstances in which the rule would be applied.[16] As discussed in the next section, the treatment of choice-of-law clauses must consider the sensitive tradeoffs in different circumstances between the relative costs and benefits of contracts and regulation. Accordingly, we propose a federal choice-of-law statute, which is presented below. First, however, we discuss the need for clear rules regarding the enforcement of choice-of-law clauses.

The Importance of Clarity

The law market can create value by enabling people and firms to choose the law that best suits their needs. However, enforcing choice-of-law clauses also can enable firms to evade mandatory rules that promote a society's interests. Indeed, many different state regulations can be compromised by a single choice-of-law clause. The policy challenge is to find a way to enforce some choice-of-law clauses without unduly eroding the states' regulatory power. How can a statutory rule accommodate these competing considerations while still providing clarity and predictability?

The current lack of clarity is costly for the law market. We have shown that the law market generally tends to move the law in the right direction from society's standpoint. As we have discussed throughout this book, parties have some ability to manipulate jurisdictional contacts and choose the adjudicator so as to promote jurisdictional choice. This mobility, or the buyers' side of the law market, can then activate interest groups on the sellers' side to motivate judges and legislatures to enforce contractual choice of law. In other words, the law market encourages legislators not only to consider the welfare of pro- and antiregulation interest groups, but also to take account of costs imposed on mobile interstate firms, at least to the extent that these firms react by entering or leaving the state. However, the market does not function perfectly. A key problem is that the supply and demand forces of the law market are muted by the ambiguity of the rules on enforcing choice-of-law clauses. Given this ambiguity, parties may not be certain at the time of making the contract, or at the time of deciding where to establish connections, whether their choice-of-law clauses will be enforced. This prevents them from fully taking the costs of enforcement or non-enforcement into account when entering into contracts or, more important for our purposes, when deciding where to establish connections.

We propose to promote predictability by clarifying both the enforcement and non-enforcement of contractual choice of law. First, our proposed federal statute specifies the relationships among parties, regulating states, and contractually chosen law that matter to whether the choice-of-law clause is enforced. Second, rather than having a court determine at the time of adjudication whether a regulating state's policy is "fundamental," our proposed rule would require state legislatures to declare prior to the formation of a contract whether their regulations have super-mandatory effect.

A Federal Choice-of-Law Statute

Here, we show how Congress or another federal or international body might promote the law market by enacting a statute that enhances the enforcement of choice-of-law clauses while specifying the situations where states will not enforce them. A statutory mandate that provides clarity at the time that the parties enter into their contracts helps them to price the contract, design supplementary contract terms, and avoid litigation.

Here is our proposed statute:

A. Subject to section B, a court shall enforce, without regard to rules or principles of conflict of laws, a written agreement between the parties expressly providing for the application to the contract of the laws of a state designated pursuant to such provision (the "designated state"). Except to the extent the contract provides otherwise, all issues relating to the contract shall be governed by or construed under the laws of the designated state.

B. Section A shall not apply to an agreement if enforcement of the choice-of-law clause is prohibited by:

    (1) a state statute enacted after [the effective date of this statute] that explicitly applies to the type of agreement involved in the case; or

    (2) a statute or judicial rule that applies to the agreement involved in the case, and that would have applied to the agreement prior to the enactment of this statute,

        if *in either case* the party or a third party protected by the statute resides, at the time of entering into the agreement, in the regulating state.

C. This law shall not affect the validity of any contract or contract provision other than the one described in sections A or B.

The proposed statute raises several issues that deserve discussion.

The Statute as a Default Rule of Enforcement

This statute explicitly validates certain clauses, but does not *invalidate* clauses that the statute does not cover. In particular, the statute does not prevent a state from providing for the *enforcement* of choice-of-law clauses even though it could provide for *non-enforcement* under section B. In other words, the proposed statute never limits states' abilities to apply their own laws, but it also never limits their ability to defer to the parties' choice of an alternative state's law.

The statute's effect on a particular type of regulation would depend on the general structure of the law market, which includes both party mobility and states' approaches to contractual choice of law. States can be generally grouped into three categories:

    (1) *Active* competitors that welcome law business, including by broadly enforcing contractual choice of law.

    (2) *Passive* competitors that participate in the law market to the extent at least of not driving firms away through excessive regulation or a refusal to enforce contractual choice of law.

(3) *Noncompetitors* that aggressively regulate interstate transactions because local pro-regulatory groups are stronger than antiregulatory and exit-affected groups combined. One reason that a state may be a noncompetitor is that pro-regulatory interest groups in the state know that the state's markets are so large that firms cannot retaliate by avoiding local contacts.

The proposed statute adopts a default position that active competitors would always accept and passive competitors would often accept. However, noncompeting and passive states may object to a federal requirement that they enforce choice-of-law clauses. The proposed statute enables these states to opt out of enforcing choice-of-law clauses with statutes that explicitly prohibit enforcement in order to protect a state's specific regulations. The statute therefore generally tracks the law market. Its main function is to facilitate the law market's operation by protecting parties from non-enforcement in noncompeting states *unless* antiregulatory interest groups in those states can muster enough support in the legislature to obtain explicit statutory support for the policy. The statute thereby preserves a core area in which the market for law can operate without cutting off the potential for jurisdictions to experiment with broader or narrower authorization of choice-of-law clauses. In addition, the statute is designed to accommodate congressional reluctance to trample traditional state regulatory authority.

Connection Requirements

The proposed statute provides for the enforcement of choice-of-law clauses even if no party resides in the designated state. This is consistent with several contractual choice-of-law statutes applicable to large commercial contracts, as discussed in chapter 3 (which do not require any connection with the designated state), but differs from the general Second Restatement rule (which requires a connection with the designated state, or at least a "reasonable basis" for the choice).

As discussed in chapter 4, a connection requirement has several useful functions. In particular, it gives regulators more incentive to adopt desirable laws in order to attract large firm assets and job opportunities. Moreover, requiring a local connection makes it more likely that other states will enforce choice-of-law clauses. However, the proposed statute rejects requiring the designated state to have a connection-based "interest" in the contract in order to enforce the contract. As we discussed in chapter 4, lawyers and other interest groups in the designated state can pressure states to enforce choice-of-law clauses wherever the parties to the contracts reside.

Of course, the state whose law is chosen can limit the effect of its law. If the contracting parties choose a state's law, they take that law with its limitations. And, with this proposed congressional statute, states no longer need to limit enforcement to contracts with connections to the state in order to get general cooperation from other states.

To the extent that a state has a regulatory interest to protect, *that* state can always pass a statute to limit the enforcement of the choice-of-law clause. And *that* state could provide for enforcement only on condition of the presence of a specified connection with the designated state. The point here is that the state chosen need not have a significant connection as a prerequisite to enforcement. But by limiting the effect of a super-mandatory rule to a regulating state's residents, our proposal maximizes the potential for party choice while fully preserving the legitimate regulatory interests of states whose residents could be hurt by the transaction.

Legislative Invalidation of Choice of Law

As discussed above, a significant feature of the proposed statute is that it forces clarity regarding when the choice-of-law clause will *not* be enforced. Recall that the Second Restatement, section 187, directs courts to decide when enforcing the choice-of-law clause would contravene a state's "fundamental policy." By contrast, the proposed statute requires the regulating legislature to determine when local policy concerns are sufficiently weighty so that they should be given super-mandatory effect over other states' laws.

Insisting that any limits on contractual choice of law be specified by the legislature has at least three salutary effects. First, it seats the public policy decision in the regulating state rather than asking some other state's court to determine whether the regulating state might have a fundamental public policy conflict. Second, legislative determination provides predictability so that the parties know what rules will govern the performance of their contract. Third, the rule forces pro-regulatory interest groups to expend extra lobbying costs to, in effect, "pay" for prohibitions that will trump contractual choice of law. This is important because a group's willingness to devote resources in order to enact a law reflects the benefits that the members of the group will reap from the law. The higher the benefits of the winning group, the greater the likelihood that the total benefits to society will outweigh the total costs. While giving the decision on contractual choice of law to the legislature does not guarantee that every law will be efficient, it is designed to increase the *average* quality of laws by engaging more affected interests in the decision-making process. In contrast to legislatures, courts have little ability to gauge popular support for the law and must act on their vague and subjective impression of whether the law represents a fundamental policy of the state. Judges may be subject to political discipline, especially if they are elected, but this does not necessarily give them insight into what the electorate wants with respect to particular issues.

When Must States Designate Super-Mandatory Rules?

The proposed choice-of-law statute gives super-mandatory effect to rules either (1) that are explicitly designated as such in state statutes enacted after the federal law goes into effect; or (2) that courts believe should receive super-mandatory effect given the nature of the statutory or judicial rules that pre-existed the federal law. The former category reflects our objective discussed above to force state legislatures to clarify super-mandatory effect. The latter category recognizes that there is already a large body of law on the effect of choice-of-law clauses that could be upset by forcing legislatures to return to previously enacted legislation to specifically address choice-of-law clause enforcement. Of course, the problem with the grandfathering exception is that it preserves uncertainty for the parties and courts as to which preexisting mandatory rules have super-mandatory effect when those laws are silent on choice-of-law clauses. We nevertheless advocate the slower route to certainty regarding preexisting laws in order to avoid wholesale reversal of state policy decisions regarding which laws should have super-mandatory effect.

One might object that the proposed statute imposes an undue burden on state legislatures by requiring them to specifically designate regulations as super-mandatory. In particular, a legislature might not be expected to know what sorts of regulatory obligations might be made the subject of contracts, including choice-of-law clauses. Thus, perhaps, the proposed statute should reverse the default rule as to particular types of choice-of-law clauses, or for choice-of-law clauses in particular types of contracts. This would be similar in effect to the Defense of Marriage Act, which provides that the states need not recognize out-of-state same-sex marriages, but does not preclude the states from doing so. Examples of possible broader exceptions would include cases that are not currently regarded as subject to contract, such as product liability claims (see chapter 7) and marriage, birth, and death arrangements that have profound social implications (see chapter 8).

These differences among types of laws do not trouble us. As we have argued throughout this book, the law market itself provides a dynamic process for working out these issues. State legislatures likely would react quickly to novel but unwelcome attempts to access the law market. Legislatures, informed by interest groups, can understand the potentially evasive effects of procedural clauses in contracts and act to prevent evasion where they deem prevention to be appropriate. And, importantly, a choice-of-law clause does not work unless some other state first chooses not to regulate. Thus, a state often need not *anticipate* novel types of contracts, but rather only *react* to these contracts. For example, states had little reason to be concerned about same-sex marriages until Hawaii threatened to become the first state to authorize them. Similarly, states would not have to worry about enforcing an attempt to opt out of liability for a defective product until some other state permitted such an opt-out.

Scope of the Super-Mandatory Effect

The proposed statute does not leave it entirely up to the enacting legislature to determine the effect of a super-mandatory law. Under our proposal, a state's mandatory law trumps the designated rule only if a person or entity protected by the law "resides" in the regulating jurisdiction. Unless this condition is met, the state lacks an interest in the matter sufficiently large to justify interfering with the operation of the law market.

This may sound a bit too much like Currie's interest analysis (discussed in chapter 3) because it assumes that states have "interests" only in residents. However, our focus on state interests here is based on the political considerations discussed in chapter 4. Linking the application of a regulation to the residence of protected parties encourages people and firms to avoid regulating states if they want to avoid regulation. A regulating state's loss of residents and investments may induce local exit-affected groups to oppose the regulation. This, in turn, encourages states to take the costs of their regulation into account. The particular connection of residence is important because a state's more transitory contacts with the transaction or the parties may not be enough to ensure that legislators will take into account both the costs and benefits of regulating the transaction.

A problem with the focus on residents is that contracting parties may not be able to determine the residence of their counterparties at the time of contract. This may interfere with the statute's objective to give the parties' timely knowledge of their rights at the time of making contracting or location decisions. However, companies will be placed on notice when some states refuse to enforce their choice-of-law clauses and then could inquire into their customers' residences if necessary to protect themselves. Moreover, it may be possible to create certainty by more precisely defining *residence* in various contexts. For example, the state statute regarding enforcement might specify that the home address for individuals is presumed to be the shipping or credit card billing address and that the relevant location for a firm is presumed to be its principal place of business as disclosed in the bill or other contract.[17]

Finally, keep in mind that section C of the proposed statute would let a state refine its prohibitions as long as it does not violate section B's restrictions. The proposed choice-of-law statute forbids only a state's attempt to impose a super-mandatory rule on behalf of a nonresident plaintiff and against a nonresident defendant when no harmed third parties reside in the state. Thus, while a state *may* prohibit the enforcement of a contractual choice of law to protect its residents, it *need not* do so, as where the regulated party also resides in the designated state.

The Choice-of-Law Clause

The proposed statute includes provisions to govern the required terms and formalities of the choice-of-law clauses as prerequisites to providing them with protected status. First, the statute provides for the enforcement of only express and written, not oral, choice-of-law clauses. This enhances predictability and certainty by encouraging the parties to clearly designate their governing law and the issues they want it to cover. Moreover, the formality of a written choice-of-law clause helps to serve the cautionary function of contract law by encouraging parties to think carefully about the import of their contract terms.[18] Second, the contract would apply to all issues relating to the contract unless the parties specify a more limited application. This reduces uncertainty regarding what issues are covered by the clause (see chapter 3).

Third, the proposed statute applies to any express written "agreement." From the standpoint of our theory, the term should be defined as broadly as possible to include any type of consensual relationship. Therefore, we use the term in its ordinary sense rather than limiting the scope of party choice to the presence of an actual contract. However, we recognize that there will be some controversy about what relationships enable party choice. We cover a few debatable situations in this book, such as marriage and business associations, and others will no doubt arise.

The main question about the scope of the term *agreement* in the proposed statute is whether and to what extent it should be determined by state law. In general, leaving this issue to state law could undercut the statute's goal of bringing clarity to the enforcement of choice-of-law clauses. Instead, federal law should be used to determine the scope of agreement. One might worry that this empowers Congress to weigh in on contentious issues, such as same-sex marriage. However, under our proposal, Congress merely decides the scope of agreement, while preserving explicit state policy judgments regarding the enforcement of those agreements. For example, federal law might define marriage as an agreement, but states would remain free to refuse enforcement, including by refusing to recognize marriage as an agreement for purposes of the statute.

Fourth, the statute does not distinguish between business and consumer agreements. As discussed in chapter 7, there are arguably reasons for distinguishing between business-to-business and business-to-consumer contracts. However, the statute's general approach is to leave such distinctions to the state legislatures.

Fifth, the statute may raise particular questions about the interaction between the proposed statute and the corporate internal affairs doctrine (IAD). As discussed in chapter 6, we believe that corporate internal governance arrangements are best viewed for choice-of-law purposes just like other contracts. Thus, *agreement* would include this situation. The statute may therefore conflict with the IAD if it enables the parties to select by separate contract a law other than that of the incorporating state to apply to a corporate governance matter. A state accordingly may want to settle this conflict by providing by statute that local incorporation constitutes a contract to apply that state's law notwithstanding any other agreement between the parties.[19]

Finally, the statute provides for the application not only of a particular state law identified in the agreement, but of a state law designated *pursuant to* a provision in the contract. This implicitly permits "floating" choice-of-law clauses, where the contract empowers one or both of the parties to choose the governing law at the time of litigation. This type of clause may be useful because the parties cannot easily foresee what types of disputes will arise and therefore what sort of law they would want to govern the dispute. There is no reason for the federal statute to exclude these agreements, since they provide another mechanism for the parties to agree on the governing law. However, the agreement may not be enforceable if an explicit state prohibition applies pursuant to section B of the statute.

Forcing the Bundling of a Designated State's Entire Law

The proposed statute provides for the application of "the laws of a state," which requires that the parties choose the law of only a single state. This provision requires that the parties choose among states' laws as bundles rather than cherry-picking particular desired provisions from across a number of states' laws. Some states appear to permit this multiple-state choice. For example, the Oregon statute provides that "the contractual rights and duties of the parties are governed by the law *or laws* that the parties have chosen."[20]

A problem with this bundling requirement is that it restricts parties' choices to a more limited number of bundles of rules as compared with the vast range of combinations offered by the mixing of individual rules of all possible jurisdictions. For example, the parties might want different states' laws to govern different portions of the contract in order to take advantage of different states' areas of expertise. Also, requiring the parties to select entire bundles rather than particular laws gives states the ability to retain inefficient mandatory rules by combining them with desirable default rules. Although the parties can, in effect, supply their own default rules by including them in the contract, they may want to choose a state's evolving bundle of default rules—such as Delaware's corporate laws—but without the mandatory rules included in that bundle.

On the other hand, the bundling requirement is a way to police choice-of-law clauses without relying on a court to distinguish good and bad law choices. Powerful interest groups are sometimes able to successfully lobby for the enactment of legal rules that benefit them at the expense of poorly organized groups, such as consumers. But this sellout to interest groups is less likely to have occurred for an entire body of law related to a contract than for a single rule. Requiring firms to choose a single state's law inhibits business interests from capitalizing on their legislative victories in multiple states by cherry-picking favorable provisions.

Note that, even if a firm cannot choose multiple laws for a single contract, it can choose different laws for different contracts. For example, it might choose to organize under Delaware LLC law but to follow New York commercial law for specific contracts between the firm and its suppliers. The bundling rule thus provides a reasonable compromise between the parties' need for flexibility and the state's need to regulate contracts.

Procedural Restrictions on Enforcement

Rather than wholly invalidating contractual choice of law, a state might condition the enforcement of the choice-of-law clause on compliance with procedural requirements, such as full disclosure of the implications of the choice. Recall that a particular concern with contractual choice is that parties' rights and liabilities can be affected in ways not apparent on the face of the contract. This lack of transparency may be a problem particularly in a contract between a business and consumers. Procedural restrictions that target potential abuse of contractual choice might be preferable to a complete prohibition that eliminates all of the potential benefits of contractual choice.

Although the proposed statute does not specifically treat disclosure requirements, section B of the proposed statute permits a state to condition the enforcement of choice-of-law clauses in particular types of contracts on compliance with procedural requirements. For example, a state law might provide that choice-of-law clauses may circumvent its mandatory provisions only if the agreement clearly discloses material differences between the regulation and the chosen law. Alternatively, the legislature could require disclosures of whether the designated law offers critical protections. Leaving these issues to the states would facilitate experimentation and possibly even competition regarding optimal disclosure requirements.

11

Summary and Implications

We have described a surprisingly broad market for law that is based on parties contracting for or otherwise choosing the law of a particular state. We have shown how this market can discipline lawmaking by forcing states to compete with each other. Moreover, contractual choice of law better enables states to experiment with alternative solutions to difficult policy problems. Enforcing choice-of-law clauses will help legal improvements to evolve more quickly and effectively. Spurred by parties' ability to move among states and adjudicators, the market for law arises despite state officials' efforts to protect their lawmaking authority. We have also discussed a mechanism for limiting the law market to prevent the undue erosion of lawmakers' power.

We close the book with thoughts on some of the broader implications of our analysis. After first discussing some limitations on our proposal, we emphasize its potential breadth. The law market can change one's view of regulation. What really matters to whether regulations are binding is not whether a rule is mandatory, but whether it is super-mandatory, in the sense of withstanding parties' ability to contract for more permissive laws. The law market also has implications for the future of the law of subordinate jurisdictions in larger, often federal, systems. The globalization of business has profoundly undermined the territorial basis of lawmaking. The law market replaces territory with contract, thereby breathing new life into lawmaking by the subordinate jurisdictions. Finally, although we have tended to emphasize the market for law within the United States, we close by emphasizing that our analysis applies equally to international law markets.

The Limits of the Law Market

Most chapters in this book have focused on the law market for conventional contracts and business associations. In chapter 8, we ventured beyond the conventional sphere into marriage, birth, and death by drawing contract analogies. Any voluntary relationship potentially can be analyzed as a contract. Indeed, in chapter 8, we discussed living wills, which do not involve a "relationship" at all but rather simply an individual's unilateral act.

It is not clear how far the contract approach should be carried and, therefore, the extent to which human affairs can or should be ordered through a law market. As indicated in chapter 8, there are problems with separating voluntary associations and seemingly private decisions from their sometimes significant moral, political, philosophical, and sociological implications. Similarly, the more a conventional contract affects people other than the direct parties, the less appropriate it is to allow these parties to determine the legal consequences of their acts.

Moreover, even where the contract seems only to affect the parties, there may be good reasons not to let them decide which government can regulate their relationship. Consider, for example, the sale of a product that injures a purchaser. Should the court enforce a clause in the sale contract that provides for the application of a given state's law, or for arbitration? As discussed in chapter 7, the choice-of-law or -forum clause is likely dictated by the manufacturer or other seller and may not be subject to effective marketplace discipline. Moreover, society as a whole has an interest in ensuring the manufacture of safe products, especially given that dangerous products can threaten the lives of bystanders and other nonpurchasers.

In making judgments about the appropriate extent of the law market, it is important to keep in mind that the potential costs involved in the law market must be compared to the benefits and to the costs of alternative solutions. Even if the contracts that underpin the law market seem to be one-sided, they are often disciplined in competitive markets. Firms are constantly seeking an edge in these markets by burnishing their reputations and can ill afford to look like they are using questionable legal tactics in their dealings with customers. Moreover, the alternative to enforcing choice-of-law clauses is often to let the plaintiff unilaterally choose the adjudicator, which also may have perverse consequences. Solving these problems by effectively moving all regulation of national and international markets to federal authorities eliminates the benefits of competition and experimentation. In short, the law market, for all of its potential defects, might be the best of several imperfect solutions to regulating global markets.

For these reasons, we think it appropriate for states to start with the default rule that choice-of-law clauses are to be enforced. To protect unsophisticated parties, third parties, or society at large, states should be able to refuse to enforce choice-of-law clauses that impose harms on their citizens. But states should have to make this non-enforcement clear in their statutes. Placing the power over the law market in legislators' rather than judges' hands will help to marshal competing interest groups to discipline state assertions of authority while helping contracting parties to order their affairs.

Mandatory and Super-Mandatory Rules

The law market changes the way that we must think about state contract regulation. Traditionally, one thinks of contract rules as either default rules, which the parties can replace by writing their own rules into the contracts, or mandatory rules, which the contract may not displace. A single state's decision to impose a rule that the parties cannot contract around might not actually have mandatory effect if the parties may contract to apply the law of a more permissive state to their transaction. In analyzing whether state law really has a regulatory bite, it is therefore necessary to distinguish between mandatory rules that simply trump customized contract terms and super-mandatory rules that also trump choice-of-law clauses.

State franchise laws provide an important illustration of the significance of the distinction between mandatory and super-mandatory rules. A franchise contract gives the franchisee, who owns a local store, the right to use the trademarks of the franchisor in operating her business. Franchise contracts benefit franchisees because they enable these entrepreneurs to run a unit of an already successful business. At the same time, trademark owners can expand their operations while maintaining the incentives of the unit operators. If the trademark owner simply hired employees to manage its stores, these workers might have an incentive to shirk because they do not share in the profits. The franchise contract lets the franchisee keep any profits that remain after she pays her operating costs, including royalty fees, to the franchisor.

A significant potential problem with these contracts is that the franchisee might be tempted to cut her costs and render low-quality service because the appeal of the trademark will still attract customers. The franchisee might earn more profits, but her conduct can reduce the value of the trademark, a harm inflicted mainly on the franchisor and other franchisees. In other words, franchisees may try to free ride off the efforts of others to build the brand.

Franchisors can minimize these costs by, among other things, including termination provisions that threaten to end the rights of a franchisee who fails to satisfy the company's expectations. But these provisions expose the franchisee to the risk of opportunistic conduct by the franchisor. Specifically, the franchisor might use its termination power to engage in "cream skimming," that is, it might take over profitable franchises even where the franchisee is not free riding. This, in effect, allows the franchisor to experiment with territories, taking over the ones that prove to be successful while saddling the franchisees with the failures.

Franchisee groups sometimes persuade state legislators to prevent franchisor opportunism by regulating these termination provisions. However, this regulation can hurt both franchisors and franchisees to the extent that it prevents franchisors from efficiently disciplining franchisee shirking. The regulation can also hurt society by foreclosing profitable business opportunities if the regulation has the effect of deterring future franchised units in the state.

In assessing the effect of this regulation, the important question is whether restrictions on franchise termination protect franchisees from cream skimming without restricting franchisors' ability to police free riding. If the laws unduly favor franchisees, they will cause a reduction in the use of franchised units. If franchisors are unable to profitably operate new stores on their own, then the total number of stores in industries with high levels of franchising also should fall. There is evidence that each of these results have followed state imposition of franchise regulation.[1]

More interesting for present purposes is the role of the law market in driving these empirical results. In particular, one study found that state restrictions on termination, standing alone, have little effect on employment in industries where franchising is common.[2] This suggests that the termination restrictions, by themselves, are not causing a reduction in outlets in these industries. Termination restrictions do negatively affect employment when they prohibit waiver of the restriction in the franchise contract. Most important, when the statute also restricts choice-of-law or choice-of-forum clauses, it increases the negative effect on employment. A restriction on *both* choice-of-law and choice-of-court clauses has a still greater effect on employment. Further, restricting choice-of-law clauses alone has almost twice the effect of restricting only choice-of-court clauses. This is consistent with the fact that even the chosen forum might apply the restrictive law if the franchise contract fails to specify the governing law.

This study bolsters the intuitive notion that the distinction between mandatory and super-mandatory laws can matter in determining the effect of regulations. Future studies of state or even national regulation should also take account of distinctions between mandatory and super-mandatory rules. Also, state legislatures should consider these contract options when crafting regulations.

Several state franchise statutes specify whether choice-of-law or choice-of-court clauses can be used to circumvent the termination provisions. More often, state statutes provide that their rules are mandatory but do not address whether they are super-mandatory. To determine whether a choice-of-law clause can be used to circumvent a mandatory rule when the statute is silent on this issue, the U.S. state courts typically seek guidance from the Second Restatement. Recall that it provides that the clause should not be enforced if application of the law chosen contravenes a "fundamental policy of a state" whose law would apply but for the choice-of-law clause and if that state has "a materially greater interest than the chosen state in the determination of the particular issue." In other words, the extent of the statute's super-mandatory effect depends on the nature of the regulatory policy and the regulating state's interest in effectuating that policy in the particular case.

The problem with this Second Restatement inquiry is that it often remains unclear until final adjudication what constitutes a fundamental policy, or whether one state's regulatory interest trumps another's laissez-faire approach in a particular case. Given that the enforcement of these clauses significantly affects how parties react to regulation, legislatures should clearly specify whether their statutes have mandatory or super-mandatory effect. To promote clarity, we proposed in chapter 10 a federal statute designed to force states to address this issue. Because the choice will significantly affect the interests of the competing interest groups, the statutory language is likely to reflect the outcome of the battle between regulation-affected and exit-affected interest groups. Clarity also can enable the parties to take the statute's super-mandatory effect into account when deciding where to locate and how to craft their transactions.

The Future of State Law

One might suppose that the increasing globalization of business would be rendering local lawmaking authority obsolete. After all, why should Delaware, or even New York or California, regulate a multinational corporation just because the state is the location of incorporation, or even of the firm's head-quarters, especially when most of the costs and benefits of regulation would be felt outside that state? Our analysis indicates that it is time to reexamine the role of state law in a globalizing world. More specifically, the law market has four important implications for the future of state law.

First, we have shown how contractual choice of law can help to promote the efficiency of state law. The parties to a contract can force jurisdictions to bear both the costs and benefits of regulation by designating the governing law in the contract.

Second, the law market has the potential to bolster the clout of states and other subordinate jurisdictions. If even the Lilliputian state of Delaware can provide the law for most major U.S. corporations, there is no reason that small jurisdictions could not supply law for other types of interstate or international contracts or business organizations. Similarly, the appeal of otherwise barren locales might rise significantly through the provision of high-quality laws.

Third, the law market might revolutionize the relationship between legis-lation and physical territory. As discussed in chapter 3, choice-of-law analysis historically emphasized territorial considerations. In a global economy with mobile actors, territory is no longer always the primary legitimizing factor for choice of law. Our analysis implies that, often, the regulation of international business is more soundly based on contract rather than the physical connection between the legislature and the regulated party. If so, then to a significant extent state legislatures can become exporters rather than local providers of law.

Fourth, we showed in chapter 10 that our approach can be an alternative perspective from which to view the need for federal and uniform state laws. Federal law is increasingly viewed as the way to reduce spillovers of regulatory costs by better aligning the beneficiaries of state regulation and those who pay the costs. For example, when state class actions threatened to let tiny "litiga-tion mills" in rural courthouses influence how products were made and sold across the country, Congress enacted the Class Action Fairness Act to enable litigation over national transactions to occur in the federal courts. For similar reasons, an increasing variety of problems has been deemed to be appropriate for federal solutions.[3] It often seems that the only way that states can fight the federal onslaught is by coordinating around uniform laws that effectively provide a national solution but are given force through the state legislatures and courts. Uniform laws are a poor solution to some spillovers, since they eliminate state competition while providing an uneasy compromise of states' political objectives.[4] An alternative and often superior way to address spillover problems is through the enforcement of choice-of-law clauses. These contracts at least theoretically enable the contracting parties to allocate regulatory costs among themselves. States that must pitch their laws to both parties to a contract rather than just one, such as plaintiffs, are more likely to enact laws that balance the parties' interests.

To be sure, the overenforcement of choice-of-law clauses in situations involving unsophisticated consumers and poor market discipline could result in a race to the bottom. Imagine, for example, Nevada becoming the Delaware of payday loans. We discussed limitations on the enforcement of choice-of-law clauses in chapter 7. But for a wide variety of contracts, which are disciplined in strong and efficient markets without third-party effects, contractual choice of law is a viable regulatory approach. Policymakers therefore should compare the costs of state competition for law with the costs of empowering a single federal decision maker that lacks the discipline imposed by a law market. Federal regulation sometimes can provide the best solution, but in other cases state competition will produce better results.

One might ask whether, if contracts are going to separate regulation from its territorial foundation, there is any further need for state governments. We saw in chapter 5 that substantial private lawmaking is already often enforced in arbitral proceedings. Why not dispense with, or significantly reduce the role of, government lawmakers and outsource the provision of law to private providers?

A definitive answer to this question is beyond the scope of this study. However, it is worth noting that, to some extent, lawmaking is a public good in the sense that it is costly to make those who benefit from laws pay for these benefits. For example, the parties to future litigation may gain from a judicial opinion in a case even if the parties to the case incur significant litigation and publicity costs. It therefore might be worthwhile to maintain a public judiciary at taxpayer expense. Similarly, while the public as a whole gains from laws that provide security or reduce environmental hazards, it is impossible to charge the beneficiaries for these benefits.

Notwithstanding the importance of public lawmaking, there may be an increasing role for private lawmaking as well. Our general analysis of the law market is not limited to public lawmakers. Indeed, in referring to the supply of and demand for law, we have analogized public law to a privately produced product. Clearly, these concepts apply to a market for private law and adjudication. Lawyers and others may gain by earning fees for their services in private legislation and adjudication. This may give them incentives to develop and promote their services and the private law systems to which these services are related. Thus, there is competition not only among jurisdictions, but among private lawmakers and between public and private lawmakers.[5] That said, however, states may be more likely to defer to choice-of-law clauses when another state provides the alternative law than when a private individual or group provides the governing rules.

Implications for International Law

We have focused substantially but not exclusively on competition among U.S. states, but we wish to make clear that our law market analysis applies also to competition among nations. Indeed, we have seen in chapters 2 and 6 that international competition for the cross-listing of securities has put pressure on U.S. securities regulation. International competition has also heavily influenced national arbitration laws and is increasingly influencing country laws regarding shipping regulations, trusts, and other subjects.

Similarly, while our discussion of jurisdictional competition within a federal system has mostly been confined to the U.S. federal system, much of what we have said applies to states and countries in other federal systems, both within nation-states, such as Germany and Canada, and among nations, particularly including the European Union. Leaving lawmaking to the states can better enable quality legal innovations than can federal regulation.

One might wonder whether the law market operates better within federal systems or across nations. Federal systems can be conducive to competition among the states. They share common constitutional and statutory constraints and often share legal histories and common cultural and economic challenges. These commonalities limit the likelihood that any state will enact laws that impose significant costs on the others. And, if a state did impose such costs, the federal government could step in to correct the problem. Indeed, the distinguishing feature of a federal system is the existence of a federal government to maintain balance among the subordinate jurisdictions.

On the other hand, a federal government is not necessarily essential or conducive to jurisdictional competition. Nations can self-coordinate, just as can states in a federal system. Moreover, a federal government may actually impede jurisdictional competition. Interest groups unhappy with jurisdictional choice can always lobby the federal government to squelch the operation of the law market across the subordinate jurisdictions. Firms wanting to avoid bad laws would then have to exit larger markets than if the states were not bound in a federal system. Perhaps some law markets should operate within federal systems while others should operate across nations.[6] We hope we have started a debate on these issues rather than pronounced the last word.

Notes

Chapter 1

1. Actually, Madison County has recently fallen off the American Tort Reform Association's list of biggest "judicial hellholes," leaving Cook County as the only remaining Illinois county left on its list. Madison County is on the association's current watch list, however. See http://www.atra.org/reports/hellholes.

2. As will be described in chapter 4, the current vague standards that govern the enforceability of choice-of-law clauses give federal courts significant discretion to enforce (or not to enforce) choice-of-law clauses, and available empirical evidence indicates that the federal courts use this discretion to enforce choice-of-law clauses more often than do the state courts.

3. Albert O. Hirschman, *Exit, Voice, and Loyalty: Responses to Decline in Firms, Organizations, and States* (Cambridge, MA: Harvard University Press, 1970).

4. Charles M. Tiebout, "A Pure Theory of Local Expenditures," 64 *J. Pol. Econ.* 416 (1956).

5. As will be discussed in chapters 3 and 4, this ability is not complete, since the enforcement of choice-of-law clauses may depend on connections between the parties or their transaction and the designated state.

Chapter 2

1. Mancur Olson, *The Logic of Collective Action: Public Goods and the Theory of Groups* (Cambridge, MA: Harvard University Press, 1965).

2. See ibid.

3. Paul B. Stephan, "Global Governance, Antitrust, and the Limits of International Cooperation," 38 *Cornell Int'l L.J.* 173, 185–86 (2005).

4. *Austin v. New Hampshire*, 420 U.S. 656, 662 (1975) (discussing the problem of nonrepresentation of nonresidents).

5. See Gary S. Becker, "A Theory of Competition among Pressure Groups for Political Influence," 98 *Q.J. Econ.* 371 (1983).

6. See James A. Brickley, "Royalty Rates and Upfront Fees in Share Contracts: Evidence from Franchising," 18 *J.L. Econ. & Org.* 511 (2002) (data indicating that franchisors charge more for franchises located in states with franchise protection laws).

7. See Jonathan R. Macey, "Promoting Public-Regarding Legislation through Statutory Interpretation: An Interest Group Model," 86 *Colum. L. Rev.* 223, 251 (1986).

8. See *Judicial Selection in the United States*, http://www.ajs.org/js/SC.htm (accessed June 20, 2007).

9. John H. Beisner and Jessica Davidson Miller, "They're Making a Federal Case Out of It...in State Court," 25 *Harv. J.L. & Pub. Pol'y* 143, 205 (2001). For a discussion of the politics of rural districts that have been notorious centers of state class-action litigation, see American Tort Reform Association, *Judicial Hellholes* (2006), http://www.atra.org/reports/hellholes/report.pdf.

10. We will return to this problem in chapter 6.

11. The potential problem was raised in *Hartford Fire Ins. v. California*, 509 U.S. 764 (1993).

12. *Armstrong v. Accrediting Council*, 980 F. Supp. 53, 59 (D.D.C. 1997). We will return to this problem in chapter 7, where we discuss the use of choice-of-law clauses to enable vendors in electronic commerce to conduct their businesses according to a single state's laws.

13. Lynn M. LoPucki, *Courting Failure: How Competition for Big Cases Is Corrupting the Bankruptcy Courts* (Ann Arbor: University of Michigan Press, 2005).

14. Albert O. Hirschman, *Exit, Voice, and Loyalty: Responses to Decline in Firms, Organizations, and States* (Cambridge, MA: Harvard University Press, 1970).

15. Charles M. Tiebout, "A Pure Theory of Local Expenditures," 64 *J. Pol. Econ.* 416 (1956).

16. See Richard A. Epstein, "Exit Rights under Federalism," 55 *J.L. & Contemp. Probs.* 147 (1992).

17. See Roberta Romano, "Law as Product: Some Pieces of the Incorporation Puzzle," 1 *J.L. Econ. & Org.* 225 (1985).

18. In chapter 10, we will discuss how this constraint might be incorporated into a federal choice-of-law statute.

19. William A. Reese, Jr., and Michael S. Weisbach, "Protection of Minority Shareholder Interests, Cross-Listings in the United States, and Subsequent Equity Offerings," 66 *J. Fin. Econ.* 65 (2002).

20. See generally Larry E. Ribstein, "Cross-Listing and Regulatory Competition," 1 *Rev. L. & Econ.*, no. 1 (2005), art. 7, available at http://www.

bepress.com/rle/v011/iss1/art7 (reviewing the cross-listing literature and discussing how cross-listing may affect the laws of both home and host jurisdictions).

21. The outcry was reflected to some extent in the comments by representatives of foreign firms in response to the SEC's rule making on the audit committee requirements. These comments are collected at http://www. sec.gov/rules/proposed/s70203.shtml and summarized at http://www.sec. gov/rules/extra/s70203summary.htm#P1121_88452.

22. See Kate Litvak, "Sarbanes-Oxley and the Cross-Listing Premium," 105 *Mich. L. Rev.* 1857 (2007); Kate Litvak, "The Effect of the Sarbanes-Oxley Act on Non–U.S. Companies Cross-Listed in the U.S.," *J. Corp. Fin.* (forthcoming).

23. See 17 CFR §240.10A-3.

24. *Interim Report of the Committee on Capital Markets Regulation* (November 30, 2006), available at http://www.capmktsreg.org/highlights.html (accessed June 20, 2007).

25. Committee on Capital Markets Regulation, *The Competitive Position of the U.S. Public Equity Market* (December 4, 2007), available at http://www. capmktsreg.org/pdfs/The_Competitive_Position_of_the_US_Public_ Equity_Market.pdf (accessed February 2, 2008) (showing, among other things, significant increases in the delisting of foreign companies from U.S. markets and in U.S. companies going public abroad).

26. There has been controversy regarding the cause of the decline in cross-listings. For example, there is evidence that the firms avoiding the United States could not have met listing requirements in the United States even before SOX. See Craig Doidge, G. Andrew Karolyi, and René M. Stulz, *Has New York Become Less Competitive in Global Markets? Evaluating Foreign Listing Choices over Time* (Fisher College of Business, Working Paper No. 2007-03-012, 2007), available at http://www.ssrn.com/abstract=982193; Joseph D. Piotroski and Suraj Srinivasan, *The Sarbanes-Oxley Act and the Flow of International Listings* (January 2007), available at http://papers.ssrn. com/so13/papers.cfm?abstract_id=956987. However, the actual cause of the decline is not significant. Indeed, the actual effect of regulation is seldom clear. For the purpose of showing the political effect of exit on regulation, it is enough that the perception that the decline was attributable to regulatory costs triggered a demand to reduce the regulatory burden.

27. Steven J. Burton and Melvin A. Eisenberg, eds., *Contract Law: Selected Source Materials* (St. Paul, MN: West, 2005), 413.

28. For a history and analysis of these developments, see Larry E. Ribstein, "The Evolving Partnership," 26 *J. Corp. L.* 819 (2001).

29. William L. Cary, "Federalism and Corporate Law: Reflections upon Delaware," 83 *Yale L.J.* 663 (1974).

30. See *Seasteading: Frequently Asked Questions,* http://seastead.org/ commented/paper/faq.html (accessed June 20, 2007).

31. Henry Hansmann, Reinier Kraakman, and Richard Squire, "Law and the Rise of the Firm," 119 *Harv. L. Rev.* 1333, 1401 (2006).

32. The *Franchise Law Journal* serves this function in the franchising industry.

33. We will discuss the doctrine of unconscionability in more detail in chapter 7.

34. Lucian A. Bebchuk and Richard A. Posner, "One-Sided Contracts in Competitive Consumer Markets," 104 *Mich. L. Rev.* 827 (2006).

35. Alan Schwartz and Louis L. Wilde, "Intervening in Markets on the Basis of Imperfect Information: A Legal and Economic Analysis," 127 *U. Pa. L. Rev.* 630 (1979).

36. See Alan Schwartz and Robert E. Scott, "Contract Theory and the Limits of Contract Law," 113 *Yale L.J.* 541 (2003).

Chapter 3

1. J. Beale, *A Treatise on the Conflict of Laws,* vol. 1 (New York: Baker, Voorhis & Co., 1935), 6.

2. Vested rights had been articulated for a century prior to Beale's contributions. A brief history of the vested rights concept is provided in Lea Brilmayer, *Conflict of Laws,* 2nd ed. (Boston: Little, Brown, 1995), 16–17.

3. For criticisms of Beale's approach, see Walter Wheeler Cook, *The Logical and Legal Bases of the Conflict of Laws* (Cambridge, MA: Harvard University Press, 1942); Brainerd Currie, *Selected Essays on the Conflict of Laws* (Durham, NC: Duke University Press, 1963); Roger J. Traynor, "Law and Social Change in a Democratic Society," 1956 *U. Ill. L.F.* 230; William F. Baxter, "Choice of Law and the Federal System," 16 *Stan. L. Rev.* 1 (1963); Brilmayer, *Conflict of Laws,* §§1.3–1.5.

4. The First Restatement provides that "[a]ll matters of procedure are governed by the law of the forum." Although the First Restatement specifies some types of rules that should be classified as procedural, the list is far from exhaustive. *Restatement (First) of Conflict of Laws* (1934), §585.

5. Lea Brilmayer and Jack Goldsmith, *Conflict of Laws: Cases and Materials,* 5th ed. (New York: Aspen, 2002), 114–19.

6. Section 612 of the First Restatement provides that "[n]o action can be maintained upon a cause of action created in another state the enforcement of which is contrary to the strong public policy of the forum." Although this provision does not by its terms direct courts to substitute foreign law with the more preferred forum's law, courts often interpret section 612 as giving them the right to do so. Monrad G. Paulsen and Michael I. Sovern, "'Public Policy' in the Conflict of Laws," 56 *Colum. L. Rev.* 969, 980–81 (1956).

7. *Mertz v. Mertz,* 271 N.Y. 466, 3 N.E.2d 597 (1936).

8. *Holzer v. Deutsche Reichsbahn-Gesellschaft*, 277 N.Y. 474, 14 N.E.2d 798 (1938).

9. Lea Brilmayer, *Conflict of Laws: Cases and Materials*, 4th ed. (Boston: Little, Brown, 1995), 312–13.

10. Symeon C. Symeonides, "Choice of Law in the American Courts in 2005: Nineteenth Annual Survey," 53 *Am. J. Comp. L.* 559, 595–96 (2005).

11. Currie, *Selected Essays*, 3.

12. Brilmayer, *Conflict of Laws: Cases and Materials*, criticizes Currie's definition of state interests as applied to corporations in this manner.

13. For a discussion of the differing arguments regarding the appropriate determination of legislative intent, see Maxwell L. Stearns, *Public Choice and Public Law: Readings and Commentary* (Cincinnati: Anderson, 1997), 553–723.

14. Daniel B. Rodriguez and Barry R. Weingast, "The Positive Political Theory of Legislative History: New Perspectives on the Civil Rights Act and Its Interpretation," 151 *U. Pa. L. Rev.* 1417 (2003) (advocating this approach).

15. See Brilmayer, *Conflict of Laws*. Empirical studies have confirmed Brilmayer's accusations; see Patrick J. Borchers, "The Choice-of-Law Revolution: An Empirical Study," 49 *Wash. & Lee L. Rev.* 357 (1992); Michael E. Solimine, "An Economic and Empirical Analysis of Choice of Law," 24 *Ga. L. Rev.* 49 (1989); Stuart E. Thiel, "Choice of Law and the Home-Court Advantage: Evidence," 2 *Am. Econ. L. Rev.* 291 (2000).

16. This was the outcome of *Lilienthal v. Kaufman*, 395 P.2d 543 (Ore. 1964), the case from which we draw our debtor example.

17. See Erin Ann O'Hara, "Opting Out of Regulation: A Public Choice Analysis of Contractual Choice of Law," 53 *Vand. L. Rev.* 1551, 1559 (2000) (discussing assertions that choice-of-law reform in the United States was at least partially motivated by a desire to speed tort reform).

18. Baxter, "Choice of Law and the Federal System."

19. David F. Cavers, "A Critique of the Choice-of-Law Problem," 47 *Harv. L. Rev.* 173 (1933).

20. Elliott E. Cheatham and Willis L. M. Reese, "Choice of the Applicable Law," 52 *Colum. L. Rev.* 959 (1952).

21. Robert A. Leflar, "Choice-Influencing Considerations in Conflicts Law," 41 *N.Y.U. L. Rev.* 367 (1966).

22. See William A. Reppy, Jr., "Eclecticism in Choice of Law: Hybrid Method or Mishmash?" 34 *Mercer L. Rev.* 645 (1983).

23. For an especially complex situation, consider the surrogacy contract discussed in chapter 8.

24. Hillel Y. Levin, "What Do We Really Know about the American Choice-of-Law Revolution?" 60 *Stan. L. Rev.* 247, 259–60 (2007).

25. U.S. Constitution, art. IV, §1.

26. U.S. Constitution, art. I, §8.

27. The Defense of Marriage Act, 28 U.S.C.A. §1738c (2007), provides that "[n]o State...shall be required to give effect to any public act, record, or judicial proceeding of any other State...respecting a relationship between persons of the same sex that is treated as a marriage under the laws of such other State."

28. National Bank Act, 12 U.S.C.A. §85 (2007). In *Marquette Nat'l Bank v. First Omaha Serv. Corp.*, 439 U.S. 299 (1978), the Supreme Court determined that a bank was located in the state where it was chartered for purposes of this section.

29. Samuel Issacharoff and Erin F. Delaney, "Credit Card Accountability," 73 *U. Chi. L. Rev.* 157 (2006).

30. Amanda K. S. Hill, "State Usury Laws: Are They Effective in a Post-GLBA World?" 6 *N.C. Banking Inst.* 411, 427 (2002).

31. Class Action Fairness Act of 2005, Pub. L. No. 109-2, 119 Stat. 4 (2005).

32. See Richard Allen Nagareda, "Bootstrapping in Choice of Law after the Class Action Fairness Act," 74 *U.M.K.C. L. Rev.* 661 (2006).

33. Pub. L. No. 109-2, 119 Stat. 4 (2005). Section 4 of the act provides that federal courts may exercise diversity jurisdiction over any class action in which "any member of a class of plaintiffs is a citizen of a State different from any defendant" so long as the claims aggregated total more than $5 million.

34. Stephen B. Burbank, "The Class Action Fairness Act of 2005 in Historical Context: A Preliminary View," draft manuscript, available at http://www.ssrn.com/abstract=1083785.

35. See *Erie R.R. v. Tompkins*, 304 U.S. 64 (1938).

36. *Klaxon Co. v. Stentor Elec. Mfg.*, 313 U.S. 487 (1941).

37. See Nagareda, "Bootstrapping in Choice of Law."

38. Samuel Issacharoff, "Settled Expectations in a World of Unsettled Law: Choice of Law after the Class Action Fairness Act," 106 *Colum. L. Rev.* 1839 (2006).

39. These options are explored in chapters 2 and 7.

40. Enforcing choice-of-law clauses may have the effect of promoting class actions by overcoming the choice-of-law impediment to class certification. This might seem to be counter to the CAFA's concern with class actions. On the other hand, choice-of-law clauses may provide a way to balance defendants' concerns about abusive class actions against the objective of providing a remedy for plaintiffs' small-value claims.

41. See U.S. Constitution, art. IV, §1 ("Full Faith and Credit shall be given in each State to the public Acts, Records, and judicial Proceedings of every other State. And the Congress may by general Laws prescribe the Manner in which such Acts, Records and Proceedings shall be proved, and the Effect thereof").

42. See U.S. Constitution, amend. XIV, §1 ("No state shall...deprive any person of life, liberty, or property, without due process of law").

43. Section 1 of the Fourteenth Amendment also provides that states may not deny any person within their jurisdiction the equal protection of the laws.

44. Article IV, section 2, of the Constitution provides that "[t]he citizens of each State shall be entitled to all Privileges and Immunities of Citizens in the several States."

45. See U.S. Constitution, art. I, §8.3 (providing that Congress has the power "[t]o regulate Commerce...among the several states"). The clause has also been interpreted to prevent states' regulation of interstate commerce. This negative aspect of the Commerce Clause is often referred to as the Dormant Commerce Clause.

46. *N.Y. Life Ins. v. Dodge*, 246 U.S. 357 (1918).

47. *Home Ins. Co. v. Dick*, 281 U.S. 397 (1930).

48. *John Hancock Mut. Life Ins. v. Yates*, 299 U.S. 178 (1936).

49. *Watson v. Employers Liab. Assur. Corp.*, 348 U.S. 66 (1954).

50. *Clay v. Sun Ins. Office, Ltd.*, 377 U.S. 179 (1964).

51. U.S. Constitution, art. IV, §1.

52. Robert H. Jackson, "Full Faith and Credit: The Lawyer's Clause of the Constitution," 45 *Colum. L. Rev.* 1, 17 (1945).

53. See Arthur T. Von Mehren and Donald T. Trautman, "Constitutional Control of Choice of Law: Some Reflections on *Hague*," 10 *Hofstra L. Rev.* 35, 49 (1981); Frederic L. Kirgis, Jr., "The Roles of Due Process and Full Faith and Credit in Choice of Law," 62 *Cornell L. Rev.* 94, 120 (1976).

54. See, e.g., *Order of United Commercial Travelers v. Wolfe*, 331 U.S. 586 (1947); *Sovereign Camp of Woodmen of the World v. Bolin*, 305 U.S. 66 (1938); *Modern Woodmen of America v. Mixer*, 267 U.S. 544 (1925); *Supreme Council of the Royal Arcanum v. Green*, 237 U.S. 531 (1915).

55. See *N.Y. Life Ins. Co. v. Cravens*, 178 U.S. 389 (1900).

56. *Modern Woodmen*, at 551.

57. See *Wolfe*, at 609.

58. See Robert A. Sedler, "Constitutional Limitations on Choice of Law: The Perspective of Constitutional Generalism," 10 *Hofstra L. Rev.* 59, 99–100 (1981).

59. *Wolfe* (dissenting opinion).

60. *Allstate Ins. Co. v. Hague*, 449 U.S. 302 (1981).

61. Ibid., 308n10.

62. Ibid., 318n24.

63. *Phillips Petroleum Co. v. Shutts*, 472 U.S. 797 (1985).

64. Ibid., 822.

65. The courts have never scrutinized choice-of-law decisions under either the Equal Protection or Privileges and Immunities clauses. This void is

probably due to the fact that the Supreme Court's scrutiny of choice-of-law decisions has been confined to limiting state courts' *application* of forum law. Challenges based on these two clauses would involve a state court's *declining* to apply forum law for the benefit of a foreign party.

66. *S. Pac. Co. v. State of Arizona*, 325 U.S. 761, 767 (1945).

67. *Kassel v. Consol. Freightways Corp.*, 450 U.S. 662 (1981); *Raymond Motor Trans., Inc. v. Rice*, 434 U.S. 429 (1978).

68. See *Bibb v. Navajo Freight Lines, Inc.*, 359 U.S. 520 (1959).

69. *Edgar v. MITE*, 457 U.S. 624 (1982).

70. Brilmayer, *Conflict of Laws*, §4.5.3.

71. Larry Kramer, "On the Need for a Uniform Choice of Law Code," 89 *Mich. L. Rev.* 2134 (1991).

72. Uniform Commercial Code §1-105(1) (2001) (hereafter UCC).

73. Twenty-three states have enacted the amended UCC, article 1, though many states altered portions of the amended text. See http://www.nccusl.org/Update/uniformact_factsheets/uniformacts-fs-ucc1.asp.

74. UCC §1-301(f).

75. UCC §1-301(e)(2).

76. Cal. Civil Code §1646.5 (West 2002); Del. Code Ann., tit. 6, §2708 (1999); Fla. Stat. Ann. §685.101 (West 1990); 735 Ill. Comp. Stat. Ann. 105/5-5 (West 2002); N.Y. Gen. Oblig. Law §5-1401 (McKinney 2001); Tex. Bus. & Comm. Code Ann. §§35-51–35-52 (Vernon 2002). The Texas statute also provides for the enforcement of choice-of-law clauses that choose other states' laws provided that the transaction has a connection with the state whose law is chosen.

77. La. Civ. Code, art. 3540; Ore. Rev. Stat. §81.120 (2005).

78. William J. Woodward, "Constraining Opt-Outs: Shielding Local Law and Those It Protects from Adhesive Choice-of-Law Clauses," 40 *Loy. L.A. L. Rev.* 9, 59n227 (2006).

79. See Commission of the European Communities, *Proposal for a Regulation of the European Parliament and the Council on the Law Applicable to Contractual Obligations*, COM(2005), 650 final 2005/0261 (COD) (June 17, 2008), art. 3 (hereafter Rome I Regulation).

80. Ibid., art. 9(3).

81. EC Convention on the Law Applicable to Contractual Obligations (consolidated version in 1998 O.J. [C 27], 34 et seq.), art. 7(1) (hereafter EC Convention). For an analysis highlighting the similarities between U.S. law and European law under the Rome Convention, see Giesela Ruhl, *Party Autonomy in the Private International Law of Contracts: Transatlantic Convergence and Economic Efficiency* (CLPE, Research Paper No. 4/2007), available at http://papers.ssrn.com/so13/papers.cfm?abstract_id=921842.

82. EC Convention, art. 3(3). This provision also requires the application of the mandatory rules of the place where all of the elements of the contract are connected.

83. Rome I Regulation, introductory clause 37.

84. For a comparison of European and U.S. choice-of-law rules and institutions, see Erin A. O'Hara and Larry E. Ribstein, "Rules and Institutions in Developing a Law Market: Views from the U.S. and Europe Rules," 82 *Tul. L. Rev.* 2147 (2008).

85. Russell J. Weintraub, *Commentary on the Conflict of Laws*, 3rd ed. (Mineola, NY: Foundation Press, 1986), 377.

86. 1939 A.C. 277 (P.C. 1938).

87. See also *Radioactive, J.V. v. Manson*, 153 F. Supp. 462 (S.D.N.Y. 2001) (enforcing the selection of New York law, citing New York's "significant experience with music industry contracts").

88. This ground of non-enforcement is discussed in *Restatement (Second) of Conflict of Laws* (1971), §187, comment b.

89. See Eugene F. Scoles and Peter Hay, *Conflict of Laws*, 2nd ed. (St. Paul, MN: West, 1992), §18.10n3 (citing cases).

90. *Restatement (Second) of Conflict of Laws* (1971), §187.

91. See Scoles and Hay, *Conflict of Laws*, 965–73; Ruhl, *Party Autonomy* (describing European enforcement patterns).

92. *Tele-Save Merch. Co. v. Consumers Distributing Co.*, 814 F.2d 1120 (6th Cir. 1987).

93. *Wright-Moore Corp. v. Ricoh Corp.*, 908 F.2d 128 (7th Cir. 1991).

94. *Bush v. Nat'l Sch. Studios, Inc.*, 407 N.W.2d 883 (Wis. 1987).

95. *Application Group, Inc. v. Hunter Group, Inc.*, 72 Cal. Rptr. 2d 73 (Cal. Ct. App. 1998).

Chapter 4

1. See U.S. Constitution, amend. V; *World-Wide Volkswagen Corp. v. Woodson*, 444 U.S. 286, 297 (1980).

2. *Asahi Metal Indus. Co. v. Superior Ct.*, 480 U.S. 102, 111–12 (1987).

3. *Helicopteros Nacionales de Columbia, S.A. v. Hall*, 466 U.S. 408, 414–15 (1984). For a general discussion of the constraints on jurisdiction in the United States and Europe, see Russell J. Weintraub, *Commentary on the Conflict of Laws*, 4th ed. (Mineola, NY: Foundation Press, 2001), §4.

4. See Richard A. Epstein, "Exit Rights and Insurance Regulation: From Federalism to Takings," 7 *Geo. Mason L. Rev.* 293 (1999) (discussing these moves and some states' use of exit taxes to prevent them).

5. Jonathan Klick et al., *The Effect of Contract Regulation: The Case of Franchising* (2007), available at http://www.ssrn.com/abstract=951464.

6. 28 U.S.C. §1332(a) (2000).

7. Ibid.

8. Ibid., §1332(c)(1).

9. Ibid., §1441(a)–(b).

10. *Klaxon Co. v. Stentor Elec. Mfg.*, 313 U.S. 487 (1941).

11. See Larry E. Ribstein, "From Efficiency to Politics in Contractual Choice of Law," 37 *Ga. L. Rev.* 363 (2003).

12. The choice of a federal forum, and therefore the enforcement of choice-of-law clauses, may get a boost from the Class Action Fairness Act, which was discussed in chapter 3. The CAFA gives federal courts diversity jurisdiction over large class actions in which any class member is a citizen of a state different from any defendant. This makes it easier to get into federal court on a state cause of action than under the standard diversity rule, which requires *complete* diversity among all plaintiffs and all defendants.

13. Note that there may be interpretation issues regarding whether the clause specifies an *exclusive* forum, or whether the clause merely permits suit in the court specified. Some interpretation issues are discussed in Eugene F. Scoles et al., *Conflict of Laws*, 3rd ed. (St. Paul, MN: West, 2000), §11.6.

14. Kevin M. Clermont and Theodore Eisenberg, "Exorcising the Evil of Forum-Shopping," 80 *Cornell L. Rev.* 1507 (1995).

15. See Lee Goldman, "My Way and the Highway: The Law and Economics of Choice of Forum Clauses in Consumer Form Contracts," 86 *Nw. U. L. Rev.* 700 (1992); Linda S. Mullenix, "Another Choice of Forum, Another Choice of Law: Consensual Adjudicatory Procedure in Federal Court," 57 *Fordham L. Rev.* 291 (1988).

16. Although commentators agree that the clauses are usually enforced, they disagree about which states constitute exceptions. See Leandra Lederman, "Viva Zapata! Toward a Rational System of Forum-Selection Clause Enforcement in Diversity Cases," 66 *N.Y.U. L. Rev.* 422, 449n172 (1991) (listing Alabama, Georgia, and Missouri as states that will not enforce clauses); Michael E. Solimine, "The Quiet Revolution in Personal Jurisdiction," 73 *Tul. L. Rev.* 1, 17 and n. 107 (1998) (discussing non-enforcement in Alabama and Georgia). Note that Alabama now enforces reasonable forum-selection clauses. See also *Prof'l Ins. Corp. v. Sutherland*, 700 So. 2d 347 (Ala. 1997). For a few other states that may or may not enforce forum-selection clauses, see Scoles et al., *Conflict of Laws*, §11.5nn5–6.

17. *M/S Bremen v. Zapata Off-Shore Co.*, 407 U.S. 1, 15 (1972).

18. Ibid., 13–14.

19. For a criticism of enforcement in this context, see Paul D. Carrington and Paul H. Haagen, "Contract and Jurisdiction," 1996 *Sup. Ct. Rev.* 331.

20. *Carnival Cruise Lines, Inc. v. Schute*, 499 U.S. 585, 593–94 (1991).

21. See Eugene F. Scoles and Peter Hay, *Conflict of Laws*, 2nd ed. (St. Paul, MN: West, 1992), §11.3.

22. A study of merger agreements shows that, of the contracts that specified a forum, 23.4 percent of them specified a federal forum for litigation. See Theodore Eisenberg and Geoffrey P. Miller, "Ex Ante Choices of Law and Forum: An Empirical Analysis of Corporate Merger Agreements," 59 *Vand. L. Rev.* 1975 (2006).

23. *Stewart Org., Inc. v. Ricoh Corp.*, 487 U.S. 22 (1988).

24. *Bremen*, 15.

25. "Convention on Choice of Court Agreements" (June 30, 2005), *Hague Conference on International Law*, available at http://www.hcch.net/index_en.php?act=conventions.pdf&cid=9.

26. Indeed, Congress might need to pass such a statute, given that the uncertain enforcement of choice-of-court clauses in U.S. state courts would place the United States at a relative competitive disadvantage vis-à-vis other nations that might adopt the convention. For a discussion of enforcement difficulties in U.S. state courts, see William J. Woodward, Jr., "Saving the Hague Choice of Court Convention," 29 *U. Pa. J. Int'l L.* 657 (2008).

27. See Eisenberg and Miller, "Ex Ante Choices of Law and Forum." However, only about half of these contracts have choice-of-court clauses, though all of them have choice-of-law clauses. It is not clear why this is the case, or whether the same result would hold for other types of contracts.

28. See Klick et al., *The Effect of Contract Regulation, supra* note 5 and accompanying text.

29. See Larry E. Ribstein, "Lawyers as Lawmakers: A Theory of Lawyer Licensing," 69 *Mo. L. Rev.* 299 (2004).

30. See Jonathan R. Macey and Geoffrey Miller, "Toward an Interest-Group Theory of Delaware Corporate Law," 65 *Tex. L. Rev.* 469 (1987).

31. See Eisenberg and Miller, "Ex Ante Choices of Law and Forum."

32. Chapter 6 will discuss the special circumstances of the corporate law market and the factors that contribute to Delaware's dominance.

33. See the discussion of *Restatement (Second)*, §187(2), in chapter 3.

34. See http://ronald.cori.missouri.edu.

35. The database includes several categories of contracts, searchable by category, specific type of contract, or type of collection. The categories are business recombinations, business transactions, compensation and employment agreements, financial agreements, franchise agreements, governance, litigation documents, bankruptcy, securities agreements, utilities such as cable and electricity, and miscellaneous. The search was conducted on September 1, 2006, using as search expressions the standard contractual language "laws of the state of" (for finding the existence of a choice-of-law agreement) and "laws of the state of X," where X was a particular law selected by the contract.

36. See Eisenberg and Miller, "Ex Ante Choices of Law and Forum."

37. In chapter 6, we will discuss Delaware's competition in the corporate and noncorporate law markets.

38. These statutes were discussed in chapter 3.

39. Ribstein, "From Efficiency to Politics in Contractual Choice of Law."

40. The search, which was completed on June 29, 2006, looked for decided cases that cited "Restatement & Conflicts W/3 187" after June 1, 2002.

41. In the remaining cases, the courts held either that the clause was not applicable (for example, the clause related only to contractual issues and the case involved a tort or procedural matter) or that the law of the forum state was the same as that of the chosen state. These techniques give the courts some leeway to refuse to enforce the clause without actually saying so, which arguably skews the results somewhat toward enforcement.

Chapter 5

1. In practice, postdispute arbitration agreements are pretty rare. See Peter B. Rutledge, "Whither Arbitration?" 6 *Geo. J.L. & Pub. Pol'y* (forthcoming 2008) (discussing this issue and citing empirical studies).

2. Klaus Peter Berger, *International Economic Arbitration* (Boston: Kluwer Law and Taxation, 1993), 8n62; Alessandra Casella, "On Market Integration and the Development of Institutions: The Case of International Commercial Arbitration," 40 *Eur. Econ. Rev.* 155, 156–57 (1996); Christopher R. Drahozal and Richard W. Naimark, "Commentary," in *Towards a Science of International Arbitration: Collected Empirical Research*, ed. Drahozal and Naimark (New York: Kluwer Law International, 2005), 57, 59 (hereafter *Towards a Science*) (discussing research that found that almost 90 percent of studied international joint venture agreements contained arbitration clauses).

3. Yves Dezalay and Bryant G. Garth, *Dealing in Virtue: International Commercial Arbitration and the Construction of a Transnational Legal Order* (Chicago: University of Chicago Press, 1996), 6 and n. 4; Drahozal and Naimark, *Towards a Science*, appendix; Hong Kong International Arbitration Centre Statistics, available at http://www.hkiac.org/HKIAC/ HKIAC_English/main.html.

4. See Theodore Eisenberg and Geoffrey Miller, "The Flight from Arbitration: An Empirical Study of Ex Ante Arbitration Clauses in the Contracts of Publicly Held Companies," 56 *DePaul L. Rev.* 335 (2007).

5. See Phillip J. McConnaughay, "The Risks and Virtues of Lawlessness: A 'Second Look' at International Commercial Arbitration," 93 *Nw. U. L. Rev.* 453 (1999) ("virtually all developed nations" participate in the convention requiring a permissible stance toward arbitration in international contracts).

6. Remarks of Patricia Shaughnessy at Arbitration and Regulation Workshop, Vanderbilt Law School, February 8, 2007; Gary B. Born, *International Arbitration and Forum Selection Agreements: Planning, Drafting and Enforcing* (Boston: Kluwer Law International, 1999), 61–62. The next section discusses the law that is applicable in arbitration.

7. See Edward Brunet, "Replacing Folklore Arbitration with a Contract Model of Arbitration," 74 *Tul. L. Rev.* 39, 52 (1999) (noting that "[t]he conditions for competitive rivalry are excellent in the arbitration field. There are numerous buyers and sellers of arbitration. The field is growing in both supply and demand. Entry into arbitration is easy; barriers to entry are minimal. Arbitrators are generally unregulated by the state. Lawyers relatively inexperienced in private arbitration can hold themselves out as arbitrators. Arbitration experience can be gained readily by serving as an arbitrator in the vast number of state and federal cases now subject to mandatory arbitration").

8. See Christopher R. Drahozal and Keith N. Hylton, "The Economics of Litigation and Arbitration: An Application to Franchise Contracts," 32 *J. Legal Stud.* 549 (2003).

9. See International Arbitration Rules of the American Arbitration Association, art. 28(1) (as amended and effective on April 21, 1997).

10. See chapter 4 (which notes that this is also a reason for choice-of-court clauses).

11. See the text accompanying note 80.

12. The parol evidence rule provides a classic example. According to the law of every state, where the parties intend a writing to represent a final and complete expression of their agreement, no outside evidence may be admitted to add to or change the terms of that agreement. Outside evidence is, however, always admissible to interpret the writing. If the contract provides for the application of South Carolina law, a California court might honor the clause but conclude that the parol evidence rule is the same in both states. It turns out, however, that South Carolina holds that a writing is final and complete by reference to the writing itself, while California courts consider outside evidence in making the determination of whether the writing is final and complete. California precedents also make it much easier for a court to determine that outside evidence will be used to interpret (not change) the terms of the agreement. In reality, then, it is much easier to introduce outside evidence under California's view of the law. A California court most likely will miss these subtle but important differences. Instead, because the most general statement of the law is the same in both states, the California court likely will proceed with its own interpretation of the rule.

13. Lisa Bernstein, "Opting Out of the Legal System: Extralegal Contractual Relations in the Diamond Industry," 21 *J. Legal Stud.* 115 (1992).

14. See Lisa Bernstein, "Merchant Law in a Merchant Court: Rethinking the Code's Search for Immanent Business Norms," 144 *U. Pa. L. Rev.* 1765 (1996). Outside of industry-specific arbitration, however, relatively few contracting parties appear to want anational rules applied to their dispute. See 16 *ICC Ct. Bull.*, no. 1, 11 (2005) (reporting that only 8 of the 561 contracts associated with new arbitration filings in 2004 requested anational rules).

15. For example, U.S. and Mexican parties to commercial contracts can opt out of the Convention on Contracts for the International Sale of Goods (CISG) and replace them with the UNIDROIT principles. See Richard E. Speidel and Linda J. Rusch, *Commercial Transactions: Sales, Leases and Licenses* (St. Paul, MN: West, 2001), 24.

16. United Nations Convention on Contracts for the International Sale of Goods, art. 6 (1980). Note, however, that parties to contracts other than international contracts for the sale of goods may not be able to opt into the CISG as the parties' governing law regime.

17. See Bernstein, "Opting Out of the Legal System."

18. See McConnaughay, "The Risks and Virtues of Lawlessness."

19. Eisenberg and Miller, *The Flight from Arbitration* (37 percent); Stewart J. Schwab and Randall S. Thomas, "An Empirical Analysis of CEO Employment Contracts: What Do Top Executives Bargain For?" 63 *Wash. & Lee L. Rev.* 231, 257 (2006) (41.6 percent).

20. Linda J. Demaine and Deborah R. Hensler, "'Volunteering' to Arbitrate through Predispute Arbitration Clauses: The Average Consumer's Experience," 67 *L. & Contemp. Probs.* 55, 55–56 (2004).

21. See Queen Mary University of London, School of International Arbitration, *International Arbitration: Corporate Attitudes and Practices* (London: Pricewaterhouse Coopers, 2006) (hereafter Queen Mary study) (a survey of lawyers involved in transborder transactions who listed the ability to select an arbitrator with sufficient experience as one of the top reasons for choosing arbitration).

22. See Christopher R. Drahozal, "Arbitration Clauses in Franchise Agreements: Common (and Uncommon) Terms," 22 *Fall Franchise L.J.* 81 (2002).

23. See William W. Park, "Arbitration in Banking and Finance," 17 *Ann. Rev. Banking L.* 213, 215–16 (1998) (listing reasons that banks historically have preferred courts to arbitration but detecting a slight trend toward experimenting with arbitration).

24. Kenneth Martin et al., *Arbitration Clauses in CEO Contracts* (2008) (draft manuscript on file with authors).

25. See Christopher R. Drahozal, "'Unfair' Arbitration Clauses," 2001 *U. Ill. L. Rev.* 695.

26. See Drahozal and Hylton, "The Economics of Litigation and Arbitration." In addition, since the value of firms rests largely on the validity of their

trademark rights, these disputes are likely to be "bet the company" disputes, which could lead the company to prefer courts to arbitration. See note 44 and accompanying text.

27. See Geoffrey Miller, *The Market for Contract* (October 2006), 40–43, available at http://ssrn.com/abstract=938557.

28. Actually, arbitration can be a mechanism for avoiding undesired court biases of any form. See Bruce L. Benson, "To Arbitrate or to Litigate: That Is the Question," 8 *Eur. J.L. & Econ.* 91 (1999).

29. See Christopher R. Drahozal, "New Experiences of International Arbitration in the United States," 54 *Am. J. Comp. L.* 233 (2006).

30. See Lisa B. Bingham, "On Repeat Players, Adhesive Contracts, and the Use of Statistics in Judicial Review of Employment Arbitration Awards," 29 *McGeorge L. Rev.* 223 (1998) (finding that the repeat-player employer advantage relative to non-repeat-player employers is primarily due to the differences in the underlying contracts involved in the arbitrated disputes).

31. See Queen Mary study (flexibility of the procedure was the most widely indicated advantage to arbitration).

32. See Kevin M. Clermont and Theodore Eisenberg, "Exorcising the Evil of Forum-Shopping," 80 *Cornell L. Rev.* 1507 (1995).

33. See Stephen J. Ware, "Default Rules from Mandatory Rules: Privatizing Law through Arbitration," 83 *Minn. L. Rev.* 703 (1999); Brunet, "Replacing Folklore Arbitration."

34. The International Arbitration Rules for the American Arbitration Association have become more legalistic during the very period in which the organization has experienced dramatic growth. Brunet, "Replacing Folklore Arbitration."

35. See Christian Buhring-Uhle, "A Survey of Arbitration and Settlement in International Business Disputes," in Drahozal and Naimark, *Towards a Science*, 25, 33 (51 percent of those surveyed thought that arbitration has no cost advantage over litigation).

36. See *Disciplinary Counsel v. Alexicole, Inc.*, 105 Ohio St.3d 52 (2004); Cal. Civ. Proc. Code §1282.4(c), (d) (2007) (permitting out-of-state attorneys to represent clients in California arbitration as long as procedural requirements are met and a member of the California bar is appointed as the attorney of record).

37. Brunet, "Replacing Folklore Arbitration."

38. Comments of Stanimir Alexandrov at Arbitration and Regulation Workshop, Vanderbilt Law School, February 8, 2008.

39. See Miller, *The Market for Contract.*

40. For example, a study of 75 franchise agreements showed that about three-fourths of the standard contracts that opted for arbitration also precluded

relief for punitive damages. See Drahozal, "Arbitration Clauses in Franchise Agreements," 737–38.

41. See, e.g., *Mastrobuono v. Shearson Lehman Hutton, Inc.*, 514 U.S. 52 (1995) (interpreting rules of the National Association of Securities Dealers to permit their arbitrators to award punitive damages); American Arbitration Association, International Arbitration Rules, art. 28(5) (default rule that punitive damages are unrecoverable).

42. See Clayton P. Gillette and Steven D. Walt, *Sales Law: Domestic and International*, rev. ed. (2002), 360–79 (discussing differing views on the contractibility for specific performance).

43. See Samuel Issacharoff and Erin F. Delaney, "Credit Card Accountability," 73 *U. Chi. L. Rev.* 157 (2006).

44. Christopher R. Drahozal and Quentin R. Wittrock, "Is There a Flight from Arbitration?" (draft manuscript dated January 21, 2008, on file with authors), 9.

45. See Brunet, "Replacing Folklore Arbitration," 52.

46. The Full Faith and Credit Clause of the U.S. Constitution requires each state to give full faith and credit to the judicial proceedings of the other states. For a more detailed description of states' obligations under the clause, see Eugene F. Scoles et al., *Conflict of Laws*, 3rd ed. (St. Paul, MN: West, 2000), §§24.8–24.32.

47. See Federal Arbitration Act, §9.

48. Thomas E. Carbonneau, *Cases and Materials on the Law and Practice of Arbitration*, 3rd ed. (Huntington, NY: Juris, 2002), 768.

49. Convention on Choice of Court Agreements, full text available at http://www.hcch.net/index_en.php?act=conventions.text&cid=98.

50. See Stephen B. Burbank, "Federalism and Private International Law: Implementing the Hague Choice of Court Convention in the United States," *J. Priv. Int'l L.* (forthcoming). Effectively implementing the Hague Convention in the United States may be complicated by the existence of multiple court systems. William J. Woodward, Jr., "Saving the Hague Choice of Court Convention," 29 *U. Pa. J. Int'l L.* 657 (2008).

51. Gary Born lists the leading international arbitration institutions: International Chamber of Commerce, American Arbitration Association, London Court of International Arbitration, Stockholm Chamber of Commerce Arbitration Institute, Singapore International Arbitration Centre, Hong Kong International Arbitration Centre, and World Intellectual Property organization. He also lists approximately 30 other well-known international arbitration institutions. Gary B. Born, *International Arbitration and Forum Selection Agreements: Planning, Drafting and Enforcing* (Boston: Kluwer Law International, 1999), 151–59.

52. Miller, *The Market for Contract*.

53. Ibid., 23 and n. 64.

54. Bruce L. Benson, "An Exploration of the Impact of Modern Arbitration Statutes on the Development of Arbitration in the United States," 11 *J.L. Econ. & Org.* 479, 481 (1995).

55. Benson, "An Exploration of the Impact of Modern Arbitration Statutes," offers an alternative history of the Federal Arbitration Act, stressing the competition to courts provided by purely private arbitration.

56. The provisions of the FAA bind federal courts when they exercise both federal question and diversity jurisdiction. The FAA applies in state courts in federal question cases and in state law cases that involve interstate commerce. See Carbonneau, *Cases and Materials on the Law and Practice of Arbitration*, 55.

57. The 138 member states are listed at http://www.uncitral.org/uncitral/en/ uncitral_texts/arbitration/NYConvention_status.html.

58. Convention on the Recognition and Enforcement of Foreign Arbitral Awards, June 10, 1958, 21 U.S.T. 2517, 330 U.N.T.S. 3, art. II (hereafter New York Convention).

59. Ibid., art. III.

60. Occasionally, international contracting parties will complain about a nation's restrictive interpretation of the convention's obligations. China and India apparently have each received criticism in the past (though not in the present). For an argument that the U.S. Supreme Court has completely rewritten the FAA, see Margaret L. Moses, "Statutory Misconstruction: How the Supreme Court Created a Federal Arbitration Law Never Enacted by Congress," 34 *Fla. St. U. L. Rev.* 99 (2006).

61. A description of these laws can be found in William W. Park, *International Forum Selection* (Boston: Kluwer Law International, 1995), 128–29. Belgian law has changed since the publication of Park's book. See William W. Park, "The Specificity of International Arbitration: The Case for FAA Reform," 36 *Vand. J. Transnat'l L.* 1241, 1267 (2003) (describing Belgian law reform).

62. See Carbonneau, *Cases and Materials on the Law and Practice of Arbitration*, 12–13 (noting that increased lawyer involvement in arbitration has created a trend toward more formal and more adversarial procedures).

63. Benson, "To Arbitrate or to Litigate," 496 and n. 23.

64. Drahozal, "Arbitration Clauses in Franchise Agreements." However, the economic effects of arbitration law are unclear. See Christopher R. Drahozal, "Regulatory Competition and the Location of International Arbitration Proceedings," 24 *Int'l Rev. L. & Econ.* 371 (2004) (finding that arbitration law reform increases the demand for ICC arbitrations to be held in the reform country but finding very small economic benefits from reform); Christopher R. Drahozal, "Arbitrator Selection and Regulatory Competition in International Arbitration Law," in Drahozal and Naimark, *Towards a Science*, 167 (finding that the number of both party-appointed

and presiding arbitrators from a country increases after the country upgrades its arbitration law).

65. Section 11028(a)(2) of Pub. L. 107–273, 116 Stat. 1836 (2002).

66. S. 91, 108th Cong., 1st sess. (2003).

67. S. 1782, Arbitration Fairness Act, Cong. rev. S. 9144 (July 12, 2007).

68. See Ware, "Default Rules from Mandatory Rules."

69. Carbonneau, *Cases and Materials on the Law and Practice of Arbitration*, 274.

70. However, international and domestic parties might be differently situated when it comes to award enforcement. In domestic cases, arbitration awards will not be enforced if the award shows a manifest disregard for the governing law. Richard E. Macneil et al., *Federal Arbitration Law* (Boston: Little, Brown, 1995), §40.7. It is not clear whether courts can similarly scrutinize international commercial arbitrations for manifest disregard of the law. See Hans Smit, "Is Manifest Disregard of the Law or the Evidence or Both a Ground for Vacatur of an Arbitral Award?" 8 *Am. Rev. Int'l Arb.* 341, 342 (1997) (discussing the lack of basis under the New York Convention for a manifest-disregard review by the courts). The Second Circuit has decided that manifest disregard of the law cannot be the basis for international or foreign awards. See *Yusuf Ahmed Alghanim & Sons v. Toys "R" Us, Inc.*, 126 F.3d 15 (2nd Cir. 1997).

71. See *Buckeye Check Cashing, Inc. v. Cardegna*, 126 S. Ct. 1204 (2006). The Court, however, can determine the validity of the arbitration provision.

72. Christopher R. Drahozal, "*Buckeye Check Cashing* and the Separability Doctrine," *ADR and the Law* app. B (forthcoming 2008).

73. S. 1782, 110th Cong., 1st sess., §4 (2007); H.R. 3010, 110th Cong., 1st sess., §4 (2007).

74. *Preston v. Ferrer*, 128 S. Ct. 978 (February 20, 2008).

75. *Mitsubishi v. Soler Chrysler-Plymouth, Inc.*, 473 U.S. 614 (1985).

76. *Scherk v. Alberto-Culver, Co.*, 417 U.S. 506 (1974).

77. *Shearson/American Express, Inc. v. McMahon*, 482 U.S. 220 (1987).

78. *Gilmer v. Interstate/Johnson Lane Corp.*, 500 U.S. 20 (1991) (age discrimination claims are arbitrable).

79. For a discussion of the issues involved when arbitrators render decisions in disputes that involve mandatory rules of law, see Donald F. Donovan and Alexander K. A. Greenawalt, "*Mitsubishi* after Twenty Years: Mandatory Rules before Courts and International Arbitrators," in *Pervasive Problems in International Arbitration*, ed. Loukas A. Mistelis and Julian D. M. Lew (Alphen aan den Rijn: Kluwer Law International, 2006), 11.

80. However, under the convention, courts can deny the enforcement of arbitration awards that would violate the public policy of the enforcing state, and they might also be reviewable in U.S. courts for manifest disregard of the law, so there is some potential peril to using arbitration to

end-run state regulation. For a discussion of the standards of reviewability, see Ware, "Default Rules from Mandatory Rules."

81. New York Convention, art. V, §2(b).

82. *Restatement (Second) of Conflict of Laws* (1971), §80, comment a.

83. See, e.g., *E. Gerli & Co. v. Cunard S.S. Co.*, 48 F.2d 115, 117 (2nd Cir. 1931) (Learned Hand).

84. The United States was not an original signatory to the New York Convention, however, and it did not join the convention until 1970, 12 years after it was concluded.

85. See http://www.hcch.net/index_en.php?act=conventions.pdf&cid=98 (June 30, 2005).

86. Drahozal, "*Buckeye Check Cashing* and the Separability Doctrine."

Chapter 6

1. Roberta Romano, "Law as Product: Some Pieces of the Incorporation Puzzle," 1 *J.L. Econ. & Org.* 225 (1985). In 1974, William Cary famously asserted that corporate law was a "race to the bottom" that Delaware had won by catering to corporate managers. William L. Cary, "Federalism and Corporate Law: Reflections upon Delaware," 83 *Yale L.J.* 663 (1974). Although scholars have vigorously debated this conclusion, and many have argued that corporate law is instead the product of a "race to the top," most agree that there is at least some kind of a market for corporate law.

2. See *Restatement (Second) of Conflict of Laws* (1971), §§304, 307. Other rules recognize the application of the law of the state of incorporation concerning particular matters: ibid., §296 (requirements for incorporation); ibid., §297 (states' recognition of foreign incorporations); ibid., §303 (determination of who is a shareholder); ibid., §306 (liability of majority shareholder).

3. For a discussion of the arguments for and against the contractual theory of the corporation, see Henry N. Butler and Larry E. Ribstein, "Opting Out of Fiduciary Duties: A Response to the Anti-Contractarians," 65 *Wash. L. Rev.* 1 (1990). For an application of the contractual theory of the corporation to choice of law, see Larry E. Ribstein, "Choosing Law by Contract," 18 *J. Corp. L.* 245 (1993).

4. See Frederick Tung, "Before Competition: Origins of the Internal Affairs Doctrine," 32 *J. Corp. L.* 33 (2006).

5. See Larry E. Ribstein, "The Constitutional Conception of the Corporation," 4 *S. Ct. Econ. Rev.* 95 (1995).

6. See P. John Kozyris, "Some Observations on State Regulation of Multistate Takeovers: Controlling Choice of Law through the Commerce Clause," 14 *Del. J. Corp. L.* 499, 509–11 (1989).

7. See Henry N. Butler, "Nineteenth Century Jurisdictional Competition in the Granting of Corporate Privileges," 14 *J. Legal Stud.* 129 (1985).

8. See Alfred Chandler, *The Visible Hand* (1977).

9. See Tung, "Before Competition," 63–65.

10. See Butler, "Nineteenth Century Jurisdictional Competition."

11. See Christopher Grandy, "New Jersey Corporate Charter-Mongering, 1875–1929," 49 *J. Econ. Hist.* 677 (1989).

12. Ibid., 680–81.

13. See Ron Chernow, *Titan* (San Francisco: Berrett-Koehler, 1999), 332–33.

14. See Lawrence Mitchell, *The Speculation Economy: How Finance Triumphed over Industry* (2007), ch. 2. Mitchell notes that New Jersey offered other advantages, including protecting officers and directors from actions brought in New Jersey under other states' laws.

15. See ibid.

16. See Grandy, "New Jersey Corporate Charter-Mongering," 689.

17. See, generally, Cary, "Federalism and Corporate Law."

18. See Lucian Arye Bebchuk and Assaf Hamdani, "Vigorous Race or Leisurely Walk: Reconsidering the Competition over Corporate Charters," 112 *Yale L.J.* 553 (2002); Maureen Milford, "Delaware's Corporate Dominance Threatened: Federal Intervention Could Put at Risk a Third of State's Budget: 'Overnight We Would Go Broke,'" *News Journal* (March 2, 2008), available at http://www.delawareonline.com/apps/pbcs. dll/article?AID=/20080302/NEWS/803020319/1006/NEWS (noting the estimate that taxes and fees paid by corporations, money from abandoned property, and personal and business taxes paid by lawyers and others in the incorporation industry amounts to 40 percent of the yearly state revenue).

19. See Marcel Kahan and Ehud Kamar, "The Myth of State Competition in Corporate Law," 55 *Stan. L. Rev.* 679 (2002); Bebchuk and Hamdani, "Vigorous Race or Leisurely Walk."

20. See Mitchell, *The Speculation Economy*, 39–42.

21. See Curtis Alva, "Delaware and the Market for Corporate Charters: History and Agency," 15 *Del. J. Corp. L.* 885, 896–98 (1990); William J. Carney, "The Production of Corporate Law," 71 *S. Cal. L. Rev.* 715, 722–28 (1998); Larry E. Ribstein, "Delaware, Lawyers, and Choice of Law," 19 *Del. J. Corp. L.* 999 (1994); Jonathan R. Macey and Geoffrey Miller, "Toward an Interest-Group Theory of Delaware Corporate Law," 65 *Tex. L. Rev.* 469 (1987).

22. See Alva, "Delaware and the Market for Corporate Charters."

23. See Ehud Kamar, "A Regulatory Competition Theory of Indeterminacy in Corporate Law," 98 *Colum. L. Rev.* 1908 (1998).

24. See Kahan and Kamar, "The Myth of State Competition."

25. See Romano, "Law as Product," 274–75.

26. Plans for federal chartering of corporations early in the twentieth century are discussed below at n. 36.

27. Some California cases are discussed later in this chapter. New York has incentives similar to California's and indeed has sought to regulate pseudo-foreign corporations. See P. John Kozyris, "Corporate Wars and Choice of Law," 1985 *Duke L.J.* 1, 66–67 (discussing New York statutes that apply New York corporation law to foreign corporations).

28. See John C. Coates IV, "The Legal Origins of the (Unimportant) U.S. Market for Corporate Charters" (draft manuscript of October 18, 2004, on file with authors) (discussing the potential influence of these interest groups).

29. See Henry Hansmann, Reinier Kraakman, and Richard Squire, "Law and the Rise of the Firm," 119 *Harv. L. Rev.* 1333 (2006).

30. Indeed, the only situation where a firm's creditors might need equal treatment outside of individual contracting is in the context of bankruptcy, where the laws are designed to achieve a parity of rights among creditors of the same class.

31. See Uniform Securities Act, §414, 7B U.L.A. 672.

32. See Roberta Romano, "Empowering Investors: A Market Approach to Securities Regulation," 107 *Yale L.J.* 2359, 2406 (1998). Romano argues that this distinction is flawed because, since a firm's common shares are the same everywhere, it is "arbitrary" to apply different state laws according to where shareholders live. While this is true, it is no truer of securities than of any nationally marketed product. The policy underlying the IAD concerns the special difficulty of applying different rules rather than the absence of a justification for different rules.

33. See Jonathan R. Macey and Geoffrey P. Miller, "The Origin of the Blue Sky Laws," 71 *Tex. L. Rev.* 347 (1991) (discussing the influence of small banks and local industries on the enactment of blue sky laws).

34. For a discussion of the effects and politics of these rules in the law firm setting, see Larry E. Ribstein, "Ethical Rules, Law Firm Structure and Choice of Law," 69 *U. Cin. L. Rev.* 1161 (2001).

35. See Larry E. Ribstein, "Ethical Rules, Agency Costs and Law Firm Structure," 84 *Va. L. Rev.* 1707 (1998).

36. See Mark Roe, "Delaware's Competition," 117 *Harv. L. Rev.* 588 (2003) (discussing the increasing federalization of corporate law).

37. See Charles M. Yablon, "The Historical Competition for Corporate Charters and the Rise and Decline of New Jersey: 1880–1910," 32 *J. Corp. L.* 323 (2007).

38. Roe, "Delaware's Competition," presents a darker picture of the federal government's role, arguing that encroaching federal regulation prevents full-fledged state competition. For a response to Roe, see Roberta Romano, "Is Regulatory Competition a Problem or Irrelevant for Corporate Governance?" 21 *Oxford Rev. of Econ. Pol'y* 212 (2005).

39. See Henry Hansmann, "Corporation and Contract," 8 *Am. L. & Econ. Ass'n Rev.* 1 (2006).

40. See Charles J. Goetz and Robert E. Scott, "The Limits of Expanded Choice: An Analysis of the Interactions between Express and Implied Contract Terms," 73 *Cal. L. Rev.* 261, 286–89 (1985).

41. See Bebchuk and Hamdani, "Vigorous Race or Leisurely Walk."

42. For a formal model of the attributes of the market for corporations, which stresses the difference between firms that do and do not demand significant infrastructure, see Oren Bar-Gill, Michal Barzuza, and Lucian Bebchuk, "The Market for Corporate Law," 162 *J. Inst. Theo. Econ.* 134 (2006).

43. See Roberta Romano, "The States as a Laboratory: Legal Innovation and State Competition for Corporate Charters," 23 *Yale J. Reg.* 209 (2006) (showing the rapid diffusion of corporate law changes, but the resistance to anti-takeover laws in Delaware as compared with states where labor has more influence); Carney, "The Production of Corporate Law."

44. See Romano, "Law as a Product."

45. Theodore Eisenberg and Geoffrey P. Miller, "Ex Ante Choices of Law and Forum: An Empirical Analysis of Corporate Merger Agreements," 59 *Vand. L. Rev.* 1975 (2006).

46. 11 Cal. Rptr. 2d 330, 834 P.2d 1148 (Cal. 1992).

47. See Jennifer Johnson, "Risky Business: Choice-of-Law and the Unincorporated Entity," 1 *J. Small Emerging Bus. L.* 249 (1997); Ribstein, "Choosing Law by Contract"; Thomas Rutledge, "To Boldly Go Where You Have Not Been Told You May Go: LLCs, LLPs, and LLLPs in Interstate Transactions," 58 *Baylor L. Rev.* 205 (2006).

48. See Alan R. Bromberg and Larry E. Ribstein, *Bromberg & Ribstein on Partnership* (Boston: Little, Brown, 1988 and Supp.), §1.04. However, in the absence of a clear statutory rule, the common law of conflict of laws may apply. The common law may apply the general contract choice-of-law rule rather than the IAD if the firm is a partnership, though probably not if it is an LLC. See *Restatement (Second) of Conflict of Laws* (1971), §298 (defining "corporation" for choice-of-law purposes). It is conceivable that applying the contract rule may mean that partner's liability is governed by the law of the plaintiff's residence rather than that of the state of formation. See ibid., §298. See, generally, Rutledge, "To Boldly Go," 238–42.

49. See Larry E. Ribstein and Robert R. Keatinge, *Ribstein & Keatinge on Limited Liability Companies*, 2nd ed. (Eagan, MN: Thomson/West, 2004), ch. 13.

50. See Ian Ayres, "Judging Close Corporations in the Age of Statutes," 70 *Wash. U. L.Q.* 365 (1992); Bar-Gill et al., "The Market for Corporate Law" (showing evidence that larger firms are more likely than smaller firms to incorporate outside their home states).

51. Roberta Romano, "State Competition for Close Corporation Charters: A Commentary," 70 *Wash. U. L.Q.* 409, 413 (1992) (arguing that there is less competition for closely held than for publicly held firms).

52. See Jens C. Damann and Matthias Schundeln, *The Incorporation Choices of Privately Held Corporations*, available at http://ssrn.com/abstract=1049581.

53. See Larry E. Ribstein, "Statutory Forms for Closely Held Firms: Theories and Evidence from LLCs," 73 *Wash. U. L.Q.* 369, 392–94 (1995); Carol R. Goforth, "The Rise of the Limited Liability Company: Evidence of a Race between the States, but Heading Where?" 45 *Syracuse L. Rev.* 1193 (1995) (showing evidence that lawyers and others participated in competition regarding LLC laws); Bruce H. Kobayashi and Larry E. Ribstein, "Evolution and Spontaneous Uniformity: Evidence from the Evolution of the Limited Liability Company," 34 *Econ. Inquiry* 464 (1996) (showing evidence of the evolution of state LLC statutes toward an efficient level of uniformity).

54. Specifically, in 2005, Florida had 123,437 new formations, followed by Delaware at 87,360. Data on LLC formations are compiled by the International Association of Corporate Administrators, www.iaca.org. Delaware and Florida LLC formations do not reflect their standings in population relative to other states. Other leading states include California (59,431), Texas (53,101), New Jersey (51,668), Arizona (48,663), New York (48,564), Colorado (45,302), Georgia (41,063), and Ohio (40,180). Florida is fourth in population after California, Texas, and New York. See U.S. Census 2000, Resident Population, available at http://www.census.gov/population/www/cen2000/respop.html.

55. The Florida homestead exemption, which is ensconced in a state constitutional provision, protects an unlimited value of real property provided that it occupies no more than a half acre within a municipality or 160 acres outside of a municipality. See Florida Constitution, art. X, §4.

56. Florida revised its statute in 1998 and 2002 to increase its usability, particularly for small firms and as retirement and debtor protection vehicles. These revisions, among other things, clarified provisions for single-member LLCs, clarified veil-piercing standards, removed the requirement to estimate capital contributions, ensured lack of marketability and minority interest discounts for use in estate planning, and offered debtor protection by denying creditors the right to foreclose on charging orders. See, generally, Fla. Stat. §608.401 et seq. (2000). See also Florida Asset Protection Blog, http://floridaassetprotection.blogs.com/alperlaw (accessed January 11, 2005) (noting that "the Florida legislature changed the law to specifically permit a single member LLC"); Fla. Stat. §608.701 (applying corporate veil-piercing case law to the LLC context); Fla. Stat. §608.4211 (removing a requirement

to estimate capital contributions); Fla. Stat. §608.433 (denying creditors the right to foreclose on charging orders). On nonforeclosure on charging orders as an asset protection provision, see Larry E. Ribstein, "Reverse Limited Liability and the Design of Business Associations," 30 *Del. J. Corp. L.* 199 (2005).

57. See Division of Corporations, Annual Statistics, http://www.dos.state.fl.us/doc/corp_stat.html (accessed November 26, 2006).

58. See, generally, John Goodgame, "Master Limited Partnership Governance," 60 *Bus. Law.* 471 (2005).

59. Robert H. Sitkoff, "The Rise of the Statutory Business Trust" (manuscript in progress) shows that, in 2005, Delaware had 14,164 of these firms, Massachusetts 10,535, and Connecticut 1,529, though Delaware had far more formations of these firms than both other states: 3,200, compared to a total of 262 in the other states.

60. Ibid. (relying on data from the Investment Company Institute). Many closed-end funds are Delaware limited partnerships, bringing Delaware's total entity share in that category close to the shares of Massachusetts and Maryland.

61. See David M. Einhorn, Adam O. Emmerich, and Robin Panovka, "REIT M&A Transactions: Peculiarities and Complications," 55 *Bus. Law.* 693 (2000).

62. See National Association of Real Estate Investment Trusts, *The REIT Story*, http://investinreits.com/learn/reitstory.cfm (accessed November 26, 2006). REITs are actually corporations formed under a special section of the Maryland Corporations and Associations Code, §8-101 et seq. However, Maryland REITs share features with unincorporated firms. See Larry E. Ribstein, "Uncorporating the Large Firm" (manuscript on file with author).

63. 15 U.S.C. §80a-1 et seq. (2000).

64. See 26 U.S.C. §856 (2000) (providing rules for the qualification of REITs for pass-through taxation).

65. Case C-212/97, *Centros Ltd. v. Erhvervs-og Selskabsstyrelsen*, 1999 E.C.R. I-1459 (1999), 2 C.M.L.R. 551 (1999).

66. Case C-208/00, *Überseering B. V. v. Nordic Construction Company Baumanagement GmbH* (NCC), 2002 E.C.R. I-9919 (2002).

67. Case C-167/01, *Kamer van Koophandel en Fabrieken voor Amsterdam v. Inspire Art Ltd.* (September 30, 2003), 2003 E.C.R. 1-10155 (2003).

68. European countries can still inhibit jurisdictional competition if it is justified "on grounds of public policy, public security or public health" under article 46 of the Treaty of Rome. Countries can also regulate outside of company law, such as by imposing legal capital-type regulations under insolvency laws. See John Armour, "Who Should Make Corporate Law? EC Legislation versus

Regulatory Competition" (ECGI, Working Paper No. 54/2005, June 2005), available at http://papers.ssrn.com/paper.taf?abstract_id=860444. They can also limit firms' ability to reincorporate in other countries, which would be a real constraint on the charter market. See *The Queen and HM Treasury and Commissioners of Inland Revenue ex parte Daily Mail and General Trust PLC*, case 81/87 (O.J. 1973, L 172, 14) (holding that the right of establishment did not prevent the United Kingdom from blocking the transfer of a company's headquarters to another country to keep the company from avoiding payment of capital gains tax).

69. See Marco Becht, Colin Mayer, and Hannes F. Wagner, *Corporate Mobility and the Costs of Regulation* (September 2006), available at http://ssrn. com/abstract=906066 (finding an increase in UK incorporations of firms not physically located in the United Kingdom, mostly coming from other EU countries subject to the *Centros* rule). Specifically, they found that the average number of European private limited companies incorporating in the United Kingdom increased from 4,600 firms per year before *Centros* to 28,000 firms per year afterward, totaling over 120,000 firms between 1997 and 2006, including 48,000 from Germany.

70. Ibid.

71. See Martin Gelter, "The Structure of Regulatory Competition in European Corporate Law," 5 *J. Corp. L. Stud.* 247–84 (2005) (discussing the use of UK corporations in Germany and the Netherlands).

72. See Directive on Indirect Taxes and the Raising of Capital, 69/335 EEC (1969), O.J. L 249/25. For analyses of the significance of this restriction, see Armour, "Who Should Make Corporate Law?"; Gelter, "The Structure of Regulatory Competition"; Ehud Kamar, "Beyond Competition for Incorporations," 94 *Geo. L.J.* 1725 (2006).

73. See Gelter, "The Structure of Regulatory Competition." Note that Liechtenstein is not subject to the limitation on charter fees, but it competes mainly as a tax haven rather than for incorporations. For other discussions of the unlikelihood that a European country would have Delaware-type incentives to actively drive corporate charter competition, see Töbias H. Troger, "Choice of Jurisdiction in European Corporate Law: Perspectives of European Corporate Governance," 6 *Eur. Bus. Org. L. Rev.* 3, 63 (2005); Marco Ventoruzzo, " 'Cost-Based' and 'Rule-Based' Regulatory Competition: Markets for Corporate Charters in the U.S. and in the EU," 3 *N.Y.U. J.L. & Bus.* 91, 130 (2006).

74. See Armour, "Who Should Make Corporate Law?"

75. European countries not only allow for some jurisdictional choice of securities laws (in contrast to the United States), but also to some extent bundle the choice of securities regime with the choice of corporate law. See Luca Enriques and Tobias H. Troeger, *Issuer Choice in Europe*, available at

http://ssrn.com/abstract=1032281 (discussing European choice of law for securities regulation and the potential benefits of unbundling the choice of corporate and securities law regimes).

76. See Romano, "State Competition for Close Corporation Charters."

77. *Lipcon v. Underwriters at Lloyd's, London*, 148 F.3d 1285 (11th Cir. 1998); *Richards v. Lloyd's of London*, 135 F.3d 1289 (9th Cir. 1998); *Haynsworth v. Corp.*, 121 F.3d 956 (5th Cir. 1997); *Allen v. Lloyd's of London*, 94 F.3d 923 (4th Cir. 1996); *Bonny v. Society of Lloyd's*, 3 F.3d 156 (7th Cir. 1993); *Roby v. Corporation of Lloyd's*, 996 F.2d 1353 (2nd Cir. 1993); *Riley v. Kingsley Underwriting Agencies, Ltd.*, 969 F.2d 953 (10th Cir. 1992).

78. For an analysis of the role of stock exchanges in the competition for securities law, see Chris Brummer, "Stock Exchanges and the New Market for Securities Law," *U. Chi. L. Rev.* (forthcoming 2008).

79. See U.S. Constitution, art. IV, §1 ("Full Faith and Credit shall be given in each State to the public Acts, Records, and judicial Proceedings of every other State. And the Congress may by general Laws prescribe the Manner in which such Acts, Records and Proceedings shall be proved, and the Effect thereof").

80. See U.S. Constitution, amend. XIV, §1 ("No state shall...deprive any person of life, liberty, or property, without due process of law").

81. See U.S. Constitution, art. I, §8.3 (providing that Congress has the power "[t]o regulate Commerce...among the several states").

82. The Equal Protection and Privileges and Immunities clauses arguably also constrain choice-of-law approaches that discriminate in favor of state residents or against out-of-state residents. However, the Privileges and Immunities Clause applies only to persons, not entities, and the Equal Protection Clause has never been used to strike a state's choice-of-law policies. We therefore do not consider these clauses in our analysis.

83. *Broderick v. Rosner*, 294 U.S. 629, 643–44 (1935). Notably, the Court cited one of the fraternal benefit association cases, *Modern Woodmen of America v. Mixer*, 267 U.S. 544, 551 (1925).

84. 449 U.S. 302 (1981).

85. 472 U.S. 797 (1985).

86. Ibid., 822.

87. See Donald H. Regan, "The Supreme Court and State Protectionism: Making Sense of the Dormant Commerce Clause," 84 *Mich. L. Rev.* 1091 (1986) (suggesting that the Court should merely prevent states from engaging in purposeful economic protectionism).

88. 457 U.S. 624 (1982).

89. Ibid., 640–43.

90. 481 U.S. 69 (1987).

91. See *Vantagepoint Venture Partners 1996 v. Examen, Inc.*, 871 A.2d 1108, 1116 (Del. 2005); *McDermott, Inc. v. Lewis*, 531 A.2d 206 (Del. 1987).

92. See *Wilson v. Louisiana-Pacific Resources, Inc.*, 138 Cal. App. 3d 216 (Ct. App. 1982).

93. Cal. Corp. Code §2115 (2001).

94. *Wilson*, 138 Cal. App. 3d at 226–27.

95. 481 U.S. 69, 89 (1987).

96. *Merrill Lynch, Pierce, Fenner & Smith, Inc. v. Dabit*, 126 S.Ct. 1503, 1509 (2006). See Larry E. Ribstein, "*Dabit*, Preemption and Choice of Law," 2006 *Cato S. Ct. Rev.* 141 (analyzing the case and its preemption issue).

97. See Butler and Ribstein, "Opting Out of Fiduciary Duties."

98. 607 A.2d 465, 468–69 (Del. Ch. 1991).

99. See Ribstein, "Delaware, Lawyers, and Choice of Law," 1022–25.

100. 114 Cal. App. 4th 434, 8 Cal. Rptr. 3d 56 (2003).

101. 134 Cal. App. 4th 693, 36 Cal. Rptr. 3d 558 (2005), *cert. denied, Moores v. Friese*, 127 S.Ct. 138 (2006).

102. 278 F. Supp. 2d 1079 (N.D. Cal. 2003).

103. 35 Cal. Rptr. 3d 58, *review granted and superseded by Grosset v. Wenaas*, 127 P.3d 27, 38 Cal. Rptr. 3d 609 (2006), *affirmed on other grounds*, 42 Cal. 4th 1100, 175 P.3d 1184, 72 Cal. Rptr. 3d 129 (2008).

104. *Grosset v. Wenaas*, 42 Cal. 4th 1100, 175 P.3d 1184, 72 Cal. Rptr. 3d 129 (2008).

105. See Erin A. O'Hara and Larry E. Ribstein, "From Politics to Efficiency in Choice of Law," 67 *U. Chi. L. Rev.* 1151, 1199–2000 (2000) (proposing this rule for choice-of-law clauses).

106. This refers to the enactment of the Securities Litigation Uniform Standards Act, discussed in Ribstein, "*Dabit*, Preemption and Choice of Law."

Chapter 7

1. See, for example, Jean R. Sternlight, "Creeping Mandatory Arbitration: Is It Just?" 57 *Stan. L. Rev.* 1631, 1649 (2005); Christine Jolls and Cass R. Sunstein, "Debiasing through Law," 35 *J. Legal Stud.* 199, 204 (2006).

2. Alan Schwartz and Louis L. Wilde, "Intervening in Markets on the Basis of Imperfect Information: A Legal and Economic Analysis," 127 *U. Pa. L. Rev.* 630 (1979).

3. Lucian A. Bebchuk and Richard A. Posner, "One-Sided Contracts in Competitive Consumer Markets," 104 *Mich. L. Rev.* 827 (2006).

4. Robert A. Hillman, *Online Consumer Standard-Form Contracting Practices: A Survey and Discussion of Legal Implications*, available at http://ssrn.com/abstract=686817.

5. Uniform Commercial Code §1-105.

6. Uniform Commercial Code, revised, §§1-301(c) and (f) provide for the application of even unrelated law in this context as long as application of

the designated law would not be contrary to the fundamental policy of the state whose law would otherwise apply.

7. See, for example, *Jett Racing and Sales, Inc. v. Transamerica Commercial Fin. Corp.*, 892 F. Supp. 161 (S.D. Tex. 1995); *Kinley Corp. v. Integrated Resources Equity Corp.*, 851 F. Supp. 556 (S.D.N.Y. 1994); *Karl Rove & Co. v. Thornburgh*, 824 F. Supp. 662 (W.D. Tex. 1993); *American Honda Fin. Corp. v. GLOMC, Inc.*, 820 F. Supp. 1157 (E.D. Ark. 1993); *Capital Center Equities v. Estate of Gordon*, 137 B.R. 600 (Bankr. E.D. Pa. 1992); *Sumner Realty v. Willcott*, 499 N.E.2d 554 (Ill. App. Ct. 1986).

8. For a comparison of our approach and that of European choice-of-law rules, see Erin A. O'Hara and Larry E. Ribstein, "Rules and Institutions in Developing a Law Market: Views from the U.S. and Europe," 82 *Tul. L. Rev.* 2147 (2008).

9. William W. Park, *International Forum Selection* (1995), 155–56.

10. 499 U.S. 585 (1991).

11. For a persuasive economic defense of the *Shute* case, see Michael Solimine, "Forum-Selection Clauses and the Privatization of Procedure," 25 *Cornell Int'l L.J.* 51 (1992). For criticism of the case, see Patrick Borchers, "Forum Selection Agreements in the Federal Courts after *Carnival Cruise*: A Proposal for Congressional Reform," 67 *Wash. L. Rev.* 55 (1992); Linda Mullenix, "Another Easy Case, Some More Bad Law: *Carnival Cruise Lines* and Contractual Personal Jurisdiction," 27 *Tex. Int'l L.J.* 323 (1992).

12. 70 F. Supp. 2d 691 (E.D. Texas 1999).

13. 90 Cal. App. 4th 1 (1st App. Cal. 2001); see also *America Online, Inc. v. Pasieka*, 870 So.2d 170 (Fla. App. Ct., 1st Dist. 2004) (Florida court striking the same choice-of-forum provision for similar reasons).

14. 805 A.2d 1007 (D.C. Ct. App. 2002).

15. Christopher R. Drahozal, "Unfair Arbitration Clauses," 2001 *U. Ill. L. Rev.* 695.

16. For example, a study of 52 consumer contracts containing arbitration clauses used in several industries found that, in 49 of the contracts, the arbitration was to take place either near the consumer's residence or the place where the consumer receives services. The three exceptions included two online businesses and one tour operator. See Linda J. Demaine and Deborah R. Hensler, "Volunteering to Arbitrate through Predispute Arbitration Clauses: The Average Consumer's Experience," 67 *L. & Contemp. Probs.* 55, 70 (2004).

17. Federal Arbitration Act, 9 U.S.C. §2.

18. See, generally, E. Allan Farnsworth, *Contracts*, 4th ed. (New York: Aspen, 2004), §4.28.

19. To be sure, markets give consumers a choice of competing products, and competitors have incentives to advertise superior terms. We do not argue for or against the regulation. Rather, our purpose here is only to note the

basis for regulating these contracts and how the law market operates to mitigate this regulation.

20. Other problems with arbitration clauses can cause courts to strike them on the grounds of unconscionability. For example, sometimes courts will strike arbitration clauses that force one party to arbitrate while enabling the drafting party to pursue court litigation. Also, a court struck down a provision that required the purchasers of a home to pay for all of the seller's legal expenses as a prerequisite to bringing any claims against the seller. See *State ex rel. Gayle Vincent v. Schneider*, 194 S.W.3d 853 (2006). In *Alterra Healthcare Corp. v. Bryant*, 2006 WL 2612769 (Fla. App., 4th Dist. 2006), the court removed a provision in the arbitration clause that purported to completely waive the right of an assisted living facility resident to appeal the arbitrator's decision.

21. *Discover Bank v. Superior Court*, 113 P.3d 1100, 1110 (Cal. 2005); see also *Aral v. Earthlink, Inc.*, 36 Cal. Rptr. 3d 229 (Cal. Ct. App., 2nd Dist. 2005).

22. *Muhammad v. County Bank of Rehoboth Beach, Delaware*, 2006 WL 2273448 (N.J. 2006).

23. *Livingston v. Associates Finance, Inc.*, 339 F.3d 553 (7th Cir. 2003).

24. *Strand v. U.S. Bank National Association ND*, 693 N.W.2d 918 (N.D. 2005).

25. *Snowden v. Checkpoint Check Cashing*, 290 F.3d 631 (4th Cir. 2002).

26. *Johnson v. West Suburban Bank*, 225 F.3d 366 (3rd Cir. 2000); see also *Randolph v. Green Tree Financial Corp., Alabama*, 244 F.3d 814 (11th Cir. 2001) (adopting a similar analysis).

27. *Leonard v. Terminix International Co.*, 854 So.2d 529 (Ala. 2002) (striking down the class action prohibition coupled with a prohibition on the recovery of "indirect, special, or consequential damages"); *State ex rel. Dunlap v. Berger*, 567 S.E.2d 265 (W. Va. 2002) (striking down an arbitration clause with a class action prohibition coupled with both a prohibition on the recovery of punitive damages and a clause requiring the equal division of arbitration costs between the parties).

28. See American Arbitration Association, Consumer Focus Area, available at http://www.adr.org/sp.asp?id=21902.

29. Consumer Due Process Protocol, principle 5, available at http://www.adr.org/sp.asp?id=22019.

30. Ibid., principle 6.

31. *Supplemental Procedures for Consumer-Related Disputes*, effective September 15, 2005, available at http://www.adr.org/sp.asp?id=222014.

32. S. 1782, Arbitration Fairness Act, Cong. rev. S. 9144 (July 12, 2007).

33. This flat ban may hurt the very parties whom the bill is intended to protect. See Peter B. Rutledge, "Whither Arbitration?" 6 *Geo. J.L. & Pub. Pol'y* (forthcoming 2008) (arguing that the ban could actually hurt the consumers who are the bill's intended beneficiaries).

34. The CAFA was discussed in chapter 3 and is also discussed below.
35. National Banking Act, 12 U.S.C. §85.
36. *Marquette National Bank v. First Omaha Service Corp.*, 439 U.S. 299 (1978).
37. *Smiley v. Citibank*, 517 U.S. 735 (1996).
38. The office of the comptroller of the currency, which regulates national banks, has aided in the broad interpretation of the term "interest rate" in its post-*Smiley* regulations. 12 CFR 7.4001(a) (2005).
39. See *Watters v. Wachovia Bank, N.A.*, 127 S. Ct. 1559 (2007) (holding that subsidiaries have the same rights to engage in real estate mortgage lending free from state regulation as do national banks because both are already regulated by the federal government through the office of the comptroller).
40. These cases are described in Samuel Issacharoff and Erin F. Delaney, "Credit Card Accountability," 73 *U. Chi. L. Rev.* 157 (2006).
41. See, for example, *Discover Bank v. Superior Court*, 36 Cal. 4th 148, 30 Cal. Rptr. 3d 76 (2005); *Knepp v. Credit Acceptance Corp.*, 229 B.R. 821 (N.D. Ala. 1999).
42. Issacharoff and Delaney, "Credit Card Accountability." A study of corporate contracts indicated that, although more than three-quarters of the consumer agreements provided for mandatory arbitration, fewer than 10 percent of the same firms' material, nonconsumer, and nonemployment agreements included arbitration clauses. Theodore Eisenberg et al., *Arbitration's Summer Soldiers: An Empirical Study of Arbitration Clauses in Consumer and Nonconsumer Contracts*, available at http://ssrn.com/abstract=1076968. This suggests that firms use arbitration clauses primarily in order to avoid class action consumer litigation. However, there are other possible explanations. For example, there are many merger and finance agreements in which the parties would want to be able to seek provisional or injunctive relief in courts. Also, there is other evidence that suggests that sellers do not use these clauses strategically against consumers. Florencia Morotta-Wurgler, "'Unfair' Dispute Resolution Clauses: Much Ado about Nothing?" in *Boilerplate: Foundations of Market Contracts*, ed. Omri Ben-Shahar (2007), available at http://papers.ssrn.com/s013/papers.cfm?abstract_id=1093293, which studies end-user licensing agreements, finds that sellers are as likely to include choice-of-dispute-resolution clauses in business-oriented products as in consumer-oriented products.
43. Issacharoff and Delaney, "Credit Card Accountability."
44. Paige Marta Skiba and Jeremy Tobacman, "Measuring the Individual-Level Effects of Access to Credit: Evidence from Payday Loans" (2006 draft manuscript on file with authors).
45. Ibid.

46. Michael Stegman, "Payday Lending," 21 *J. Econ. Perspectives* 169 (Winter 2007).

47. Paige Marta Skiba and Jeremy Tobacman, "The Profitability of Payday Lending" (2006 draft manuscript on file with authors).

48. Robert Lawless, *Credit Slips* (March 13, 2007), available at http://www.creditslips.org/creditslips/payday_lending/index.html (stating that at least one employee credit union has offered payday loans at a 12 percent annual rate of interest).

49. The Web site www.cashcentral.com has even introduced its own "state-licensed" logo to attract consumers.

50. Idaho Code Ann. 28-46-412; N.H. Rev. Stat. 399-A.13; S. Dak. Cod. L. 54-4-66.

51. Ore. Stat. 725.622; N.H. Rev. Stat. §399-A.13; Kan. Stat. Ann. §16a-2-404.

52. Ore. Stat. 725.622; Idaho Code Ann. §28-46-413. Under South Dakota law, rollovers are permitted only if the consumer pays off at least 10 percent of the outstanding principal on the loan. S. Dak. Cod. L. §54-4-65.

53. 815 Ill. Comp. Stat. 122, §2-20; N.H. Rev. Stat. §399-A.13; Idaho Code Ann. §28-46-412; Kan. Stat. Ann. 16a-2-404.

54. Ore. Stat. 725.622 (no hold-harmless clauses, no confessions of judgments, and no waiver of rights to claims, defenses, or rights to notice or opportunity to be heard); Kan. Stat. Ann 16a-2-404 (similar prohibitions); N.H. Rev. Stat. §399-A.13 (similar prohibitions, plus the agreement may not authorize the lender or a third party to bring suit against the borrower in a court outside the state); 815 Ill. Comp. Stat. 122, §4-5 (listing extensive restrictions).

55. Idaho Code Ann. §§28-46-402 and 28-46-409; 815 Ill. Comp. Stat., art. 3.

56. 815 Ill. Comp. Stat. 122, §§2.15–2.17.

57. See www.20cash.com (located in Delaware); www.paydayloantoday.com (choosing Nevada law); www.littleloanshoppe.com (choosing Nevada law).

58. For example, www.nationalpayday.com; www.mypaydayloan.com.

59. McCarran-Ferguson Act, 15 U.S.C. §1012(b).

60. This was a risk created by the Supreme Court's decision the year before the McCarran-Ferguson Act was passed, in *United States v. South-Eastern Underwriters Ass'n*, 322 U.S. 533 (1944).

61. Arkansas, Georgia, Hawaii, Kentucky, Louisiana, Maine, Massachusetts, Missouri, Montana, Nebraska, Oklahoma, South Carolina, South Dakota, Vermont, Virginia, Washington, Puerto Rico, and the U.S. Virgin Islands all appear to prohibit the arbitration of insurance contracts. Kansas also prohibits the arbitration of direct insurance contracts but permits arbitration clauses in reinsurance contracts. Rhode Island prohibits the use of arbitration clauses in life insurance contracts. Maryland prohibits their use in life, health, and annuity contracts. Colorado, California, and Utah all regulate but do not flatly prohibit the use of arbitration provisions in

insurance agreements. Alabama's Department of Insurance also attempted to regulate arbitration clauses, but because the department failed to follow established state rule-making procedures, those regulations do not have the force of law. A description of state laws on this subject appears in Susan Randall, "Mandatory Arbitration in Insurance Disputes: Inverse Preemption of the Federal Arbitration Act," 11 *Conn. Ins. L.J.* 253 (2005).

62. Jill A. Douthett, "Forum Selection as a Threshold Issue," 25 *Fall Brief* 14, 16 (1995).

63. Richard A. Epstein, "Exit Rights and Insurance Regulation: From Federalism to Takings," 7 *Geo. Mason L. Rev.* 293 (1999).

64. Ibid.

65. For reviews of current proposals, see Elizabeth F. Brown, *The Fatal Flaw of Proposals to Federalize Insurance*, available at http://ssrn.com/abstract=1008993; Henry N. Butler and Larry E. Ribstein, "A Single License Approach to Regulating Insurance" (May 2008), available at http://papers.ssrn.com/sol3/papers.cfm?abstract_id=1134792; William J. Warfel, "Insurance Regulatory Reform: An Evaluation of Options for Expanding the Role of the Federal Government," *CPCU* e-journal (forthcoming 2007), available at http://ssrn.com/abstract=946457.

66. Another modification would include market-based minimum federal standards for insurer solvency. See Butler and Ribstein, "A Jurisdictional Competition Approach."

67. See Warfel, "Insurance Regulatory Reform."

68. Ibid.

69. Robert A. Hillman and Jeffrey J. Rachlinski, "Standard-Form Contracting in the Electronic Age," 77 *N.Y.U. L. Rev.* 429, 445–54 (2002).

70. See, for example, Jeffrey R. Brown and Austan Goolsbee, "Does the Internet Make Markets More Competitive? Evidence from the Life Insurance Industry" (NBER, Working Paper No. W7996, 2000), available at http://papers.ssrn.com/paper.taf?abstract_id=248602 (showing evidence that Internet comparison shopping for life insurance has caused general price decreases across demographic groups).

71. See Erin Ann O'Hara, "Choice of Law for Internet Transactions: The Uneasy Case for Online Consumer Protection," 153 *U. Pa. L. Rev.* 1883 (2005).

72. Hillman, *Online Consumer Standard-Form Contracting Practices*.

73. By contrast, Europe has embraced a general rule in these transactions that applies the law of the seller's jurisdiction. See Directive 2000/31/EC of the European Parliament and of the Council of June 8, 2000, on certain legal aspects of information society services, in particular electronic commerce, in the Internal Market (Directive on Electronic Commerce) (2000), O.J. L 178/1.

74. A critique of these choice-of-law provisions can be found in Bruce H. Kobayashi and Larry E. Ribstein, "Uniformity, Choice of Law and Software Sales," 8 *Geo. Mason L. Rev.* 261 (1999).

75. See Jack L. Goldsmith and Tim Wu, *Who Controls the Internet? Illusions of a Borderless World* (New York: Oxford University Press, 2006); Jack L. Goldsmith and Alan O. Sykes, "The Internet and the Dormant Commerce Clause," 110 *Yale L.J.* 785, 811 (2001).

76. Joel R. Reidenberg, "Technology and Internet Jurisdiction," 153 *U. Pa. L. Rev.* 1951 (2005).

77. Tribunal de Grande Instance de Paris, May 22, 2000, available at www.lapres.net/html/yahen.html (translation by Daniel Lapres).

78. See, e.g., Richard A. Posner, *Overcoming Law* (Cambridge, MA: Harvard University Press, 1995), 533–34; George J. Stigler, "An Introduction to Privacy in Economics and Politics," 9 *J. Legal Stud.* 623, 628–33 (1980).

79. See Richard S. Murphy, "Property Rights in Personal Information: An Economic Defense of Privacy," 84 *Geo. L.J.* 2381, 2405 (1996) (citing an Equifax survey that showed that 78 percent agreed that "because computers can make use of more personal details about people, companies can provide more individualized services than before").

80. See Paul H. Rubin and Thomas M. Lenard, *Privacy and the Commercial Use of Personal Information* (Boston: Kluwer Academic, 2002), 23&NDASH;24; Privacy in the Commercial World: Hearing before the Subcommittee on Commerce, Trade and Consumer Protection of the House Committee on Energy and Commerce, 107th Cong. (2001), 47 (testimony of Paul H. Rubin, professor of economics and law, Emory University).

81. See Richard A. Posner, "Privacy," in *The New Palgrave Dictionary of Economics and the Law*, ed. P. Newman (New York: Stockton Press, 1998), 103–8.

82. See *Restatement (Second) of Torts* (1976), §§652A–C (providing that the right of privacy is invaded by unreasonable intrusion upon the seclusion of another, appropriation of the other's name or likeness, unreasonable publicity given to the other's private life, or publicity that unreasonably places the other in a false light before the public).

83. See Frank H. Easterbrook and Daniel R. Fischel, "Contractual Freedom in Corporate Law," 89 *Colum. L. Rev.* 1416, 1433 (1989); Charles J. Goetz and Robert E. Scott, "The Mitigation Principle: Toward a General Theory of Contractual Obligation," 69 *Va. L. Rev.* 967, 971 (1983); but see Ian Ayres and Robert Gertner, "Filling Gaps in Incomplete Contracts: An Economic Theory of Default Rules," 99 *Yale L.J.* 87 (1989) (arguing that default rules that force disclosure by informed parties can be efficient).

84. See Paul H. Rubin, "Courts and the Tort-Contract Boundary in Product Liability," in *The Fall and Rise of Freedom of Contract*, ed. Durham, NC: Duke University Press, F. H. Buckley (1999), 119 (proposing contract treatment for product liability cases).

85. See Regulation of the European Parliament and of the Council on the Law Applicable to Non-Contractual Obligations, art. 14(1)(b), adopted July 11, 2007, effective January 11, 2009.
86. See Cindy Skrzycki, "Trial Lawyers on the Offensive in Fight against Preemptive Rules," *Washington Post* (September 11, 2007), D2 (noting how federal agencies are creating "silent tort reform" or "stealth preemption" by expanding federal regulations to preempt aggressive trial lawyers and state attorneys general).

Chapter 8

1. Indeed, two authors have made the comparison explicit by proposing a Uniform Domestic Partnership Law, which is based on the Uniform Partnership Act. See Jennifer Ann Drobac and Antony Page, "A Uniform Domestic Partnership Act: Marrying Business Partnership and Family Law," 41 *Ga. L. Rev.* 349 (2007).
2. See Joseph William Singer, "Same Sex Marriage, Full Faith and Credit, and the Evasion of Obligation," 1 *Stan. J. C.R. & C.L.* 1, 3–4 (2005).
3. For a discussion of these and other marriage restrictions, see, generally, Eugene F. Scoles and Peter Hay, *Conflict of Laws*, 2nd ed. (St. Paul, MN: West, 1992), §§13.8–13.12.
4. See *Restatement (Second) of Conflict of Laws* (1971), §284.
5. See ibid., §283 and comments j–k.
6. See Scoles and Hay, *Conflict of Laws*, §13.13.
7. See Joanna L. Grossman, "Resurrecting Comity: Revisiting the Problem of Non-Uniform Marriage Laws," 84 *Ore. L. Rev.* 433 (2005); Tobias Barrington Wolff, "Interest Analysis in Interjurisdictional Marriage Disputes," 153 *U. Pa. L. Rev.* 2215 (2005).
8. *Baehr v. Lewin*, 852 P.2d 44 (Haw. 1993) (holding that the state bears the burden of showing discrimination to be not unconstitutional); *Baehr v. Miike*, No. 91-1394, 1996 WL 694235 (Haw. Cir. Ct. December 3, 1996) (concluding that the state failed to satisfy its burden).
9. See Hawaii Const., art. 1, §23 (1998); *Baehr v. Miike*, No. 20371, 1999 Haw. LEXIS 391 (December 9, 1999) (holding that the amendment mooted plaintiff's challenge to Hawaii's marriage law).
10. See *Restatement (Second)*, §284, comment c.
11. See Frank Buckley and Larry E. Ribstein, "Calling a Truce in the Marriage Wars," 2001 *U. Ill. L. Rev.* 561 (discussing the different normative implications of allowing celebrations of marriage locally and enforcing foreign marriages).
12. Society's interests might be accommodated in this context by outlawing "tramp" marriages, that is, by not allowing parties to travel from their state of residence solely to take advantage of another state's marriage law.

Note that the only state that recognizes same-sex marriage, Massachusetts, extends its recognition only to Massachusetts residents because of a much earlier statute, Mass. Gen. Laws, ch. 207, §§11–12 (2006). A problem with such a restriction is that it removes a potentially important mechanism for state competition, that is, competition for marriage-celebration business. Massachusetts recently eliminated its restriction on "tramp" marriages. See note 19 below.

13. See Buckley and Ribstein, "Calling a Truce in the Marriage Wars," 598–99.

14. These contracts were first enforced in *Marvin v. Marvin*, 557 P.2d 106 (Cal. 1976). See Lenore J. Weitzman, *The Marriage Contract: Spouses, Lovers, and the Law* (New York: Free Press, 1981), 395–415.

15. See Larry E. Ribstein, "A Standard Form Approach to Same-Sex Marriage," 38 *Creighton L. Rev.* 309 (2005).

16. *Goodridge v. Dep't of Public Health*, 798 N.E.2d 941 (Mass. 2003); *Lewis v. Harris*, 188 N.J. 415, 908 A.2d 196 (2006); *Baker v. Vermont*, 744 A.2d 864 (Vt. 1999); *In re Marriage Cases*, 43 Cal.4th 757, 183 P.3d 384, 76 Cal.Rptr.3d 683 (2008).

17. 15 Vt. Stat. Ann. §1201 (2005).

18. See the Human Rights Campaign Web site, available at http://www.hrc. org (detailing state laws related to rights for lesbian, gay, bisexual, and transgender individuals).

19. Chapter 216 of the Acts of 2008 (signed July 31, 2008).

20. See, e.g., Jonathan Finer, "At Expo, Few Disagreements on Gay Marriage," *Washington Post* (May 3, 2004), A3; Robert Strauss, "Philadelphia Invites Gay Tourists in TV Ad," *Washington Post* (July 3, 2004), A3.

21. Thirty-eight states include these prohibitions. See the Human Rights Campaign Web site, http://www.hrc.org (providing the current status of each state's laws). The political dynamic has been complicated by the incentives of Republican politicians to use referendums on same-sex marriage to attract their voter base to the polls.

22. Virginia Affirmation of Marriage Act, 2004 Va. H.B. 751. A Virginia court refused to honor a Vermont civil union. See S. Mitra Kalita, "Vt. Same-Sex Union Null in Va., Judge Says," *Washington Post* (August 24, 2004), B1; see also the Human Rights Campaign Web site, http://www.hrc.org (providing the legal treatment of same-sex marriage by state).

23. See David Tuller, "The Basics: 'Gay Divorce?' A Knottier Knot for Gay Couples," *New York Times Week in Review* (November 12, 2006) (discussing the legal problems of dissolving same-sex marriages since most states do not recognize their formation).

24. Commission of the European Communities Green Paper, *On Conflict of Laws in Matters concerning Matrimonial Property Regimes, including the Question of Jurisdiction and Mutual Recognition* (2006), available at http://www.law.duke.edu/cicl/choiceoflaw/literature.

25. A state might attract permanent residents by refusing to extend its liberal law to nonresidents. Massachusetts took this approach until recently. See notes 12 and 19.

26. Pub. L. No. 104-199, 110 Stat. 2419, codified at 28 U.S.C. §1738C and 1 U.S.C. §7 (2000).

27. See Patrick Joseph Borchers, "The Essential Irrelevance of the Full Faith and Credit Clause to the Same-Sex Marriage Debate," 38 *Creighton L. Rev.* 353 (2005).

28. See text accompanying note 20.

29. 539 U.S. 588 (2003).

30. For a discussion of the potential effect of *Lawrence*, see Ribstein, "Standard Form Approach."

31. *Lawrence*, 539 U.S. at 578.

32. Ibid., 567.

33. Ibid., 578.

34. Ibid., 585.

35. See Nelson Lund and John O. McGinnis, "*Lawrence v. Texas* and Judicial Hubris," 102 *Mich. L. Rev.* 1555, 1583 (2004) (noting that the case "certainly points toward the abolition of all laws denying any of the benefits of marriage, including the dignitary benefits associated with the term 'marriage,' to homosexual couples").

36. See Ribstein, "Standard Form Approach."

37. *Lawrence*, 539 U.S. at 571.

38. Ibid. (quoting *Planned Parenthood of Southeastern Pa. v. Casey*, 505 U.S. 833, 850 [1992]).

39. Ibid., 604.

40. See Edward Stein, "The Story of *Goodridge v. Department of Public Health*: The Bumpy Road to Marriage for Same-Sex Couples," in *Family Law Stories*, ed. Carol Sanger (Mineola, NY: Foundation Press, 2005) (discussing the role of the Gay and Lesbian Advocates and Defenders in devising litigation strategies for several same-sex marriage cases, including the Massachusetts decision that struck down the state's same-sex marriage ban).

41. See Federal Marriage Amendment, S.J. Res. 40, 108th Cong. (2004) (proposing a constitutional amendment providing that "[m]arriage in the United States shall consist only of the union of a man and a woman. Neither this Constitution, nor the constitution of any State, shall be construed to require that marriage or the legal incidents thereof be conferred upon any union other than the union of a man and a woman").

42. See Ribstein, "Standard Form Approach."

43. *Williams v. North Carolina*, 317 U.S. 287, 302–3 (1942) (upholding Nevada's power to divorce a North Carolina couple when one spouse claimed a local domicile but the other spouse remained in North Carolina).

44. For a summary of these developments, see Cynthia Crossen, "Back When Divorcing Was Hard, Some States Found a Way to Profit," *Wall Street*

Journal (August 6, 2007), B1, available at http://online.wsj.com/article/
SB118635505489588702.html?mod=todays_us_marketplace.

45. It should be noted, however, that the state of the marital domicile can strike the validity of a divorce if it determines that a spouse's domicile in the divorcing state was not bona fide (i.e., the divorcing spouse returns to his home state after the divorce is granted). *Williams v. North Carolina II*, 325 U.S. 226 (1945).

46. Since 1975, every state has permitted divorce without proof of fault. See Michael Grossberg, "Balancing Acts: Crisis, Change, and Continuity in American Family Law, 1890–1990," 28 *Ind. L. Rev.* 273, 295 (1995).

47. See Leora Friedberg, "Did Unilateral Divorce Raise Divorce Rates? Evidence from Panel Data," 88 *Am. Econ. Rev.* 608 (1998). This shopping for divorce laws is not confined to the United States. For example, forum shopping along religious and geographical boundaries to obtain divorce has been documented in early twentieth-century colonial South Asia as well. Mitra Sharafi, "The Marital Patchwork of Colonial South Asia: Forum Shopping from Britain to Baroda, c. 1900" (draft manuscript on file with authors).

48. See Gary S. Becker et al., "An Economic Analysis of Marital Instability," 85 *J. Pol. Econ.* 1141 (1977); Lloyd Cohen, "Marriage, Divorce, and Quasi Rents; or, 'I Gave Him the Best Years of My Life,'" 16 *J. Legal Stud.* 267, 287–89 (1987); Elizabeth S. Scott, "Rational Decisionmaking about Marriage and Divorce," 76 *Va. L. Rev.* 9, 25–37 (1990).

49. See Niko Matouschek and Imran Rasul, "The Economics of the Marriage Contract: Theories and Evidence," 51 *J.L. & Econ.* (forthcoming 2008), available at http://ssrn.com/abstract=950688.

50. See Lynn A. Baker and Robert E. Emery, "When Every Relationship Is Above Average," 17 *L. & Hum. Behav.* 439 (1993).

51. For an analysis of the effect of divorce on children, see Judith S. Wallerstein, *The Unexpected Legacy of Divorce* (New York: Hyperion, 2000).

52. La. Rev. Stat. Ann. §9.272.

53. Ibid., §9.307.

54. See Ariz. Rev. Stat. §§25-901–906 (1998); Ark. Code Ann. §§9-11-801–811. For an analysis of covenant marriage laws in the context of the law market, see Buckley and Ribstein, "Calling a Truce in the Marriage Wars."

55. Not only have the parties signaled their expectation by choosing to marry under a covenant marriage law, but these laws include counseling requirements to ensure that parties are aware of, and have reflected on, the commitment they are making.

56. Theodore F. Haas, "The Rationality and Enforceability of Contractual Restrictions on Divorce," 66 *N.C. L. Rev.* 879, 911–14 (1988).

57. Ibid., 914–21.

58. See Margaret F. Brinig and Francis H. Buckley, "No-Fault Laws and At-Fault People," 18 *Int'l Rev. L. & Econ.* 325, 326, 328 (1998).

59. Achieving this result might require legal reforms, however, because parties cannot create court jurisdiction by contract, and current federal laws do restrict the jurisdiction of state courts in granting or modifying custody determinations.

60. 814 N.E.2d 320 (Mass. 2004).

61. 426 Mass. 501, 689 N.E.2d 790 (1998).

62. 814 N.E.2d at 326n12. Federal law may limit the contract parents' ability to take the child away from the gestation mother.

63. See *R.R. v. M.H.*, at 506–8 (discussing varying state laws).

64. See Mary Patricia Byrn, *From Right to Wrong: A Critique of the 2000 Uniform Parentage Act*, Minnesota Legal Studies, Research Paper No. 06-42, available at http://ssrn.com/abstract=928683 (discussing the failure of a uniform law to deal appropriately with these issues).

65. See James Q. Wilson, "Killing Terri," *Wall Street Journal* (March 21, 2005) (arguing that "[p]eople with [living wills] are likely to get exactly the same treatment as people without them, possibly because doctors and family members ignore the wills. And ignoring them is often the right thing to do because it is virtually impossible to write a living will that anticipates and makes decisions about all of the many, complicated, and hard to foresee illnesses you may face").

Chapter 9

1. See *Restatement (Second) of Conflict of Laws* (1971), §§270, 272.

2. See Robert H. Sitkoff and Max Schanzenbach, "Jurisdictional Competition for Trust Funds: An Empirical Analysis of Perpetuities and Taxes," 115 *Yale L.J.* 356 (2005).

3. The incidence of wealth transfer taxes is described in 26 U.S.C. §§2611–2613, 2651 (2000). Exemptions rose to $1 million through 2003, $1.5 million in 2004 and 2005, $2 million in 2006 through 2008, and $3.5 million in 2009. Ibid., §§2631(c), 2010(c). The Economic Growth and Tax Relief Reconciliation Act (EGTRRA), Pub. L. No. 107-16, 115 Stat. 38 (2001), repealed the tax on wealth transfers and the estate tax effective in 2010, but reinstates these taxes at 2001 levels for transfers occurring in and after 2011.

4. See Sitkoff and Schanzenbach, "Jurisdictional Competition for Trust Funds," 366n26 (noting that "[t]oday, because almost all life estates and future interests are created in trust rather than as legal interests, the Rule's primary modern application is to interests in trusts funded with stocks, bonds, and other liquid financial assets").

5. See ibid., 375.

6. Ibid., 355.

7. Ibid.

8. See Ira Mark Bloom, "The GST Tax Tail Is Killing the Rule against Perpetuities," 87 *Tax Notes* 569 (2000) (arguing that abolition of the RAP will lead to intergenerational inequity).

9. See Robert H. Sitkoff, "The Lurking Rule against Accumulations of Income," 100 *N.W. U. L. Rev.* 501, 514 (2006) (discussing other potentially more profitable investment mechanisms).

10. See note 3.

11. Corporate wealth is said to be twice taxed because the firm pays taxes on its profits, and then these profits are later taxed again when they are distributed to the shareholders.

12. See *Restatement (Second) of Trusts* (1959), §156, comment c.

13. See Lynn M. LoPucki, "The Essential Structure of Judgment Proofing," 51 *Stan. L. Rev.* 147 (1998); Stewart E. Sterk, "Asset Protection Trusts: Trust Law's Race to the Bottom?" 85 *Cornell L. Rev.* 1035 (2000).

14. David C. Lee, "Offshore Asset Protection Trusts: Testing the Limits of Judicial Tolerance in Estate Planning," 15 *Bankr. Dev. J.* 451, 459 (1999).

15. Eric Henzy, "Offshore and 'Other' Shore Asset Protection Trusts," 32 *Vand. J. Transnat'l L.* 739, 740 (1999).

16. See *Lawrence v. Chapter 7 Trustee*, 251 B.R. 630, 642 (Bankr. S.D. Fla. 2000); *Sattin v. Brooks (In re Brooks)*, 217 B.R. 98 (Bankr. D. Conn. 1998); *Marine Midland Bank v. Portnoy (In re Portnoy)*, 201 B.R. 685 (Bankr. S.D.N.Y. 1996).

17. See Sterk, "Asset Protection Trusts."

18. Ibid.

19. Adam J. Hirsch, "Fear Not the Asset Protection Trust," 27 *Cardozo L. Rev.* 2685 (2006).

20. See, generally, Larry E. Ribstein, "Reverse Limited Liability and the Design of Business Associations," 30 *Del. J. Corp. L.* 199 (2005).

21. See Uniform Partnership Act §18; Revised Uniform Partnership Act §401.

22. See Alan R. Bromberg and Larry E. Ribstein, *Bromberg & Ribstein on Partnership* (2005), §3.04(a)(1).

23. See RUPA §503(b).

24. See UPA §32(2); RUPA §806.

25. UPA §28; RUPA §504.

26. See *Hellman v. Anderson*, 233 Cal. App. 3d 840, 853 (Cal. Ct. App. 1991) (holding that a creditor can foreclose on charged interest without the consent of the co-partner unless the co-partner shows that foreclosure would unduly interfere with the business); but see *Madison Hills Ltd. Partnership II v. Madison Hills, Inc.*, 644 A.2d 363, 370 (Conn. App. Ct. 1994) (permitting strict foreclosure of partnership interest).

27. See Juliet M. Moringiello, "Seizing Domain Names to Enforce Judgments: Looking Back to Look to the Future," 72 *U. Cin. L. Rev.* 95 (2003).

28. UPA §6(1) (1914); RUPA §101(6) (1994).

29. Many LLC statutes permit an LLC to be organized for any lawful purpose, or similarly clarify that LLCs can be used for nonbusiness purposes. See Larry E. Ribstein and Robert Keatinge, *Ribstein & Keatinge on Limited Liability Companies*, 3d ed. (Eagen, MN: Thompson/West, 2007), §4:10; Uniform Limited Liability Corporations Act §101(3).

30. As discussed above, even under the partnership statutes, an assignee, including a charging creditor, has no right to seek judicial dissolution of a firm that is subject to an unexpired term or undertaking. Some LLC statutes do not give assignees even that limited ability to seek dissolution. See Ribstein and Keatinge, *Ribstein & Keatinge on Limited Liability Companies*, ch. 7, app. 1.

31. It is difficult to quantify the size of the LLC asset protection industry. However, it is perhaps notable that, as discussed in chapter 6, Florida, a notorious asset protection state, has become a leader in LLC formations.

32. See Ribstein, "Reverse Limited Liability" (reviewing application of these remedies).

33. Daniel Barham, "Domestic Asset Protection Trust States and Their Race to Nowhere" (December 2006 draft manuscript on file with authors).

34. See Eugene F. Scoles and Peter Hay, *Conflict of Laws,* 2d ed. (St. Paul, MN: West, 1992), §19.1.

35. See Abraham Bell and Gideon Parchomovsky, "Of Property and Federalism," 115 *Yale L.J.* 72 (2005) (discussing this issue).

36. See ibid.

37. See Thomas W. Merrill and Henry E. Smith, "Optimal Standardization in the Law of Property: The *Numerus Clausus* Principle," 110 *Yale L.J.* 1, 12–13 (2000).

38. See Bell and Parchomovsky, "Of Property and Federalism," 91.

39. On the relevance of marriage law, see ibid., 86, 87, and 107. For choice-of-law issues that arise at the intersection of property and other areas of law, see Russell J. Weintraub, *Commentary on the Conflict of Laws*, 5th ed. (New York: Foundation Press, Thompson/West, 2006), §§8.7–8.21.

40. See Weintraub, *Commentary on the Conflict of Laws*, §§8.7–8.21.

41. Thus, Scoles and Hay, *Conflict of Laws*, 804–5, note the "difficulty in making a will devising land in several states conform to the varying requirements in each."

42. See Bell and Parchomovsky, "Of Property and Federalism," 105.

43. Robert C. Ellickson, "A Private Idaho in Greenwich Village?" 115 *Yale L.J.* Pocket Part 5 (2005).

44. See Bell and Parchomovsky, "Of Property and Federalism," 89.

45. See ibid., 103.

46. See *Fall v. Eastin*, 215 U.S. 1 (1909) (the nonsitus state lacks jurisdiction to create a deed to land located in another state).

47. See ibid. (suggesting that the court could order the parties to act regarding the property even if it could not act on that property directly).

48. See Weintraub, *Commentary on the Conflict of Laws*, 548–51.

49. See chapter 4, which discusses this sort of price discrimination in the general market for law.

50. See text accompanying note 43.

51. See text accompanying note 38.

Chapter 10

1. See Larry E. Ribstein and Bruce H. Kobayashi, "Economic Analysis of Uniform State Laws," 25 *J. Legal Stud.* 131 (1996) (discussing the politics of the NCCUSL and evaluating its work).

2. Ibid., 147.

3. Bruce H. Kobayashi and Larry E. Ribstein, "Evolution and Uniformity," 34 *Econ. Inquiry* 464 (1996).

4. Bruce H. Kobayashi and Larry E. Ribstein, "Uniform Laws, Model Laws and ULLCA," 66 *Colo. L. Rev.* 947 (1995). There is also evidence that NCCUSL processes can even *interfere* with the state process of spontaneous uniformity. See Bruce H. Kobayashi and Larry E. Ribstein, *The Non-Uniformity of Uniform Laws*, available at http://papers.ssrn.com/so13/papers.cfm?abstract_id=998281.

5. These provisions are discussed in chapter 3.

6. Indeed, restatements are subject to political pressures similar to those affecting uniform laws. See Alan Schwartz and Robert E. Scott, "The Political Economy of Private Legislatures," 143 *U. Pa. L. Rev.* 595 (1995).

7. See Jonathan R. Macey, "Federal Deference to Local Regulators and the Economic Theory of Regulation: Toward A Public-Choice Explanation of Federalism," 76 *Va. L. Rev.* 265 (1990).

8. See Samuel Issacharoff and Catherine M. Sharkey, "Backdoor Federalization," 53 *U.C.L.A. L. Rev.* 1353, 1402 (2006) (discussing cases and various preemption approaches).

9. 15 U.S.C. §§77p(b) and 78bb(f)(1) (2000).

10. A problem with SLUSA is that its state law exception only applies to some actions governed by state law. This effectively preserves some types of cases for exclusively federal treatment *even if* the claims arise under state corporation law. Under our analysis, the key question should not be the type of claim, but whether the claim is covered by a state regulation that is subject to contractual choice of law. This approach might avoid the sort of line drawing involved in *Merrill Lynch, Pierce, Fenner & Smith v. Dabit*, 126 S. Ct. 1503 (2006). In that case, the Supreme Court held that SLUSA preempted a state suit in which the defendants' fraud allegedly caused plaintiff to hold onto stock even though SLUSA

prohibited only state actions in connection with the purchase or sale of securities.

11. See 12 U.S.C. §85; *Marquette National Bank v. First Omaha Service Corp.*, 439 U.S. 299 (1978) (interpreting the statute).

12. See Roberta Romano, "Empowering Investors: A Market Approach to Securities Regulation," 107 *Yale L.J.* 2359 (1998) (arguing that firms should be empowered to choose their governing securities law and that litigation involving that law should proceed in the state whose law is chosen).

13. 313 U.S. 487 (1941).

14. See Samuel Issacharoff, "Settled Expectations in a World of Unsettled Law: Choice of Law after the Class Action Fairness Act," 106 *Colum. L. Rev.* 1839 (2006).

15. Each of these problems was discussed in chapter 7.

16. The Court sometimes imposes bright-line rules in constitutional cases. The Court could promulgate in a single case our proposed federal statute as a governing bright-line rule under the Full Faith and Credit Clause. If so, the rule would bind all federal and state courts, and therefore the result would be the same as that achieved through a congressional statute. Because we think it extremely unlikely that the Court would impose this general rule, we instead advocate a congressional statute.

17. For example, the relevant location of a franchisee might (and probably should) be the location of the franchise rather than the residence of the franchise owner. This is consistent with the statute's objective of giving the legislature the right political incentives; these would likely depend on the location of the business rather than of the individual owner. Moreover, we assume that residence statutes would apply regardless of whether firms or individuals end up as plaintiffs or defendants in the litigation.

18. Lon L. Fuller, "Consideration and Form," 41 *Colum. L. Rev.* 799 (1941), makes a similar argument in favor of requiring promises to be supported by consideration.

19. A possible problem with this approach is that other states could nevertheless decide to enforce the choice-of-law clause despite the limitation in the incorporating state's statute. The incorporating state might respond by revoking the firm's charter. This would, in effect, withdraw the application of its law and thus nullify the choice-of-law clause.

20. Ore. Rev. Stat. §81.120.

Chapter 11

1. James A. Brickley et al., "The Economic Effects of Franchise Termination Laws," 34 *J.L. & Econ.* 101 (1991); Jonathan Klick et al., *The Effect of Contract Regulation: The Case of Franchising* (2007), available at http://www.ssrn.com/abstract=951464.

2. Ibid.

3. See Samuel Issacharoff and Catherine M. Sharkey, "Backdoor Federalization," 53 *U.C.L.A. L. Rev.* 1353, 1402 (2006).

4. See Larry E. Ribstein and Bruce H. Kobayashi, "Economic Analysis of Uniform State Laws," 25 *J. Legal Stud.* 131 (1996); Alan Schwartz and Robert E. Scott, "The Political Economy of Private Legislatures," 143 *U. Pa. L. Rev.* 595 (1995).

5. See Gordon Tullock, *Trials on Trial: The Pure Theory of Legal Procedures* (New York: Columbia University Press, 1980); William M. Landes and Richard A. Posner, "Adjudication as a Private Good," 6 *J. Legal Stud.* 235 (1979).

6. See, e.g., Chris Brummer, "Federalization's Competitive Edge: Corporate Law Preemption in an Age of Global Capital Markets" (manuscript, March 18, 2008, on file with authors) (arguing that securities laws should compete at the national rather than state level).

Index

choice-of-court rules, 70–73, 104, 138–40, 221; arbitration and, 151; consumer contracts and, 133–34, 144; international convention on, 105–6. *See also* choice-of-forum clauses

choice-of-forum clauses, 6, 77, 97, 134, 154, 221; enforcement of, 104

choice-of-law clauses: arbitration and, 88, 151; benefits of, 26; CAFA and, 236n12; choice-of-court clauses and, 71; circumventing state law, 35; class action suits and, 147–48, 232n40; common law and, 56, 204–5, 248n48; connection requirements and, 78–80; constitutional limits on, 55; consumer contracts and, 35, 133–38, 144; consumer protection and, 57; corporate law market and, 128; corporations and, 108, 128; court hostility to, 104; default rules and, 31–32; divorce law and, 174–75; effect on consumers of, 135; electronic commerce and, 153–54, 155; enforcement in Europe, 60; enforcement in United States, 201–2, 237n26; enforcement of, 6–10, 10, 81, 82–84, 188, 203, 219, 223, 227n2; in Europe, 137–38, 158; exit and, 29; federal courts and, 49–50, 69; First Restatement and, 40; floating, 213–14; fundamental policy exception to enforcing, 114; general partnerships and, 119; insurance law and, 150, 151; Internet privacy and, 157; judicial attitudes toward, 65–66; law market and, 14; lawyer licensing laws and, 75; mandatory laws and, 36, 205; marriage and, 11, 162, 163–65; overenforcement of, 223; product liability and, 158; property law market and, 197–98; for real property, 192–95; real seat rule and, 121; reasons for non-enforcement of, 59, 209–10; right to die and, 179; Second Restatement and, 45; state-by-state, 84; state law and, 222; substantial relationship requirement and, 60–62;

super-mandatory rules and, 201; Supreme Court rulings on, 50–55, 146, 233n65; surrogacy contracts and, 178; for trusts, 184; U.S. Congress and, 47–48; U.S. Supreme Court and, 47; written *vs.* oral, 212–13. *See also* federal choice-of-law statute; internal affairs doctrine (IAD)

choice-of-law statutes, federal. *See* federal choice-of-law statute

choice-of-law statutes, state, 47, 58, 68, 80, 82, 204

choice-of-law theories, 37

choice-of-marriage law, 162, 163–64

civil unions, 11, 166–67

class action arbitration, 141–42, 256n42

Class Action Fairness Act of 2005 (CAFA), 48–50, 144, 148, 204, 222–23; choice-of-law clauses and, 236n12

class-action lawsuits, 24, 48, 125, 140, 142, 147–48; choice-of-law clauses and, 75, 232n40; federal courts and, 144, 204; litigation havens and, 8, 222

class action waivers, 36

Clay v. Sun Insurance Office, Ltd., 53

closely held business associations, 28, 33, 117, 119–21

collective bargaining, 91

Colorado law, 92

Commerce Clause, 51, 55, 113, 124–27, 144, 233n45; federal choice-of-law statute and, 200

common law, 48, 56, 63, 123, 204–5, 248n48

conflict of laws, 4, 38, 45, 206. *See also* choice-of-law topics; First Restatement of Conflict of Laws; Second Restatement on Conflict of Laws; Third Restatement on Conflict of Laws

Congress. *See* United States Congress

Connecticut law, 152, 165

connection requirement, 60, 62, 78–80, 116–17; federal choice-of-law statute and, 208–9; trend toward eliminating, 84. *See also* substantial relationship requirement